# The CHILD and the MACHINE

# The CHILD and the MACHINE

## How Computers Put Our Children's Education at Risk

Alison Armstrong and Charles Casement

**Robins Lane Press**

*a division of Gryphon House, Inc.*

**Beltsville, Maryland**
**www.robinslane.com**

Reprinted with permission; excerpts from Theodore Roszak, *The Cult of
Information: The Folklore of Computers and the True Art of Thinking* © 1986 by
Theodore Roszak.

Reprinted with permission; excerpts from Douglas Sloan (ed.), *The Computer in
Education: A Critical Perspective* (New York: Teachers College Press © 1991 by
Teachers College, Columbia University. All rights reserved.), pp. 3, 7-8, 58.

Reprinted with permission; excerpts from Seymour Papert, *Mindstorms: Children,
Computers and Powerful Ideas* © 1980 by Basic Books, Inc.

Library of Congress Cataloging-in-Publication Data

Armstrong, Alison, 1955–
    The child and the machine: how computers put our children's education at
risk / Alison Armstrong and Charles Casement.
        p. cm.
    Includes bibliographical references and index.
    ISBN 0-87659-210-8
        1. Education–Data processing.  2. Computer-assisted
instruction.  3. Computers and children.  4. Child development.
I. Casement, Charles.  II. Title.

LB 1028.43 .A76 2000
372.133'4–dc21

00-029122

*This is for Alex, Anthony and Deirdre.*
*A.A.*

*To the children of the Parent-Child Mother Goose Program.*
*C.C.*

# CONTENTS

# PREFACE

Like many U.S. schools, the public elementary school my children attend has been preoccupied with the question of technological change. Several years ago we held a Parent–Teacher Association (PTA) meeting on computer technology. Both a representative from the board of education and another from a computer company showed up at our school to tell us we needed to prepare our children for the future. The lights went down in the gym and a screen displayed a software program designed to improve our children's math skills. The presenters told us that computers and new educational software packages were an unstoppable combination, and that "children need this technology in order to compete in the global marketplace of the future."

In the past several years, our PTA has spent tens of thousands of dollars—money often matched by government grants—on computer technology. Typically, a teacher will ask for funds to purchase new computers, printers, or software packages that they've seen advertised or heard about from a colleague or friend. Parents usually vote, often unanimously, to raise the necessary money. All across the United States, PTAs are holding spaghetti suppers, bake sales, and silent auctions to fund the purchase of the latest educational technology for their children's schools. Many millions more are spent from school and government budgets for the same purpose.

Parents routinely say things such as, "We have to prepare our children for the future and computers are part of that future…They have to learn sometime—they may as well start sooner rather than later." Or, "Computers help kids to learn the basics. We don't want them to be left behind." Or, "Computers are fun. Kids just love them." At a nearby school, parents voted to spend thousands to buy networked computers for the primary classes. A parent who tried to ask questions about the objectives behind this decision was told by another parent, "I'm a judge, and all the judges have computers."

Scenes such as this are being acted out throughout the United States and in many countries around the world in what appears to be a headlong rush to computerize classrooms and thereby equip our children for survival in the future we are creating for them. Underlying such discussions is the assumption that computer technology is the biggest boost that education can get. Parents are genuinely motivated by a belief that their children will receive a better education if they have access to computers. Missing from the discussion are questions about the quality or suitability of the material accessed through computers, as well as concern about how it will affect students physically, socially, and intellectually.

But are computers really essential to children's education? Curious to find out just what we were buying in my own school, I examined some of the software on which we were spending our scarce education dollars. I discovered much of it was little more than electronic games dressed up to look like math or language instruction. I began to ask myself how we could designate so much money to buying hardware and software, yet take so little time to evaluate them. While we were spending a bundle on computers, our library needed books, magazines, and atlases, and many classes were short on math textbooks.

I noticed that parents were often more enthusiastic about bringing computer technology into the classroom than were teachers. The parents were the ones grumbling about the failure to teach "computer literacy" in teachers' colleges and the fact that teachers needed special workshops to bring them up to speed. At one school, parents were so keen to have their children use computers that they went out and bought a lot of costly equipment, which then sat unused for most of the school year because no one knew how to install it.

Until recently, the media have been so caught up in the enthusiasm for high-tech education that it was difficult to determine where reporting ended and advertising began. Critical coverage was so hard to find (beyond the pages of specialist journals) that when I wrote a feature article for a national newspaper that questioned the benefits of computer use with young children, numerous readers responded with outrage. Several readers suggested that the problem lay not with the technology, but with the teachers. If we turned our backs on computer technology, the argument went, our children would suffer. Not only would they miss out on unique learning opportunities only possible through new technology, but they would also fall behind in a global struggle, the outcome of which would determine the course of their lives. It was heady stuff indeed.

Given the extreme response to my initial articles, I decided more needed to be written on the subject. As I began research for this book, I discovered that what had been excluded from the debate was scientific evidence. Proponents often claimed this research bolstered the argument for computer-based education, but in reality it struck a far more cautious, if not critical, note. Because the volume of research in this field is extensive, I asked Charles Casement to collaborate with me.

As we dug deeper into the history of computer-based education and researched various aspects of computer use in elementary schools, we found that many important questions were not being asked, let alone answered. I set out to visit as many schools as possible in the United States and Canada, selecting those that were recognized as exemplary in their use of computer technology, to get a feel for what was actually happening. Charles concentrated on the published research in U.S., European, and international journals. By and large, we restricted our focus to elementary schools because we believe that young children will be most affected by the current obsession with computers as a medium for learning. One question was foremost in our minds: do computers improve the quality of instruction in schools?

This question needs a clear answer, supported by real evidence. The public education system must be accountable to the citizens who pay for it—we need to do what is best for our children. So far, the most that can be said about computer-based instruction is that vast sums have been lavished on a technology whose educational potential has yet to be proven. We can only guess the long-term effects of computer use on young children's development.

We hope this book will spark a long-overdue public discussion about the role of computer technology in schools and help provide a framework for such a debate.

Alison Armstrong

## CHAPTER 1

# Educational Technology and Illusions of "Progress"

*A prudent society controls its own infatuation with "progress" when planning for its young.*

—Jane Healy[1]

*Schools will never be good places for students until they are good places for teachers. Given current trends, I'd say our schools are in danger of becoming good places for machines.*

—R. W. Burniske[2]

In April 1997, President Bill Clinton received an official visit from Canadian Prime Minister Jean Chrétien. While their husbands held talks, Hillary Rodham Clinton and Aline Chrétien went to the Burrville Elementary School in a poor neighborhood of Washington, D.C., where, as the media reported, "through the wonders of technology, they watched the students of twinned schools in Washington and Ottawa share their hopes on a live, audio-visual Internet hook-up."[3] It was the kind of photo opportunity politicians love to stage these days: virtually every public figure in the United States wants to be associated with the latest developments in information technology. In this instance, however, the scene created was a sham. The equipment had been installed for the First Ladies' visit and would be removed immediately after their departure. Before the day was over, the students would be back to taking turns on the school's single aging computer with an internet connection.

We mention this story not to underline the thorough-going cynicism of political posturing, but to draw attention to the way in which computer technology seems to have taken over public perceptions of what education is all about. It's almost as if nothing worthwhile goes on in schools unless computers are involved. Yet some of the most elementary questions about the educational use of computers remain unanswered. Why should children be exposed to computer technology from an early age? Are computers and computer software so essential to children's education? What can we expect them to gain? What do they stand to lose? Not only are these issues unresolved, but for the most part the questions themselves have never been asked.

U.S. schools are currently undergoing the most dramatic change to occur in education since the introduction of compulsory schooling in the mid-nineteenth century. A host of new and emerging computer technologies, such as intranets that allow video conferencing and multimedia presentations, are radically altering the work place and are now establishing themselves in our homes and schools, transforming the education of the young in as yet unimaginable ways. Children have become unwitting participants in what can only be described as a huge social experiment. This experiment calls for a radical restructuring of the educational system and, with it, a fundamental change in the way children learn about and experience the world.

The impetus for this reform stems largely from two beliefs. The first is that computer technology can make education more productive, relevant, and interesting for students of all ages. Students will learn more and more quickly, the argument goes, because they will be more motivated to learn. They will be more motivated because they like working with computers and because their intellectual horizons will no longer be limited by the resources of their school or the knowledge of their teachers.

The second belief is that because computers play an ever-larger role in our lives, students must understand and be able to take advantage of the potential of technology if they are to participate fully in society. Many see a familiarity with computer technology as a prerequisite for a successful career.

Arising from these beliefs is the conviction that a key part of our children's schooling is the acquisition of computer literacy, and that to be computer literate, children must have access to computers in schools. But the airy optimism and sense of certainty with which computers have been acquired for educational use are not matched by what has been happening in schools. Computer use in the classroom, in fact, has been largely a matter of trying to keep up with the pace of technological change, with educational goals running a distant second. The greater the capabilities of the technology, the more eagerly it was embraced, yet specific problems for which it could be used were seldom identified in advance. The main thing was to get the machines installed; the benefits would emerge later. As MIT professor Joseph Weizenbaum pointed out, a computer is "a solution in search of problems."[4]

When computers were first introduced into classrooms in the late 1970s and early 1980s, the computer language BASIC was in widespread use. Unlike earlier programming languages, which were taught only at universities, BASIC was simple enough to allow beginners to program a computer. Teachers from kindergarten through high school were encouraged to master BASIC in order to pass along the necessary technical skills to their students, the rationale being that it was "the language that comes with your computer."[5]

But BASIC did not remain the language that comes with your computer for long. With the development of operating systems such as MS–DOS and the graphic user interface of the Macintosh, computer operators could do all sorts of things without knowing how to program. Consequently, the advantages of learning to program in BASIC or master other languages such as Fortran, Pascal, Cobol, or PL–1 became minimal. Far from being skilled technicians, many of today's computer operators are little more than typists because the software packages they use require them to perform repetitive, machinelike tasks.

But this was not the end of teaching programming in schools. By 1984, educational reformers were swept up by a new notion of what to do with computers. Instead of merely programming a computer for the sake of acquiring technical expertise, children would use computers to teach them how to think. Educators reasoned that the step-by-step thinking involved in programming would make the computer the perfect tutor.

The idea of using computers to teach children to think originated with Seymour Papert and was put forward in his book *Mindstorms: Children, Computers and Powerful Ideas*. Back in the 1960s, Papert, who along with Marvin Minsky cofounded artificial intelligence studies at MIT, developed a new programming language called *Logo.* Dismayed by the boring, repetitive nature of computer-based instruction, which consisted mostly of drill-and-practice lessons, Papert believed that Logo could revolutionize the way children learn. Through programming, children would see computers "as instruments to work with and to think with, as the means to carry out projects, the source of concepts to think new ideas."[6]

Children programming with Logo instruct a "turtle" (a triangular cursor) to move around the screen, for example to create a square. By observing the movement of the turtle, children can see whether their program has had the desired effect. If it has not, they must go back and find out where their thinking went wrong in order to debug the program. This is a very basic example, but it illustrates the principle that made Logo such an attractive learning tool: children become aware of how they think in solving particular types of problems.

Logo played a key role in the widespread adoption of computer programming in elementary schools. Claims made for the educational value of Logo persuaded thousands of educators to see the use of computers as a tool for enhancing cognitive development in young children. Whether the use of Logo has actually had this effect is, however, greatly in doubt. Much depends on the way it is used, and although Logo was seen as a creative tool, it was often used as just another medium for drill and practice, an application that would most likely horrify Papert. (Logo is discussed in detail in chapter 3.)

The use of Logo, then, did not mean the end of drill and practice. In fact, by the mid-1980s, concern about declining test scores gave rise to renewed interest in drill-and-practice programs. Computers were seen as an ideal medium for improving test scores because they allowed for individualized instruction, provided immediate feedback to students, and never became impatient with even the most reluctant learner. Software packages such as *Math Blaster* and *Reader Rabbit,* which promised to improve math and language skills, respectively, became big sellers.

In the 1970s, students used drill-and-practice programs as a supplementary activity, often for remedial work. But as schools began to network their computers, they turned to integrated learning systems (ILSs), which provide computer-based lessons designed to be an integral part of the curriculum. Rather than having students spend short periods of time in the computer lab, they would spend hours a day at their own computers in the classroom, each student going through the lessons at his or her own pace. Although ILSs offer other forms of lessons such as word processing and simulations, their emphasis is on drill-and-practice programs in reading, writing, and math, and their success has been measured largely by their effect on standardized test scores. According to a recent report of the President's Committee of Advisors on Science and Technology, 30 percent of schools are still using these systems. The same report also notes that "computers are often employed for teaching isolated basic skills and for playing educational games."[7]

By the late 1980s, with the advent of simple word-processing programs, educators began to view the computer as a practical tool. Keyboarding has become the focus of much school computer use, even though many primary school children do not possess sufficient eye–hand coordination for the task until they are eight or nine years old.

The educational scope of "the computer-as-useful-tool" was given a dramatic boost by the development of CD–ROM technology, which greatly expanded the amount of information that could be delivered in a small package. Because CD–ROMs offered content in a wide range of subject areas, schools were encouraged to integrate their use throughout the curriculum, which meant having computers in every classroom instead of keeping them in the lab or the library. Progressive teachers dropped the "drill-and-kill" software packages in favor of simulation programs and electronic encyclopedias.

As the software became more sophisticated, interest began to focus on the "products" that students could create such as multimedia presentations. Educators thought that the creation of such products, besides demonstrating students' technical expertise, would encourage students to communicate with people all over the world. Students now often create electronic portfolios of their work and are  encouraged to produce their own CD–ROMs.

Since the mid-1990s, the focus has been on the Internet as a universal communications and research tool, which, some claim, will connect students with the real world of global telecommunications. It will also expose students to less desirable aspects of the real world, such as pornography, pedophilia, and hate literature. Thus, internet use confronts educators with a dilemma: on the one hand, the promise of greater freedom; on the other, a need for greater control.

With multimedia and the Internet, we have come a long way from the educational software of the early 1980s, and there is no sign that the pace is slowing. Each time a new technological development arises, schools will be pushed into teaching their students the corresponding skills. Our love affair with rapidly changing technology has left us breathless in our attempts to revise the school curriculum, and the end of the race is nowhere in sight.

The fact that computers have so many uses in schools is a tribute to their power and versatility, but the sheer speed of change is a serious drawback. Computer hardware and software change constantly. State-of-the-art machines become obsolete within a year. Many schools have to make do with old machines of limited usefulness.

Along with changes in the way computers are used, we have seen a continual shift in the meaning of *computer literacy*. In the early days, the term often referred to the ability simply to turn on the machine, load a disk, and get a program up and running. Computer literacy was commonly defined as proficiency in applications such as word processing and electronic spreadsheets. In high schools especially, computer literacy was equated with knowledge about how computers actually worked. Now the term is most likely to be associated with e-mail use and Internet surfing. One thing, however, is clear: there is no consensus as to what computer literacy entails.

This much has been admitted by Andrew Molnar, one-time director of the Office of Computing Activities at the National Science Foundation and the person who created the term in 1972. In a 1991 interview, by then painfully aware that computers had failed to have much positive effect on education, Molnar explained: "We started computer literacy in '72. We coined that phrase. It's sort of ironic. Nobody knows what computer literacy is. Nobody could define it, and nobody knew what it was."[8]

Despite the lack of definition, *computer literacy* became an umbrella term for more concepts than even Molnar and his colleagues could have imagined. It has provided the theme for many conferences and academic journals, and it is often invoked by politicians concerned that their schools are not performing to standard. California began a national trend in 1983 when it required all of its high school students to take computer literacy courses before they could graduate. Many states soon followed California's lead, although none was successful in defining *computer literacy*.

The arguments for computer literacy focus mainly on the wonders of the technology itself and the need for students to get their hands on it, rather than on what educational purpose it might actually serve. The public perceives that computer use is equated with high intelligence, leading-edge technology, and future success. As a result, computers tend to have what has been referred to as a "halo effect," whereby any activity or enterprise in which computers are involved acquires an intellectual luster and significance it would not otherwise have. It is as if computerizing an activity automatically improves it.

Interestingly, although Papert remains perhaps the greatest advocate for the use of computers by children, his definition of computer literacy reflects a need for balance. In Papert's view, "true computer literacy is not just knowing how to make use of computers and computational ideas. It is knowing when it is appropriate to do so."[9] By placing computers at the center of children's lives and encouraging a kind of techno-tunnel vision, we may be undermining our children's ability to make such a judgement.

Electronic media have had a profound impact on our perceptions of the world and our place in it. When communications theorist Marshall McLuhan proclaimed that "the medium is the message," he was telling us that television was not just a new source of information, it changed the nature of the information we received and thus shaped our responses to it. Indeed, it would create types of information that had not been previously considered. In a very real sense, nothing would ever be quite the same again.

A lesson we can draw from McLuhan's writings is that electronic technology can affect us in ways that are not always obvious to us. In the early days of television, no one expected that, eventually, the average American would spend four to six hours watching it every day. Certainly, no one foresaw that television would become *the* forum for election campaigns or that it would bring live coverage of warfare directly into people's living rooms. But it did, and both developments have had a profound effect.

Television has now been around long enough for us to be aware of its influence. Love it or hate it, we have learned to live with it. For many people it is a central focus in their lives. The same thing is now happening with personal computers and the new forms of communication and entertainment they make possible. Computers are beginning to rival television as a way of spending leisure time.

More than 50 percent of U.S. households now own PCs (up from approximately one-third in 1995), and the figure is even higher for families with an annual income in excess of $50,000. The multimedia capabilities are enticing. Many parents have noticed that their children prefer to spend time at their computer rather than watch television, and parents often regard this as a good thing.

Public opinion about television is generally less favorable than it is about computers. This may simply be because television has been around longer. But in the public perception, critical differences exist between television and computers. Television is *watched*; it evokes a passive response. Computers are *used*; they require active intervention. Television is seen as mindless relaxation; it produces couch potatoes. Computers are associated with skills needed for a successful career; they help to develop tomorrow's leading-edge computer scientists.

Yet in one important way computers and television are more similar than is often acknowledged: they both involve people sitting more or less motionless in front of a screen that feeds them a rapid succession of images comprising what Jerry Mander, author of *Four Arguments for the Elimination of Television*, has called "the replacement of experience."[10] Both computers and television present us with an artificial world that undermines our ability to experience the real one. We should bear this in mind when contemplating the possible effects of computer use on young children.

Children, as is now recognized, can be especially vulnerable to the effects of television because they have not built up enough real-life experience against which they can judge what they see on the screen. Moreover, once these effects have taken hold, they tend to exert a permanent influence. In Bill McKibben's evocative phrase, anyone who grew up with television has been "flavored for life."[11]

We seem to have learned little from our experience with television. No one could have predicted its pervasive influence when it was introduced; now we know better. In integrating computers into our classrooms, we should therefore proceed with caution. This is especially important in the case of young children in elementary schools who are most susceptible to the influences of electronic media.

Caution, however, has been in short supply. Governments, encouraged by the prospect of corporate partnerships, have climbed eagerly aboard the bandwagon. By 1998 there were 7.4 million computers in U.S. schools, up from 3.5 million in 1992.[12] In 1992 there was one computer for every nineteen students in U.S. schools; by 1998 the ratio had dropped to one computer for every six students. With the Clinton Administration's pledge to connect every school in the nation to the information highway, we see no sign that the pace of computerization is abating. When President Clinton, Vice President Al Gore, and a host of volunteers strung electrical wire through California classrooms on what was billed as the first "NetDay,"[13] on March 9, 1996, they were signaling the Clinton Administration's commitment to make Internet access a priority. (More than forty states duplicated this initiative later that year.) If Al Gore prevails, every school, library, and hospital in the United States will soon be online.

Government enthusiasm has been more than matched by the media. In an effort to capture more high-tech advertisers, newspapers such as the *Washington Post* and the *Los Angeles Times* have created sections devoted to glowing reports of technology in all aspects of daily life. This advertising blitz has not, until recently, been balanced by critical reporting. Rather, the media have encouraged the widespread perception that mastery of computer technology is a matter of both personal and national survival. "While there is no law saying people must become computer literate, there is a growing social and economic stigma attached to those who refuse to ride the digital rocket into cyberspace," warned one journalist. "While government, education, union, and industry spokespersons may squabble over how we should become a more computer-literate society, they agree we need to become one if we are to compete successfully in the information-based global economy."[14]

Numerous television reports have also painted glowing pictures of the educational potential of computer technology. A recent documentary called *Learn & Live*, funded by the George Lucas Educational Foundation and narrated by Robin Williams, is a good example:

> ...all over the country educators, parents, policy makers, business leaders, and community leaders and students, are all getting together and wrestling with how to reinvent the educational system, to rethink the one room schoolhouse and expand the concept so that it will be responsive to the needs of learners and society. They also recognize that technology can be a powerful tool for change in education just as it's been in the world of business, science, and entertainment.

Whereas success stories are described throughout, there is not a critical note in the whole program.

Advanced technology has become both an icon and a defining characteristic of U.S. society. The preferred solution to problems and challenges is the high-tech solution. Educators are not exempt from this technocentric approach, and they have drawn much of their inspiration from research by the U.S. military.

This is not as surprising as might at first appear. The U.S. military has long been at the forefront of research into applications of technology for the training of military personnel. Douglas Noble points out in his book *The Classroom Arsenal* that U.S. military expenditures on educational technology research far exceed what civilian agencies spend. "Each year, for example, the military spends as much on educational technology research and development as the Department (formerly Office) of Education has spent in a quarter century."[15]

When computer-based education was introduced into schools, much of the military mind-set came with it. Computers were seen as an efficient way for children to learn basic skills, using drill-and-practice programs that still account for a large proportion of school computer use. The military's need for swift information processing and decision-making lies behind the emphasis on using computer programs to develop problem-solving and decision-making skills—skills that are sometimes assessed purely in terms of successful computer use.

Some say that the computer is just a tool that can be used in good and bad ways. But this view ignores the fact that, like any other tool, computers are not neutral in their effect on the people who use them. They create their own conditions for exploiting their use. Because computers are extremely powerful and adaptable tools, they can affect a particularly wide range of human activities. And, as in society as a whole, the willingness to embrace computer technology in schools has consequences that extend well beyond the mere fact of its use. When much of students' learning takes place at a computer screen, many other things change.

In many ways, computer technology is reenacting the revolution brought about by the earlier technology of print, which has itself had profound effects on human societies. Being able to read and write changed the way people could think about things because the written word could be referred to again and again and could communicate long after it was first expressed. Literacy, as has often been pointed out, is not just a matter of acquiring the ability to read and write. Mastering the technology of print brings about a new mentality, a new way of considering things.

Computer technology has a similar effect. When children learn to use a computer, they are not just learning a skill. They are changing the relation between themselves and the world around them. The way in which information is accessed, the manner of its presentation, and the ways in which it can be manipulated all alter children's perceptions of knowing and doing.

Computer use changes perceptions in a radically different way from print, a way that is, in many respects, diametrically opposed to the effects of the older technology. Unlike print, which encourages reflection and a careful consideration of various points of view, computer software urges immediate action. Words and images on-screen invite constant change or substitution—this is, after all, one of the things the computer and the software it runs are designed to do. And the faster you can manipulate what you see on the screen, the more control you appear to have over the technology you are using. Speed and control are emphasized at the expense of thoughtfulness and understanding.

The sheer volume of information available through computer technology encourages this kind of quick-fire response. There is just too much to see, or at least too many possibilities to explore. Thus, a situation emerges in which a high-speed search for information, followed by rapid review, replaces a slower, more deliberate buildup of knowledge and the formation of ideas. Is this type of learning good for the healthy development of young minds?

Overwhelmingly a visual medium, computers deal in images, not actual things. Young children, on the other hand, need to be oriented to the world around them with its sights, sounds, smells, tastes, and textures. Many adults think that something wonderful has happened when their three- or four-year-old succeeds in making a few words appear on a computer screen. But something equally wonderful happens when that child takes pleasure in tracing patterns in the sand, makes a tower out of building blocks (and knocks it down again), or has conversations with a teddy bear. Computers cannot provide these kinds of sensory experiences, nor can they cultivate the emotional and intellectual bonds that develop between children and those who help them learn. Computers cannot match a good teacher's ability to inspire interest and excitement in learning. They cannot speak with passion and commitment about ideas. Although a computer program may post a word or two of praise when a child gives a correct answer, the computer doesn't *care* whether the answer is right or not. It knows when a child has made a mistake, but it is not interested in *why* the mistake has been made.

This technology also does little to create an environment in which children can fully develop their powers of speech. In order to learn language, children need to talk with other people. To do this successfully, they must listen attentively to what is said to them and gauge the effect of what they have said to see whether it matches their intentions. At a certain point, they learn to internalize oral language as a means of working out what their intentions are before expressing them in speech. This internalization of speech, which enables us to "hear" the content of our conscious minds, is the prelude to the ability to engage in rational thought.

Most computer software, which, like television, provides a rapid succession of powerful visual images, discourages just these kinds of mental activities. The constant stream of images that appear on the screen crowd out thoughts and reflections and undermine the ability to concentrate on quieter, more subtle experiences. Electronic technology does not allow breathing space for the mind. Instead, it induces a kind of mental congestion. Television creates intellectual apathy, whereas computer use can easily lead to a compulsive, although increasingly unproductive, persistence. It is easy to stare at a computer screen and play around with commands without doing anything constructive.

Our current obsession with computers reflects the ethos of our increasingly frantic times. The pace of life is faster than ever before, and in the current view, only through more extensive use of computer technology we will be able to keep up. Children are not being spared the effects of the accelerating treadmill we have constructed. In our schools, we appear to be creating an environment that mirrors the fast-paced adult world in which time, productivity, and instant communication are paramount. Yet there is surely an argument to be made that schooling, particularly in the elementary grades, should provide a refuge from the world and allow children time to think and wonder and get to know themselves. This is not just indulgence. Early childhood experiences have a profound and far-reaching effect on later development. Young children are already learning an enormous amount in a relatively short time. To subject them to a barrage of electronic stimuli is like trying to plug too many electrical appliances into a single outlet. Eventually, something has to give.

One significant casualty may well be the ability to develop the full potential of language as a means of regulating thought. In her book *Endangered Minds: Why Our Children Don't Think,* Jane Healy writes:

> I am convinced that a major reason so many students today have difficulty with problem solving, abstract reasoning, and writing coherently is that they have insufficiently developed mechanisms of inner speech.

On the other hand:

> Children who use inner speech effectively can remember information and
> events better. They are better at problem solving because they can "talk
> through" steps, evaluate alternatives, and speculate about possible outcomes.
> They can organize and apply information more effectively and develop
> better strategies when taking notes in class, studying for exams, and even
> understanding and remembering what they read.[17]

In other words, the development of inner speech is directly related to
the ability to think.

Learning how to think is such a basic, yet all-important, ability that
it is easy to forget that it does not occur all by itself. Teaching children
how to think—how to use their inner voices—takes time and concentration on the part of the learners. It will not be any easier if the sound
of this voice is drowned out by wave after wave of electronic noise.
Ironically, the very technology that so many champion as a means of
enhancing students' thinking may be responsible for exactly the opposite result.

It is, of course, possible that entirely new ways of thinking will
emerge, ways that are more in tune with the technological future we
are creating for our children. But this is speculation. The long-term
effects of computer use are still unknown, and whether these effects will
be beneficial remains much in doubt. Meanwhile, it is worthwhile to
look back on similar technological experiments that were conducted in
the past as we listen to the claims that computer technology can really
make a difference.

Computers are not the first technology to enter U.S. classrooms
promising increased productivity and intellectual enrichment. Attempts
to reform or revolutionize the educational system by introducing one
newly minted technology after another have been a recurring theme
over the last 100 years. The fact that none of these technologies has
lived up to its promise has done nothing to dampen the zealousness of
would-be educational reformers.

Earlier in this century, lantern slides, tape recorders, movies, radios,
overhead projectors, reading kits, language laboratories, and televisions

were all touted as promising teacher aids. Enthusiastically embraced by educational reformers, they were soon found to be ineffective by the teachers upon whom they had been foisted. In due course they were relegated to storage closets, dust-gathering footnotes in the history of education.[18]

Radio was first licensed for commercial and educational stations in the 1920s. "The central and dominant aim of education by radio," said reformer Benjamin Darrow:

> is to bring the world to the classroom, to make universally available the services of the finest teachers, the inspiration of the greatest leaders and unfolding world events which through the radio may come as a vibrant and challenging textbook of the air.

As Larry Cuban documents in *Teachers and Machines*, many major North American cities broadcast educational programs for school-children on a host of topics ranging from automobiles to farming to science. Parents dutifully raised funds to buy receivers, and school superintendents pressured teachers to incorporate radio into their teaching. Surveys were conducted to count the number of radio sets and to gauge the number of listeners. Time-and-motion studies were conducted to prove that radio was a more effective learning medium than textbooks. School districts, state departments of education, and universities produced radio shows for classroom use.[19]

In spite of the best efforts of radio enthusiasts at every level of government, radio simply did not take hold in the classroom. In 1943, a six-year study to evaluate broadcasts in schools concluded that "radio has not been accepted as a full-fledged member of the educational family."[20] By the 1950s, research on this technology, along with the initial enthusiasm, had pretty much dried up.

Television was the next technological break-through. Beginning in the early 1950s and continuing throughout the 1960s, television was used experimentally in classrooms. Electricians fished wiring through walls and installed extra fuse boxes, construction workers built production studios, and educators put out clusters of television sets on metal stands.

Convinced of the advantages of television use, the Ford Foundation set aside a substantial amount of money for grants to assist schools in the purchase of this technology.

> Students in today's classrooms can be eyewitnesses to history in the making.... They can see and hear the outstanding scholars of our age. They can have access to the great museums of art, history, and nature. A whole treasure-trove of new and stimulating experiences that were beyond the reach of yesterday's students can be brought into the classroom for today's students."[21]

Despite meticulous and costly planning and design, teachers used the technology sparingly. Standardized achievement tests were administered to compare the difference in quality of learning between televised lessons and conventional instructional methods used by classroom teachers. Results indicated that children did not learn more from the television than they did from their teachers.[22]

Will the current obsession with computer use in schools come to a similarly disillusioned end? When *Time* magazine featured a computer on the cover of the May 3, 1982, edition as the editors' choice for Man of the Year, it also included a special section called "Here Come the Microkids," heralding the start of "the information revolution." The technology needed to accomplish this revolution, however, proved to be too slow, too expensive, and too complicated to operate to make much of an impression on the school system. Now, nearly twenty years later, with the information revolution in full swing, with faster, cheaper, and (supposedly) user-friendly technology, and with billions of dollars already spent on educational hardware and software, we should bear in mind that as far as our schools are concerned, the revolution is far from achieved. Indeed, with computer technology developing so rapidly, it is unlikely that it will ever be wholly achieved.

Nevertheless, millions of parents are intent on preparing their children for electronic education. Parents rush to buy software for their toddlers and sign up preschoolers for computer courses. At a Washington, D.C., conference, sponsored by the Center for Media Education in November 1999, one manufacturer was presenting software for four- to six-month-old babies. Children are exposed to computers before they can write their names, read traffic signs, or tie their own shoelaces. Life for these "silicon kids," as they are so often called, is unfolding in a markedly different way than it did for their parents. The computer is now penetrating all spheres of human life. If current trends continue, computers will be even more influential in shaping children than television. Yet computers may prove to be just as wasteful of childhood as television, and just as harmful to a child's overall development.

The average child in the United States spends an average of twenty-five to thirty hours per week watching television (at least as much time as he or she spends in school). Most parents concede that this is a far from ideal situation: few seriously believe that television sharpens the intellect, stimulates the imagination, or even depicts a realistic view of the world. But many people now work longer hours each week than they did a decade ago; consequently, more children spend time alone at home with television, simply because their parents are not around to supervise them. As home computers become more common, they will increasingly challenge television's status as "the electronic babysitter."

Before the computer craze set in, children who did little but watch television could at least count on spending six or seven hours a day nurtured and supervised by their teacher, who would provide a variety of activities that they were not likely to get otherwise. This served as an antidote to an excess of electronic stimulation at home. But if computers are integrated into classrooms, and students work at computers for several hours per day, this balance could be upset.

Recent trends in education are not encouraging. The time devoted to classroom computer use has *increased* over the years. At the Celebration School in Celebration, Florida, a showcase high-tech school funded by Disney, Apple Computer, and others, students use computers whenever they find them to be the most effective means of completing a task. It is not unusual for grade school children to plug into their machines for two or more hours a day and access their work at home from their family's computers. It is a given that computers benefit children.

Immense effort has gone into integrating computers in the school curriculum. But just because computers *can* be used in schools is not a good enough reason for deciding that they *should* be used. In the absence of any precise educational goals, computerizing classrooms is merely an excuse to use expensive new toys.

These toys will not remain new for very long and the computer skills children learn today may well be irrelevant by the time they enter the workforce. Also uncertain is how, in a broader sense, the world will be working by the time our children are grown. The current preoccupation with computer technology is sustained by a vision of the future that may never materialize. The changes already being wrought by technology are so far-reaching that the next generation may confront completely different challenges. Are we really doing our children a favor by encouraging them to develop a computer-focused mind-set at an early age? This may well close them off from options that might otherwise be open to them. The advance of computer technology, surely one of the great success stories of the late twentieth century, is nonetheless threatening to destroy our sense of balance in the way we define and evaluate our experience of life.

We are witnessing a loss of nerve in the face of the growing influence of computers in our lives: the future, experts tell us, is already here, and we can do nothing to change it. But by doing nothing to change current attitudes, we will allow the most depressing predictions of twenty-first-century life to come true. Moreover, there are compelling reasons why, for the sake of our children, these attitudes must be challenged.

## CHAPTER 2

# White Knight or White Elephant?
# The Real Costs of
# Computerizing Education

> *Try not to be intimidated by people who claim that children*
> *will be left behind or ill prepared for the computer age unless*
> *they are exposed to the computer early on. People who say such*
> *things are invariably trying to sell you something.*
>
> —Aaron Falbel [1]

urely no school in the country projects the future of U.S. education
more optimistically than Florida's Celebration School. Serving
students from kindergarten through grade twelve, the school is part of
the model community of Celebration, designed and built by the Walt
Disney Corporation just a few miles from the gates of Disney's Magic
Kingdom. Celebration manifests what Walt Disney once called his
vision for the future, an "experimental Prototype Community of
Tomorrow." With more than 5,000 residents and growing quickly,
Celebration attracts people from all over the country with its nostalgic
urban design: period homes with mandatory verandas cluster around an
old-fashioned Main Street of shops, restaurants, and a cinema. A tiny
lake at the center of town laps gently against its oak-lined banks. A
4,700-acre "green belt" of undeveloped land insulates the town from
the rest of Florida. Making such a dream into reality is not cheap, of
course: the town's quiet streets, verdant lawns, and charming structures
cost Disney more than $2.5 billion to design and build.

Although most of the town tries to bring the quaint charm of the past to today's residents, its school—perhaps one of the most expensive ever built—brings ideas from the most visionary educators together to implement the best educational practices possible. It is the jewel of the community and the drawing card for most parents, who have uprooted their families from across the nation to share in the promise of a first-rate education for their children.

The Celebration School is a unique public/private venture, which drew its initial funding—more than $45 million in total—from sources as diverse as the Walt Disney Corporation; Apple Computer; Osceola County; Stetson University in nearby DeLand, Florida; and the State of Florida itself, which contributed $15.5 million to cover construction costs.

Celebration School is both thoughtfully conceived and technologically sophisticated. Instead of traditional single-grade classrooms, children are placed in "neighborhoods"—multiage groups designed to provide a supportive social structure and encourage team teaching and collaborative learning. Students learn at their own pace. Teachers do not issue traditional grades, but give written assessments. Included in its staff of seventy teachers are three full-time librarians, three music teachers, three art teachers, and three wellness (health and physical education) teachers. Approximately 1,000 students attend the school; its teacher-student ratio is below 1:14.

The quantity of and extent to which computers are used is a technologist's dream. The school has 1.2 computers for every student and sits at the center of a vast underground web of wiring, which links the school to the Internet as well as to homes and businesses. From any computer on campus, students can access the Media Center (the library), the music area, the art area, the cafeteria—even their own homes. The school is, in the words of Scott Muri, the school's technology specialist, "future proof.... Through our sophisticated hardware, software, and networking, we are ready for whatever technology happens in the next few years."

Celebration School also boasts a technical team that consists of a network specialist, systems engineer, systems administrator, hardware/software specialist, and six technical instructors (who train the school's teachers). The team's salaries and benefits alone cost $500,000 a year.

The county pays for two team members; the private partners—seventeen in all—pay for the rest. In Muri's view, the level of technical support is necessary. "If we didn't have eleven technical people, our technology program wouldn't be nearly as effective," he says.

The corporations that have made this possible have benefited too because they have had the opportunity to showcase their wares at a school that has generated extraordinary media attention. Since the school first opened, two books and hundreds of magazine and newspaper articles have been written about it. Television and radio items have kept both the school and the community in the spotlight. This attention has ensured that the companies that supply the school with high-tech equipment get lots of opportunities to promote their corporate logos. Celebration also houses the adjunct Celebration Teaching Academy, where teachers from all over the county and country come to improve their teaching skills and learn to use the latest educational technology.

Certainly the Celebration School has all the right conditions to make technology work. The program is well-funded, the teachers are well-trained, and the computers are integrated into the curriculum.

This chapter, however, is not the story of the Celebration School. The story of the Celebration School is not the story of how most children are educated in the United States. Celebration is a rare exception: a school with lots of money, teachers, and training. It serves to underscore the reality of most other U.S. schools: the money, staff, and time required to implement computer-based education simply do not exist.

Celebration School is also unique in the security of its corporate support. As the centerpiece of a corporate showcase community, it is not only generously provided for now, but it is also extremely unlikely to see its funding reduced any time soon. Other schools that have received corporate sponsorship (generally for a limited time only and usually from a single source) have not been so lucky—when funding for technology is withdrawn, the effects can be painful. Muri acknowledges that if funding cuts were to be made at his school, the first to go would most likely be the six instructional teachers on the technical team.

The Open Charter School in Los Angeles is a far more typical case—an example of how difficult it is for schools to sustain corporate or government funding for technology programs. From 1987 to 1992 Apple Computer used this elementary school, set in a middle-class section of the city, as a research and development (R&D) site for new educational software. Under the auspices of Apple's Alan Kay, the school undertook what was touted as the most innovative educational project of its kind—the Vivarium project.

The project involved students from kindergarten through fifth grade in the construction of an imaginary sea creature. After researching the behavior and habitats of sea animals, children at the Open Charter School pooled their research with students in San Jose, California, and Erie, Pennsylvania. Kay described the project as teaching children to "put intelligence into the heads of animals." In a number of papers that he wrote at the time, he suggested that the way to interest children in biology and environmental issues was to allow them to design "living things." These early forays into artificial intelligence could, he said, teach children a great deal about animal behavior. The result was the design of a two-dimensional electronic sea creature, which eventually took up residence on the Internet.

The small size (380 students) and status of the Open Charter School made it an ideal choice as an R&D site for Apple. The oldest charter school in Los Angeles, founded in 1977, it is run by a board of directors composed of teachers and parents. The teachers are members of the union, but they are chosen by a committee including the principal, parents, and teachers. This structure allowed the school to make autonomous decisions about its relationship with Apple.

A teacher with eighteen years' experience teaching third, fourth, and fifth grades at the Open Charter School, Betty Jo Allen-Conn was unreservedly enthusiastic when Apple approached the school. She had already tried to educate herself about what computer technology could do for her students: "I knew the twenty-first century was coming," she told me, "and we had a responsibility to make sure the kids were up on it. So I took classes in Logo and word processing."

Although the cost of establishing the project was considerable, Apple spared no expense. Allen-Conn was one of twelve teachers who spent months taking the Apple training courses. Each teacher received a bonus of $12,000 as compensation for lost vacation time. At the beginning of the project Apple flew them to the Exploratorium, a science center in San Francisco, to experience hands-on activities that would be both fun and inspiring because "Apple wanted us to see how easy science is."

The company also paid to hire four extra staff members, an expense amounting to $250,000 for each of the five years of the project. In this way, the school acquired an art teacher, a music teacher, a physical education instructor, and a gardening consultant. The extra classes they provided allowed the regular classroom teachers an extra two to three hours per week of preparation time, during the school day, to upgrade their computing skills and develop lesson plans maximizing computer use.

Apple also donated all the hardware and software. Altogether, 190 computers were available for student use, or one computer for every two students. Apple paid for ongoing technical support, as well as the cost of maintaining and repairing the equipment. The teachers received free computers and printers, which were upgraded twice during the life of the project, to ensure that their technology remained state-of-the-art. Apple finds this model of implementation works well—encouraging teachers to become comfortable with the technology by giving them their own personal computers so they become both adept and enthusiastic about using them in the classroom.

In all, the Vivarium project was a costly one. However, Apple's involvement ensured it was implemented under optimal circumstances —a large corporate donation, ongoing training and technical support, and the support of the energetic Alan Kay.

From the teachers' points of view, the experience was a positive one. They found their training stimulating and entered into their new courses with enthusiasm. The administration was pleased with the results: every child in the school was exposed to leading-edge technology, and parents felt their children were acquiring skills that would prepare them for the job market.

When Apple completed its research in 1992, the school's parent group had to find the money to maintain the equipment. With Apple no longer funding the project, the costs of computer-based learning proved to be much larger than anyone had realized.

When I visited the school in 1996, nine years after the Vivarium project was launched, the room that acted as home base for the project had become a repair shop for computers that had broken down or been abused. One monitor had a burn mark on the screen and looked as though its useful days were at an end. The only sign of life was a teacher using a blackboard to tutor three special education students. The computers, once shining white knights, had become a collection of battered old white elephants.

"Our equipment is no longer state-of-the-art," said Allen-Conn. "It is falling apart, so to speak." The principal, Dr. Grace Arnold, agreed: "Repair is the biggest issue." Most of the computers and printers at the Open Charter School date from the early days of Apple's research effort and keep running thanks only to the constant repair work of the teachers. Before it left the school, Apple provided some final training courses in the repair and maintenance of aging equipment, and it continues to give a discount on replacement parts. Because of the number of teachers who are qualified Apple technicians, the Open Charter School is, in fact, a certified Apple repair center.

After Apple left, each teacher in the six-member team (half the teaching staff) had to spend four hours each week on repairs—twenty-four hours altogether, taken from their after-school time. Allen-Conn conceded that "laboring over computer equipment counting screws, rewiring faulty connections, or cleaning screens" at the end of a long school day was difficult. She called it "a mind-boggling job."

"I don't feel very happy about this," said Arnold. "I would prefer that [the teachers] would be spending their time in curriculum and conceptual development rather than on their hands and knees on labor." Yet she noted that if the teachers did not put in the extra hours, the school could not afford to continue using the technology.

From the time Apple left until 1998, the school's board of directors raised approximately $165,000 per year to pay for the extra teaching help to which they had become accustomed when Apple was paying for it. As Allen-Conn said recently, "This has become increasingly difficult to do and each year what they are able to raise decreases." Each year, $10,000 goes to the technical team—five teachers who spend their own time working to repair and maintain the machines—and $15,000 goes to pay for a part-time technology expert. As well, $10,000 of this money is set aside for replacement parts.

Teachers continued to repair worn-out equipment until the fall of 1998, when the school received a federal technology grant of $310,000, or about $104,000 per year for three years, to buy new hardware, software, and furniture. New computer tables were designed by the school's technology coordinator at a cost of $600 each. Approximately 25 percent of this grant is set aside for staff training. Although this infusion of new technology is only a small fraction of what the Celebration School owns, it is still highly unusual for any school to have teachers with the kind of technical knowledge that the teachers at the Los Angeles Open Charter School possess.

In spite of this boom-and-bust cycle, teachers at the Open Charter School continue to be highly motivated users of technology. "We simply couldn't imagine delivering the curriculum without it," says Allen-Conn. "We train each other and we upgrade our skills at our own expense. Our part-time technology coordinator has taught all of us a lot, especially about the elaborate networking systems."

The experience of the Open Charter School is a more accurate depiction of the realities of creating and maintaining a computer-rich curriculum. Schools that accept technology from a corporation, either as a one-time grant or as part of an ongoing research project, are often short of funds when the corporation withdraws its support and the equipment starts to age. Schools that make computer purchases with a community or government grant frequently run into the same trouble. One of the hardest lessons learned at the Open Charter School was that computer systems need continual maintenance and repair.

When a company in the private sector sets up a new computer system, it allocates 30 percent of the original purchase price annually toward technical support and equipment maintenance. "Sometimes the price tag is even higher," says Skip Dye, vice president of sales and technology for Random House. "Ten to twenty percent of our gross is spent on upgrading technology each year. Training could be as high as one-third to one-half of an employee's salary." Random House is currently undergoing a complete technological upgrade, which necessitates intense employee training. Dye says he has "spent more on their training than they have earned in salary in the past three years," and inflation raises the costs even more.

George Moon is vice president of engineering for MapInfo, a multinational computer software company based in Troy, New York, and a major provider of computer mapping software. A father of two, Moon attended a parent meeting at his children's school to discuss the funding needed to purchase new computers, printers, and up-to-date software. The school was trying to raise $300,000 for this purpose, but Moon was dismayed to learn the committee had budgeted nothing for ongoing technical support, nor had they budgeted for the cost of replacing worn-out equipment, something businesses routinely take into account. "It's not a one-time expense," said Moon. "You have to plan ahead to replace equipment because it goes out of date so quickly." In Moon's experience, businesses replace their computer equipment every two to three years. Schools, however, can rarely undertake the kind of long-range financial planning necessary for such costly purchases because the funding for computer technology often comes from short-term grant allocations.

School boards, administrators, and parents are, in fact, often unaware that the initial cost of software and hardware is just the beginning. One-time grants from state governments, municipalities, or community foundations typically range from $10,000 to $250,000 and cover the cost of purchasing computers, printers, and software. Once the maintenance contract runs out (the industry standard is one year), the school district or parent association must secure additional funds to keep the equipment operating. As with a car, the older the equipment, the more expensive the repair bills. Sometimes it is impossible to repair older machines because replacement parts are no longer available.

New software is designed to be compatible with the latest computer terminals and printers, so the life of the average computer is short. In order to be current, hardware must be upgraded approximately every five years. Yet a large proportion of the computers in North American classrooms are more than five years old. In the 1997–98 academic year, for example, 8 percent of the computers used in elementary and secondary schools in the United States were Apple II models. Only about one-half of classroom computers had multimedia capabilities.[2] This is, of course, no guarantee that they can run the latest software.

The constant need to maintain and upgrade computer hardware

and acquire the latest software is having an enormous impact on school technology expenditures. If school districts are to keep up with developments in computer technology, they must continue spending. In the 1997–98 academic year, schools spent a total of $2.1 billion on computer hardware. Expenditures for 1998–99 are expected to be almost as high at $1.9 billion.[3] Spending on software, although not as high, has been increasing rapidly. School spending on software—everything from CD–ROMs, to spreadsheets and word-processing programs—rose from $670 million in 1995–96 to $822 million in 1997–98. Schools spent an additional $378 million on integrated learning systems, which are comprehensive programs where students work at their own pace on math or language skills.[4]

According to Quality Education Data, a Denver-based research company, spending on educational technology is expected to reach an estimated $6.5 billion in 1998–99, up from $5.7 billion the year before.[5] These figures, however, pale in comparison to the amount that would be spent if plans for universal access to computers in schools are implemented. In 1995, the now-defunct U.S. Office of Technology Assessment estimated the one-time installation costs of having "one personal computer per student desktop, with full, ubiquitous connection to the Internet" at anywhere from $66 billion to $145.5 billion. This does not include the necessary $4.5 billion to $11 billion in annual operating costs, which includes annual training and support for teachers.[6]

The U.S. Department of Education now recommends one computer for every five students. Even this more modest goal is costly. According to the President's Committee of Advisors on Science and Technology, the cost of networked computers (at a 1:5 ratio) in all of the nation's classrooms would cost an initial $47 billion, plus $14 billion to maintain the equipment.[7]

Installation, maintenance, and upgrading costs are not the only concern. If recent trends continue, schools may find just keeping the equipment on site increasingly expensive. Computer theft from schools has become a serious problem, and in some cases, thieves use students to garner inside information. In Sacramento County's San Juan school district which includes 48,000 students, more than $150,000 worth of computers were stolen during the 1995–96 school year. As a result, schools are forced to invest in computer security. In Dade County, Florida, most of the district's computers are "locked in place, at a cost of $100 per machine." To protect a new shipment of computers, the Canterbury Magnet and Elementary School in Arleta, California, spent more than $15,000 to install security bars on the school's windows, "money that would otherwise have been spent on instruction."[8]

Internet access also represents a significant cost, with the majority of the nation's public schools (89 percent by the fall of 1998) logged on. Many public school teachers gain free access by connecting to a university computer center where costs are assumed by a government agency or private funding source. Those who come from small, rural school districts are unlikely to have this option and, therefore, incur large long-distance phone charges. The U.S. Telecommunications Act of 1996 contains "universal service" provisions under which schools and libraries are guaranteed access to telecommunications services at "affordable rates." But the U.S. Telephone Association (USTA) has argued that funding should be limited to providing access only, and that other costs such as teacher training, software, and equipment be paid by the public. In other words, the phone companies should do no more than provide schools with basic telephone services at reasonable rates.[9]

As the USTA recognizes, in addition to affordable access, teachers need the knowledge that will enable them to use the Internet effectively. Clearly, having a lot of expensive computer technology in our schools is pointless if teachers do not know how to use it. Idle computers are a wasted resource. Yet many teachers have little or no experience with computers, and even when they receive training, they still require ongoing support to upgrade their knowledge and skills to be able to keep up with advances in technology. According to some estimates, training costs should surpass the amount spent on the technology itself.

Henry Jay Becker of the University of California at Irvine is an educational researcher who has conducted, over the course of twenty years, a detailed study of the real cost of computerizing schools. He calculates that, for an average-sized school of 800 students, it would cost $1,375 per pupil per year, or $1.1 million per school, to cover only the personnel-related costs for providing a meaningful technology program. This is more than double the corresponding cost of hardware and software, which Becker estimates at $556 per pupil per year. The largest items included in these personnel costs (but almost entirely lacking from school district estimates) are funds for teacher training, greater access to school computers for lesson preparation and other professional tasks, and the creation of smaller classes.[10]

Bob Pearlman is a former director of research in the field of educational technology for the American Federation of Teachers. He believes that greater funds are needed to train teachers in the educational use of computer technology, and he generally supports Becker's estimates. Pearlman believes that more than 50 percent of the technology budget (Becker recommends 70 percent) should be set aside for teacher training, but knows that in reality this is never done. Both Pearlman and Becker agree that, to make this technology meaningful in an educational setting, the costs will be enormous.

As an example of a high-end system, the New Haven Unified School District in California plans to spend $27 million to equip every classroom in its eleven schools with an average of seven computers per classroom. This amount covers items such as $9 million for fiber-optic cabling, $800,000 for computers and printers, $3.1 million for electrical upgrades, $300,000 for video distribution systems, $100,000 for telephone upgrades, $1.2 million for fiber-optic cabling between district headquarters and the school, $1 million for document management systems, and $750,000 for video centers. *This does not, however, cover the cost of teacher training.* To find time for teachers' in-service training, the district got permission to start classes one-and-a-half hours late each Wednesday for the first four months, which meant the additional costs came out of time meant for student instruction.

No one disputes the high costs of ongoing teacher training, yet only fourteen states require a portion of their technology budget to be spent on training. A mere 5 percent (or $266 million for 1998–99) of the total technology budget for U.S. schools is allocated to teacher training.[11]

If teachers do not receive adequate and ongoing training, money spent on computer technology will be wasted. We have seen many instances of equipment being purchased and then being used only by one or two teachers. Very often, in fact, schools buy computers because a few teachers or an administrator become interested in using them. An informal kind of training may then take place in which the "experts" share their knowledge with both students and fellow teachers. However, when these expert users leave the school, technology programs often flounder because those who remain do not have the same enthusiasm or commitment.

Teacher training will not be effective if it is confined to a one-time introductory course. Apple Computer has discovered that teachers need an average of five to six years to change their teaching methods so that they use the computers in a way that benefits students.[12] This may explain why, in a national survey, the Center for Social Organization of Schools, Johns Hopkins University, in Baltimore concluded that only 5 percent of teachers using computer technology in U.S. public schools could be counted as "exemplary" users.[13]

The survey found that teachers who were using the technology wisely—for instance, helping their students produce yearbooks or newspapers, instead of allowing them to use computers for game-playing activities—were those who had received considerable training and who were supported by both their schools and their districts in their use of computer technology. They differed from other computer-using teachers in that they were much more likely to have had a liberal arts background, as opposed to a degree in education. The single most important factor, however, was class size. Teachers with the best record of meaningful use of computer technology had, on average, classes sizes of seventeen students—20 percent smaller than the average class size.

These findings underscore educational research by Becker and others, indicating that class sizes must be kept smaller than average in order for students to derive maximum benefits from the technology. This contradicts the widespread belief that by increasing the number of computers in classrooms, teachers will be able to teach more students. Concurrent with this kind of thinking is the notion that once students are given computers, they will somehow become less dependent upon the classroom teacher for learning. In fact, introducing computers into the classroom, particularly for schools that are connected to the Internet, will make the role of the teacher, and thus adequate teacher training, more essential than ever.

Clearly, school technology costs are not going to go away, nor will they even decline significantly once computer systems are in place. The question then arises: If schools are to accommodate large expenditures on computer technology, what areas of their budgets will be reduced?

The first casualty may be building maintenance. In its 1995 report on school technology, the U.S. Office of Technology Assessment pointed out that

> school districts are facing huge costs just to bring their aging, dilapidated school buildings to where they meet basic standards. The General Accounting Office [GAO] reports that $112 billion is required for the repairs, renovations, and modernization required to restore the nation's 80,000 public schools to good condition and to comply with federal mandates related to accessibility and safety regulations, for major building features such as plumbing and environmental conditions such as ventilation, heating, lighting, or physical security.[14]

In particular, a 1995 study by the GAO found that almost half of U.S. public schools had inadequate electrical wiring for computer and communications technology.[15] More recent GAO figures indicate that 33 percent of schools have at least one building in need of major repairs.[16]

Compounding this problem is the fact that computers require more classroom space than traditional teaching materials. In 1970, an average elementary school provided 62 square feet per student. In 1995, the average space per student was 111 square feet, according to an annual report by *American School and University* magazine. One reason for this change was increased use of technology. In the view of many school planners, "the size of the standard classroom needs to increase another 25 percent to incorporate new technology into everyday instruction."[17]

Even when schools have been designed and built with computers in mind, and have received corporate funding, technology expenditures have a noticeable effect on other areas of their budgets. If schools do not find new money to support the equipment in their classrooms, they will most likely face some hard choices in the future—either scrap their computer programs or cut other areas of the curriculum.

Arts programs and teacher's aide positions are particularly at risk. The Kittridge Street Elementary School in Van Nuys, California, cut its music program in 1996 in order to hire a full-time technology coordinator. Two years later it hired a part-time music teacher. In Mansfield, Massachusetts, administrators eliminated proposed teaching positions in art, music, and physical education, then spent $330,000 on computers. One Virginia school turned its art room into a computer laboratory.[18]

Lowell Monke, a former advanced computer technology coordinator at a school district in Des Moines, says that it is often difficult to figure out what is being lost or cut back when computers enter schools. His school district eliminated 104 school jobs, including teachers and teacher's aide positions, yet obtained $2 million in state funding earmarked for technology. Monke is concerned that this increase in attention to techonology takes "time and attention" away from a teacher's regular duties. In a study written for his school district he said:

> None of the teachers I have discussed this with has doubted the enormity of time spent by staff helping each other keep their computers running. Most suggested that this peer help time is growing rapidly as the complexity of the machines and the activities increases.

A particularly vexing problem is the decline in funding for library materials—books and periodicals. Administrators justify budget cuts to libraries on the grounds that books will soon be dispensed with and that students can get all the information they need from electronic encyclopedias and the Internet. Some also believe that computers will change the roles of teachers and librarians (or, in many cases, teacher-librarians) by enabling children to learn more independently.

Experienced teacher-librarians now have to learn technical skills that are better performed by experienced technicians. In other words, highly trained teachers, especially teacher-librarians, are having their jobs turned into technical occupations. Moreover, teachers who are taking over these technical tasks are less available to students in a real teaching capacity, so students are losing out on time they could be spending with knowledgeable teachers. When teachers spend time dealing with malfunctioning equipment instead of tending to the students' needs, the real costs of using computer technology are very high indeed.

Computer technology has proven so expensive that many schools have had to put a great deal of time and energy into fundraising efforts. The Peakview Elementary School in Aurora, Colorado, for instance, has taken a novel approach to funding its computer program. Like the Open Charter School, Peakview was given new computers from Apple and supplied with technical support for a couple of years. But since the initial acquisition of equipment, Peakview has had to assume the cost of maintaining and replacing the equipment. In order to continue to pay for technical upgrades, the school's administration decided to sponsor computer workshops. Lead by Peakview's technology coordinator, these workshops attract teachers and administrators from all over the United States.

Peakview is a year-round school, where forty-five-day terms are followed by two-week breaks. The workshops are held four times a year, during break time, and cost $285 each for an average of about fifty participants. Virtually all of the money is profit. Apple Computer continues to play a role in the workshops mainly by paying for the cost of the participants' meals, but also by occasionally offering technical expertise. (This is a good deal for Apple. The company stands to benefit from future purchases because all of the instruction is done on its equipment.)

Peakview also makes other accommodations to cover the costs of its technology program. To afford a technology coordinator and a part-time assistant, it increased class sizes in every grade. In doing so, the school was able to eliminate one regular classroom teacher. The lower grades average about twenty-five students per class (fewer in the kindergarten), and the fourth, fifth, and sixth grades average about thirty students. Additionally, the school's art teacher has had to change her method of instruction because her class sizes have grown so much that large group projects (such as creating a mural of a New York City street or an installation of a life-size humpback whale) have become much more difficult.

Peakview's unique solution to the problem of funding computer technology is not available to most schools. Schools that decide to go the high-tech route clearly will have to turn increasingly to corporate sponsorship and special fundraising activities.

Not surprisingly, therefore, corporate donations, of both expertise and equipment, have reached unprecedented levels. This will most likely continue because corporations can usually write off such donations. When Steven Jobs was chairman of Apple Computer, he, among others, managed to lobby the California legislature into giving a 25 percent tax credit on corporate donations to schools. What amounted to tax savings for Apple was also a form of advertising because it gave Apple an opportunity to capitalize on the school market, thereby ensuring customer loyalty. Correspondingly, the fact that the company was saving on its taxes meant less money for the state; this at a time when spending on education in California was at its lowest point in more than a decade.

Partnerships with the corporate sector, although providing fiscally strapped schools with free or subsidized technology and a certain amount of technical support, have given teachers' unions and school districts additional headaches. Corporations donate equipment and expertise to schools to increase the profile of their companies while building customer loyalty for their products. In the quest to perfect new software, developers also benefit from observing children and how they use the software. This knowledge may be employed in a variety of ways, from debugging programs, to assessing the degree of user friendliness, to observing new uses of the software. Whereas this may benefit the corporation conducting the research, researchers are not at all clear that the students or their teachers are engaged in meaningful activities. Although the cost does not appear on a balance sheet, time spent in pursuit of activities of dubious educational value is a high price to pay for the introduction of computer technology in the elementary school years.

Plans are well under way not only to connect U.S. schools to the Internet, but also to connect classrooms around the globe. One U.S. reporter has likened the cost to the creation of another Pentagon with ultimately billions and billions of dollars being spent to wire the country. But calculating the full cost of this technology is difficult. The expense of training teachers, acquiring and upgrading systems, and the lost tax base due to corporate write-offs is only part of the equation. For a full reckoning, the cost of computer technology must also be measured in terms of the other kinds of learning it displaces. If access to libraries and printed materials is limited, if class size increases, if music and art programs are canceled or reduced in order to pay for this technology, then we must begin to question what we are losing.

The first attempt to computerize classrooms in the 1970s is considered to have been largely a failure for several reasons, one of the chief being that so little attention was paid to teacher training. The same error is in danger of being repeated. "There is a consensus," writes U.S. education activist Douglas Noble, "that except for a few futuristic demonstration projects, all of this money and hardware has had an insignificant effect on educational practice in the nation's schools."[19]

Apple Computer concurs with these findings. As early as September 1992, an article in *Macworld* described the reality of computer use in schools:

> Antiquated computers; unused computers; computers used for games and not for teaching; schools and teachers unprepared to use computers that they own; mismanaged or misdirected policies; and unknown hundreds of millions of dollars spent over the last decade for little return.[20]

Even if we could afford to computerize every classroom, we have little reason to believe that this would be money well spent. Having put more computers in schools than "anyone else on the planet," Steven Jobs has changed his thinking on this issue:

> I've had to come to the inevitable conclusion that the problem is not one that technology can hope to solve. What's wrong with education cannot be fixed with technology. No amount of technology will make a dent.[21]

If our aim is to ensure our children get the best education possible, we must first ask what kinds of experiences will most benefit children before we look to technology to provide "quick fix" solutions.

# CHAPTER **3**

# The Disembodied Brain

*I lay it down as an educational axiom that in teaching you will come to grief as soon as you forget that your pupils have bodies.*

—Alfred North Whitehead[1]

One morning while visiting an elementary school, I overheard the sweet, piping voices of a children's choir. Entering the gymnasium, I listened while the six- and seven-year-olds sang their warm-up exercises, followed by a spirited song in two-part harmony. When they finished singing, the music teacher asked them if they had memorized the lyrics to a new piece of music. "Have you put the words into your computer?" she asked twice, tapping the side of her head for emphasis.

Using the brain-as-computer metaphor in everyday speech may not, in itself, be a matter for serious concern, but it can be seen as a symptom of a more troubling tendency—to equate intellectual ability with mastery of technical skills. One of the most seductive arguments for the early introduction of computers into the lives of children is the claim that this technology will sharpen children's minds and accelerate their intellectual development. Many parents believe that computers will make children more effective thinkers and problem-solvers at an earlier age.

Some scientists think of the brain as a computer and liken the mind to the program it runs on.[2] We are not surprised, therefore, that some teachers and parents have begun to view children's minds as programmable machines. Today, the image of brain as computer surfaces commonly in everyday speech, in schools as much as anywhere else. Skills involving computers are admired especially because computers are seen as *the* leading-edge technology. Intelligence is, therefore, seen as a kind of technical mimicry in which the brain works in sync with the step-by-step procedures of the machine, while human memory becomes just another data bank.

This glorification of technical reasoning—the emphasis on the ability to understand technical functions—has eroded a more expansive view of what it means to be educated. It has also begun to diminish our understanding of how children learn. A liberal arts education, for instance, consists of far more than the acquisition of information and skills. The word education derives from the Latin educare, which means *to lead out*. Socrates believed that the role of a teacher was to draw out of a pupil the awareness, insight, and knowledge that would dispel ignorance and lead to clarity of thought. In other words, education entails the development of a certain frame of mind, one that includes the idea of meditative thinking based upon self-knowledge and careful observation of the world. This is very different from molding young minds to work like machines.

As mentioned, the idea of using computers to teach children to become better thinkers originated with Seymour Papert. Papert believed that the computer would "blow up the school," revolutionize education, and reshape the minds of children. His programming language designed especially for children was to provide the spark for this revolution. Influenced by the Swiss psychologist and philosopher Jean Piaget, with whom he studied, Papert claimed to have combined Piaget's complex theories of child development with his own work in the field of artificial intelligence. This apparent fusion led to the creation of Logo, which Papert hoped would systematize the use of computers in learning, beginning in kindergarten, if not earlier.

Papert is not alone in his assertion that the models or tools a child is given will ultimately shape how and what that child can learn. He belongs to a long line of behavioral theorists, from B. F. Skinner to the more recent, and more extreme, Glenn Doman of the Better Baby Institute in Philadelphia. (Doman has persuaded generations of parents to shine bright lights into the eyes of newborns, dangle geometric shapes over babies' cribs, and teach two-year-olds to read using scarlet-colored flashcards—the idea being that each of these techniques will accelerate cognitive development.) What differentiates Papert from Doman and others is his overwhelming reliance on a single technology.

Papert's faith in the computer as a learning tool is linked to his fascination with gearboxes when very young.

> Before I was two years old I had developed an intense involvement with automobiles. The names of car parts made up a very substantial portion of my vocabulary: I was particularly proud of knowing about the parts of the transmission system, the gearbox, and most especially the differential. It was, of course, many years before I understood how gears work; but once I did, playing with gears became a favorite pastime.[3]

Mathematical ideas entered Papert's life through his early experience of playing with gears. Gears proved an effective learning tool for several reasons. They were part of the natural "landscape" around him, objects that he could discover on his own. They were also part of the adult world to which he wanted to belong and thus a means of relating to adults. (Many children today are, of course, drawn to computers for the same reasons—because they see their parents using them.) In addition, he could use his knowledge of body movement to think about the way gears worked, and in so doing come to grips with the mathematics involved. To Papert, the differential acted as a launch pad for abstract thought and was transformed into what Papert called an "object-to-think-with."

For Papert, this was a learning tool of prime importance. Gears, however, have a specialized appeal. Few children are likely to derive significant mathematical insights from playing with the innards of an automobile. Papert had to wait until he discovered what seemed to be the ultimate, universal "object-to-think-with": the computer. Papert's thesis, then, as he states succinctly, is: "What the gears cannot do the computer might."[4]

And what might learning to use computers do for children? Nothing less, in Papert's view, than change the way they learn everything else. Many people have interpreted this to mean that the computer can be used to teach absolutely anything.

Clearly, Papert became as fascinated with computers as an adult as he was with gears when a child. Describing his work at MIT, he says that he was "playing like a child and experiencing a volcanic explosion of creativity." If this could happen to him, he wondered, "Why couldn't the computer give a child the same kind of experience? Why couldn't a child play like me?"[5] Papert was so enthusiastic about the computer's potential to educate children that he dubbed it "The Children's Machine" (which is also the title of his second book).

Papert based his approach to learning on the way in which a child learns to talk. Speech is part of the child's natural landscape, and children learn to talk "naturally" as they communicate with their parents and other family members. Make computers a part of the child's natural environment, Papert argued, and the child will seize the opportunities they offer to explore and learn. Papert believed that such spontaneous learning would make much formal education unnecessary.[6]

Infectious as Papert's enthusiasm may be, one must ask whether his emphasis on computer-based learning is an appropriate response to the needs of the vast majority of students. Dangers arise when one bases child development and educational theories on the experiences of a gifted or exceptional child, as Papert evidently was, particularly if that child has a rather unusual fixation. Gifted children often have difficulty functioning in a regular classroom because they learn more quickly, in markedly different ways, and often with less instruction than other children. Logo was intended as a universal gateway to a new form of learning, but in reality, it has created several serious roadblocks.

Decades of research into the effectiveness of Logo have shown that, for the majority of children, the process of learning how to program is far from easy. The evidence from conferences, reports, and literally hundreds of research studies also shows that Logo does not seem to enhance children's thinking and problem-solving skills. For many children, using Logo is a bewildering experience.

Papert has always favored discovery learning, where students are

largely free to experiment with Logo on their own. The problem is that
this style of learning encourages a trial-and-error approach, which
makes it difficult for children to develop an understanding of the programming language. Although this approach may eventually give students a knowledge of various commands, they are unlikely to develop
sufficient competence in the program to engage in the kind of learning Papert envisioned.

In order to create even the simplest geometric shapes on the screen,
for instance, children must first learn to conceptualize movement in
terms of direction and distance, and to do so from the turtle's (a triangular cursor) point of view rather than their own. Only then will they
be able to work out the appropriate numerical codes to enter.
Producing a square on the screen, for instance, requires that children
learn the following sequence of commands: "FORWARD 100, RIGHT
90, FORWARD 100, RIGHT 90, FORWARD 100, RIGHT 90, FOR-
WARD 100" (with a final "RIGHT 90" to have the turtle facing the
same way as when it started). If the turtle starts at the lower left-hand
side of the screen and is pointing upward, the first "FORWARD 100"
will create a line that goes from the bottom to the top of the screen;
"RIGHT 90" will turn the turtle 90° to the right; the next "FOR-
WARD 100" will create a line at a right angle to the first, going from
left to right across the top of the screen; and so on. "FORWARD 100,"
which to a child might indicate movement in one direction only, in fact
moves the turtle both up and down, and left and right; similarly,
"RIGHT 90" turns the turtle left as well as right, although from its own
perspective, the turtle in fact makes a right turn each time. Many young
children find the relation between these commands and the resulting
actions confusing. This is because they are still trying to comprehend
the concepts of left and right, up and down as they experience them
from their own point of view. Yet to be able to use Logo, children must
be able to transfer these concepts to an object whose sense of direction
differs from their own.

Children are not expected to be able to use mathematical language
to describe geometric concepts until the fifth grade. Most schools do
not expect children to understand key concepts in transformational
geometry using concrete materials and drawings until they are about

ten years old.[7] If children do not understand the concepts involved, they will find working with Logo difficult and frustrating, as was the case in a year-long study of second graders in Ontario. Leaving students to work on their own simply slowed them down to the point where they became bored. Feeling incompetent, these children soon gave up trying to solve particular problems and played around aimlessly, waiting for their turn at the computer to be over. Although the children were approximately the same age, they varied considerably in ability, which made it difficult for the teacher to provide appropriate support to the class as a whole.[8]

Researchers at the University of Stirling in Scotland who had been working with older children between ages of nine and eleven drew similar conclusions. Teachers found that allowing children to navigate what they termed "this web of complexity" on their own was simply not feasible. Allowing children to construct their own problems and solve them by testing hypotheses was a desirable goal, but in this case, it was outweighed by the "real difficulties" that arose.[9]

Working with Logo places enormous demands on teachers' time, and this fact alone makes it difficult to use. Without continual guidance and assistance, children are likely to approach Logo in a haphazard way that will do little to enhance their development. Logo may, in theory, provide opportunities for them to think about how to solve problems, but in practice, we have no guarantee that children will not use the turtle simply to fool around or play games. Many children do not understand how a computer works and fail to grasp the point of the exercise. Two Manhattan teachers who set out to use Logo with their fourth-, fifth-, and sixth-grade students discovered that the children did not have any realistic idea of what they could do with the program and could not figure out the steps involved in solving problems.[10]

On the other hand, although children appear to learn Logo more readily with a teacher to guide them each step of the way, a more structured approach can lead to a narrow focus on Logo as a programming language rather than a means of developing cognitive skills. (This is, in fact, what happened with the Manhattan teachers mentioned above.[11]) There is a kind of catch-22 at work here. Logo's desired effects require a certain competence in programming, but an emphasis on programming tends to displace the discovery learning through which these effects are to be achieved.

Teaching children to think logically or procedurally may prove more complex and elusive than first thought by proponents of Logo. As Theodore Roszak, author of *The Cult of Information*, points out, "students have to be lured into it cleverly and then work at it with great persistence." Yet all the persistence in the world may yield few results if the child is unwilling or unable to absorb this kind of thinking.

> Has it ever occurred to Logo educators that there may be a reason for the seeming strain of the exercise? It may be because the mind does not always and spontaneously solve problems in that way, especially the young and growing mind. Children may be much more absorbed at feeling their way through the major contours of mental life.... Envisioning things as meaningful wholes, choosing among them: this may be the first order of intellectual business for children. Careful, logical plotting of procedures may be premature for them, and so a distraction."[12]

In fact, researchers have found no consistent evidence that children learn to think in a logical or sequential way and develop problem-solving skills as a result of programming in Logo, or that they can then apply these skills in other situations. Problem-solving skills can be taught, but learning skills in one context does not necessarily mean children will be able to transfer them to another subject or situation, especially an unfamiliar one. Yet without the transfer of problem-solving skills, where is the intellectual boost that Logo was designed to give?

Basically, the transfer of skills can occur in two ways.[13] One occurs when a skill is practiced in a variety of situations to the point that it becomes completely automatic, such as learning to ride a bicycle. One simply transfers the skill to similar situations without having to think about it. The other type of transfer involves a conscious awareness that skills learned in one context can usefully be applied in another. This implies, of course, that we understand what we are doing. We make a deliberate rather than an automatic response. Children who learn to read music in order to play the piano can easily transfer the concepts of musical notation to learning to play the flute or reading choral music.

Mathematics, which requires an understanding of numerical patterns, is another good example. Children may to learn to add, subtract, multiply, and divide using blocks, shells, beads, or their fingers and toes. Once these patterns are understood and memorized, they can be applied in various other contexts such as counting change at the corner store or measuring correctly when baking. Transferring the concepts Logo is designed to teach would mean that children would be able to describe in words, or reproduce by hand, what was meant by a rectangle, triangle, or circle.

Is either form of transfer likely to occur with problem-solving skills learned through programming in elementary schools? Most of the evidence points to the answer "no." In order to develop the necessary knowledge and skills, students would have to spend far more time programming than most schools would allocate and would need considerable guidance from teachers who possess good understanding of programming.

We may have a better case for arguing that if children derive any real benefit from programming, that benefit comes from the kind of cooperative effort involved when several children share a computer. A number of studies have noted that children working together at a computer tend to socialize more and ask each other questions more often than when working at more traditional classroom activities (although collaboration can often lead to some degree of conflict because only one child at a time can control the keyboard). Some researchers have suggested that this kind of interaction among children is as important as anything that happens between the children and the computers.[14] But this raises the question of whether other activities could encourage socializing and questioning without the involvement of a computer.

Meanwhile, Logo and its spin-offs continue to be used widely in schools, and few teachers are entirely clear why they are using these programs or indeed what they can expect their students to accomplish. Observing a group of eight- and nine-year-olds working with Logo in a San Francisco classroom, I saw how painstaking it was for the children to key in the correct commands in order to direct the computer to copy various geometric shapes that were etched on transparencies and affixed to their computer screens. The forty-five-minute exercise seemed both laborious and tedious.

"Is it part of their geometry class?" I asked their teacher.

"No."

"Part of their math class, then?"

"No," she responded. "It teaches them to think procedurally."

"What skills do they take away from this?"

"Studies have shown," she informed me, "that the skills are not transferable."

Even if students are able to exploit the creative potential of Logo, it remains questionable whether Logo or programs like it actually promote cognitive development. Such programs may simply presuppose a level of mental development at least as high as that which they claim to encourage. As child psychologist David Elkind suggests,

> a child who really understands programming is at a sufficiently high level of mental development that learning programming is not really going to promote additional mental development.[15]

Educators have suggested, for example, that children will not really benefit from using Logo until they are about twelve years old, the age at which they develop the ability to deal with abstract concepts.[16] This ability apparently precedes the beneficial use of Logo rather than the other way around.

Piaget referred to the early stage of childhood as the "concrete" or "operational" stage of development. "Concrete" thinking is well developed by the time the child is six or seven years old. Up to this age and for some years after, children learn a great deal by using their bodies to manipulate objects in the world around them. This is a time when children learn to count using blocks, marbles, or their fingers. What Piaget called "formal" thinking usually develops around twelve years of age, although many children are well on their way to it several years before. This is a period when children begin to engage in abstract or symbolic thinking, and it marks the transition to adult modes of thought.

Here, Papert departs significantly from Piagetian psychology. Piaget and others assume a slow continuous growth with certain spurts that, in the normal course of events, occur at key stages of development. This natural pattern of development should be allowed to unfold at its own pace. It follows that certain types of learning are appropriate for children of various ages. Papert, on the other hand, believes that computers can accelerate the process of cognitive development by shifting the boundary between concrete and formal, and allowing children to make the transition to adult thinking at a much earlier age than was previously considered possible.[17]

This faster, smarter philosophy lies at the heart of computer-based learning. Its aim is to catapult children into the adult world as quickly as possible. Through the wonders of computer technology, young minds will be able to leapfrog over the tedious obstacles of childhood learning to become full members of the cyber culture their elders are so eagerly embracing. Far from being "the children's machine," the computer is very much part of an adult agenda.

This approach to learning ignores both the fact that children have bodies, and the nature of the relationship between their physical and cognitive development. Using a computer precludes the use of the full range of sensorimotor skills and inhibits a child's physical exploration of his or her environment. Advocates of computer use by young children overlook the consequences of such a sedentary form of learning, which relies almost entirely on a single (that is, visual) sense.

At the moment, we can only speculate what these consequences might be in terms of children's cognitive development. Our understanding of cognitive processes remains very rudimentary and, in many instances, highly conjectural. The little we know about the brain is dwarfed by the amount we do not know. What we do know is that sensory stimulation and physical development are critical to the cognitive development of children, and that this relationship exists from the moment of birth. Infants first bond with their mothers through their sense of smell. Almost immediately after an infant smells his or her mother's body for the first time, networks begin to form in the baby's brain.[18] Moreover, there are certain critical stages or windows of opportunity for cognitive development that, if missed, cannot be recovered later. An infant who is placed on the mother's stomach within minutes after birth will learn to crawl towards the nipple; an infant who is removed from the mother, even for a short time, will not learn to do so. The delicate relationship between mother and child can be disturbed in ways that are not fully understood.

The bonding that occurs between mother and child has profound implications for the child's physical and cognitive development. Babies, especially those born prematurely, grow faster and are healthier when they are held and cuddled. Touching babies activates their sensory systems, and they become more alert and attuned to the world. Securely bonded, well-fed children are naturally more able to learn from their surroundings. This helps to explain why a long-term study of more than 1,300 children found that the quality of child care has a significant effect on school readiness and language skills. Results of a National Institute for Child Health and Development study showed that children in high-quality child care scored higher in language ability and school readiness than children in low-quality care. High-quality settings were those where teachers or parents "had more positive physical contact with children, and were responsive to the children when they spoke."[19] Emotional stimulation, touching and talking to children, is an important part of any child's social development. Researchers who observed children on playgrounds in the United States and France reported that the American parents talked to and touched their children less than the French parents. Researchers also found children in the United States to be more aggressive toward both their parents and their peers, leading researchers to conclude that the *lack* of touching and eye contact plays a role in developing aggressive behavior.[20]

Emotional contact plays a critical role in human learning. Strong emotional experiences—a kind word or an enthusiastic response from a teacher or parent—strengthen the memory of what is being learned. As a recent article in *Educational Leadership* noted,

> when we are able to add emotional input into learning experiences to make them more meaningful and exciting, the brain deems the information more important and retention is increased.[21]

This is why teachers in Waldorf schools stay with their students for six years—because they believe that the emotional ties between teacher and student are critical to a child's success in school. Many teachers in the public school system have also noted that keeping students for two or three years enhances the learning experience for the teacher, as well.

As infants grow into toddlers, children's cognitive and physical development remain inextricably linked. Maria Montessori noted that observations of children all over the world confirm that a child's mind develops as a result of physical movement. Language development increases alongside the child's use of those muscles that are needed to form sounds and words. "Movement helps the development of mind," she wrote,

> and this finds renewed expression in further movement and activity. It follows that we are dealing with a cycle, because mind and movement are parts of the same entity. The senses also take part, and the child who has less opportunity for sensorial activity remains at a lower mental level.[22]

Continued observation of children has deepened our understanding of these intricate links. The action of finger pointing, which is unique to human babies, has recently been closely correlated with language acquisition. Babies who start to point early in life acquire words more readily than babies who do not point. Some babies may begin to speak before they learn to point, but learning to point accelerates the process of language acquisition by drawing objects to the attention of adults who can then name the objects. Pointing thus initiates conversation between adult and child, which is of crucial importance in the development of the child's oral language. One baby can also learn to point by watching another do so. The fact that babies point at things they want to have identified for them suggests a strong connection in the nervous system between those areas of the brain that control pointing and those involved in speech. The physical coordination necessary to see, hear, and point seems to stimulate the mind.[23]

The most critical structural organization of the brain takes place during infancy and childhood, up to the age of about twelve. This is when the brain is learning most actively from its environment. It shapes itself according to the sensations it experiences and can reorganize itself extremely quickly in response to changes in stimulation and environment. The first three years are especially important because that is when the foundations for thinking, language, vision, and emotional security are established. But the windows of opportunity that permit information to reach the brain and cause changes in its structure are open for only brief periods of time at various stages of a child's development. When these windows close, the brain loses much of its ability to re-mold itself. Its basic structure has now been determined.[24]

Therefore, certain kinds of sensory experiences must occur during the right period of development if the brain is to take advantage of them. We know that it is much easier to learn music or a foreign language as a young child than as an adult. On the other hand, if deprived of the right kind of stimulation, some neural pathways in the brain will simply die and, once gone, will not regenerate. For example, visual stimulation at birth is vitally important because without it, the brain cells designed to interpret vision will either wither away or be diverted to other tasks. If this happens, eyes that are perfectly healthy will never be able to see. For this reason, infants born with cataracts have them removed as quickly as possible after birth because delaying surgery could leave them permanently blind. As well, children who have amblyopia (lazy eye) must wear patches over their strong eyes to allow the weak ones to develop the appropriate neural connections in the brain. Without adequate sensory stimulation, the brain will shut off vision to the poor eye.

Children in elementary schools who spend hours a day on the computer may face similar, if less extreme, risks because they may be losing out on essential sensory experiences. If the brain needs to be activated by using the whole body, what centers in the brain are undernourished because of a lack of tactile or sensorimotor stimulation? Computer programs may be mentally stimulating in some respects, but they are lacking in terms of overall sensory experience. Placing a child in front of a computer is more physically restricting than placing a child at a desk and expecting him or her to stay there. Unlike with reading or looking at the blackboard, the eye's focal range is fixed at one distance for long periods of time. (This is discussed in chapter 9.)

The risks are all the more real when children begin using computers at a very young age. Software aimed at toddlers is a growing market, as I discovered when I attended a conference in Washington sponsored by the Center for Media Education and the University of Texas at Austin, College of Communications. The conference was called "Ensuring a Quality Children's Media Culture in the Digital Age: Setting a Research Agenda." But software developers, who were out in full force with their latest electronic offerings, appeared to have given little thought to the effect of their products on children and seemed unconcerned by the lack of research in the area. One developer even spoke excitedly about producing a reading program for three- to six-month-old babies. One child advocate was clearly taken aback at the thought of such a program. "How is this used?" she inquired incredulously. The software developer explained that parents would hold the baby on their lap in front of the computer screen. The baby would face the screen, which would display a series of colorful letters. "What will the baby get from this?" the child advocate asked with mounting disbelief. "They will learn to track," replied the developer. She meant, we presumed, that babies would follow the letters with their eyes. Although academics try to push for more research, those who make and market software are not waiting to find out whether their products are useful or perhaps even harmful.

Clearly, as these programs become available, parents are seduced into buying them by the promise that they will accelerate their child's learning. Speed, however, is not always best where children are concerned. Karl Pribram is a noted brain researcher at the University of Virginia. "People think they are doing their child a favor by getting them to learn earlier, to walk, talk, read, et cetera," he told me.

> But some skills need to be developed slowly. The speed of learning is different for different organisms. Lower organisms, like cats and rats learn faster than humans, but their repertoire is limited. [For humans] it is the level of complexity which is important.

Pribram also believes that visual art, hands-on science, music, and languages should be integral to the elementary school curriculum.

We may one day discover that accelerating the way children learn is a mistake. One teacher explained to me that she taught her first of three children to read before she began kindergarten. "I would never do this again. She is the only one of my children who now doesn't like to read." This teacher believes that her daughter's aversion to reading in an otherwise bookish household came about because she pushed her daughter too hard at too early an age.

To justify computer use at such an early age, researchers argue that very young children can learn to operate simple programs. Children two and three years old can, for example, use a computer simulation to sort objects into categories with no more difficulty than using real-world objects.[25] But it is by no means certain that working with a computer program offers any *additional* benefits compared with activities involving real-world materials; on the contrary, this method may well have significant drawbacks.

Early childhood educators have long recognized that the younger the child, the more he or she requires a range of physically diverse, "hands-on" activities. Using computers during their preschool years, which many of them do, deprives children of more stimulating kinds of learning. In their book *Engaging Children's Minds*, Lilian Katz and Sylvia Chard argue that "just because children *can* do something when they are young does not mean that they *should* do it." Certain activities, for example, may be within a child's capability but may have an adverse long-term effect if engaged in frequently. [26]

The narrow sensory range of computer-based learning should be a concern, especially in terms of its cumulative, long-term effects. Far from opening up a world of learning, as is often claimed, computers tend to restrict the arena in which children's learning takes place, emphasizing the development of abstract skills at the expense of concrete modes of learning. But the brain is, after all, part of our bodies, and the mind receives information through all our senses. Some children who do not learn to read easily, for instance, may not be strong visual learners and may learn sound–word correlations more readily when they paint the words, hear them spoken, or practice writing in sand. In an experiment in California, researchers discovered that young children become better spellers if they first say each word and letter before they spell it, and then repeat each letter as they write it. Educators found this method, called "simultaneous oral spelling," to be a better method of teaching spelling to first-grade children than simply typing letters onto a computer screen. The *combination* of seeing, hearing, and writing the words by hand seems to make children learn and remember the correct spellings.[27]

Physical forms of learning are especially important for young children who are still discovering much of the world about them through bodily contact. We find an interesting parallel here with other animal species. As John A. Livingston described in his book *The Rogue Primate*, domesticated animals such as chickens or cattle have greatly diminished sensory capabilities compared with their wild counterparts. In the domesticated animal,

> scent, hearing, vision and tactility are in varying degrees crippled. From the outset of its life the animal is poor at processing even the meager sensory information available in its simple, monotonous environment.

Similarly, children today are growing up with less potential to develop sensory acuity because of the monotony of their environments. Watching television, playing with computers, and spending extended amounts of time indoors all contribute to a lack of sensorimotor stimulation. As with domesticated animals, children do not experience the full potential of their physical selves.[28]

One critic of Logo has described its learning environment as having

> no smells or tastes, no wind or birdsong (unless the computer is programmed to produce electronic tweets), no connection with soil, water, sunlight, warmth, no real ecology (although primitive interactions with a computerized caterpillar might be arranged).[29]

It is "almost autistic" in the enclosed relationship it develops between the child and what appears on the screen, and offers far less variety of stimulation than children's playground games. The comparison with play is instructive. As well as helping to develop body coordination through physical movement, many children's games demand a high degree of visual and auditory concentration, qualities that are invaluable in the classroom, where academic failure is often associated with an inability to pay attention. They also help children discover what is and is not possible in terms of their physical capabilities and their interactions with others. Learning through direct physical experience cannot be reproduced on a computer screen.

Early childhood educators such as Maria Montessori were instrumental in changing the monotonous classroom environments in which young children were expected to learn. Thanks to her research, classrooms lost their spartan feel: wooden desks and chairs were replaced with cushions and carpets for reading corners; water tables, building blocks, dress-up corners, fish tanks, and window boxes with plants became standard features in elementary schools. In many respects, placing children in front of computer screens returns them to sensory monotony.

Papert argued that computers enable children "to carry out projects of greater complexity than is usually possible in the physical world." Children often imagine things they would like to make or do, but when they try to put their ideas into practice, they are frustrated by "the unintelligible limitations of matter and people." With a computer program, these limitations can be safely encountered. As a result, "children are able to acquire a feel for complexity."[30] Complexity, however, is not confined to computer activities. "Matter" and "people" offer not only the sensorimotor challenges that are so important to children, but also the rich social and emotional interactions that are not part of life on the screen.

Graphics programs, for example, enable children to produce more sophisticated-looking pictures than they can with paint or crayons, but the programs deny children the spontaneous, tactile experience that is essential to art. Computer graphics offer none of the concrete experience that comes from mixing your own paints or watching yellow and blue blend into green. Precision is gained at the expense of subtlety and spontaneity. On screen, children need not deal with messy imperfections or worry about spoiling what they have already done. If they make a mistake, they have only to choose "undo" or "cancel" and the error will disappear, as the preschool children in one study soon discovered.[31]

But in art, as in many other activities, "mistakes" often create opportunities for learning. This is rarely true of most software programs.

The fact that computers enable children to present their work in a professional format is not necessarily an advantage. What they may lose is their individual creativity. In many ways, a flawless computer printout depersonalizes children's work. Some judge work as more successful if it has a computer-generated neatness, like those who prefer a word-processed page to the imperfections of their students' handwriting. The heart of artistic expression, however, lies in originality. Computer-generated material gives less scope for personal creativity because a child must work within the constraints of the program. The result, says artist Konrad Bonk, is depersonalized art "unsoiled by the human hand."

Some schools do emphasize the importance of original creative work. Waldorf schools, which are now the fastest growing educational movement in the United States, provide tremendous encouragement for individual creativity. For instance, the main lesson books produced by children in a Waldorf school are remarkable because they are so personal. Each book reflects the style of its creator and no two are ever alike. Such highly original books are, in a very real sense, the handiwork of the students; one can see the amount of work, both physical and mental, that has gone into making them. Children are encouraged to stay connected to and take ownership of their work and their learning. And, like adults, children are more highly motivated when they feel an emotional and physical connection to what they do.  At Waldorf schools, computers are eschewed until high school to give a child as much scope for the creative arts as possible. Nurturing a rich imaginative life in childhood, Waldorf educators say, is the key to a successful social, emotional, and intellectual adulthood.

The physical effort and control required in working with concrete materials may, at times, make learning seem slow, but it appears to pay off in the long run. Researchers investigating the role of sensorimotor-perceptual skills in children's cognitive development were surprised to discover that certain kinds of activities, such as putting pegs into holes, solving pencil-and-paper mazes, and copying geometric shapes, were related to academic achievement not only for five year olds, but also for older children up to thirteen years of age.[32] We may well be doing a disservice to those children who are given computers because their handwriting is deemed sloppy or difficult to read. These children may, in fact, benefit from *additional* activities that employ their hands and eyes in different ways in order to develop the facility they lack.

Underlying the importance of learning through physical sensations and the use of physical materials is the fact that children are, first and foremost, creatures of sense. As the noted naturalist Diane Ackerman has written,

> There is no way in which to understand the world without first detecting it through the radar-net of the senses. What is beyond our senses we cannot know. Our senses define the edge of consciousness.[33]

Making "sense" of the world means using the senses to find meaning and sustenance in our environment. At birth, babies emerge from the Eden of the womb into a tumultuous world of new sensations in which they must try to find their bearings. From this tangle of sensations, infants slowly build an understanding of their world, a process that continues throughout childhood.

In spite of all the claims that computers offer a rich, active learning environment, the fact is that much of the software aimed at children does little more than bombard them with a lot of visual information within carefully designed parameters—just like children's television programs. Developmental theorists argue that, because some children get more information from visual images than from talking with other people, their brains are simply not being trained to understand oral language and retain what is said. Jane Healy, author of *Endangered Minds: Why Our Children Don't Think*, suggests that overemphasizing the visual sense deprives children of the opportunity to acquire listening skills, which are crucial to overall cognitive development.

> Children with poor auditory skills—whatever the reason—have a difficult time learning to read, spelling accurately, remembering what they read long enough to understand it, or retaining the internal sound of a sentence they want to write down.[34]

Language skills are built from listening to stories and rhymes and from having meaningful conversations with parents, siblings, and caregivers. When children talk with others, the conversation proceeds at a pace that enables the children to follow what is said. It also concerns topics of direct interest to them. Words that accompany the images of electronic media lack this kind of relevance, and the succession of images is so rapid that children either cannot or choose not to pay attention to what they are hearing. They may hear, but they don't listen. Children who don't learn to listen can easily develop habits that let them avoid exercising—and thus building—important auditory-processing connections in the brain. As Healy argues,

> ...*habits of the mind soon become structures of the brain*...The very act of remembering lays down physical tracks in the brain, but children can quite easily avoid having to build these systems.[35]

Too much electronic stimulation, whether from computers or television, may contribute to the rise in the incidence of learning disabilities such as auditory-processing problems and attention deficit disorder. Many teachers believe that the listening skills of children in schools today are much worse than those of previous generations, and report that children who watch television or play a lot of video games are much harder to teach because they have trouble paying attention. Their nervous systems are being trained to watch, not listen.

Children are also becoming less coordinated physically because of their increasingly sedentary habits. In research spanning several decades, child development expert Phyllis Weikart has found that children engage in less physical activity than they used to—about 75 percent less since the turn of the century. Largely because of the time pressures on parents, children are not given enough time or space to allow them to have the necessary experiences that are optimal for their growth. "Children are not encouraged to spend as much time crawling, or exploring their physical environment as they once were," she explained when I spoke with her. "We have children who are not growing up with adequate coordination. As a result, there is much more clumsiness in children."

The same was found to be true among teenagers. In her program with adolescent girls, Weikart has observed a steady decline in certain key skills. Teenagers are much clumsier physically than they were just twenty years ago, a fact she attributes to lack of key physical experience in the early years.

This clumsiness, Weikart believes, may indicate a corresponding cognitive underdevelopment.

> The body is the primary learning center for the child. We give inadequate attention to the body, so we are not building the learning foundation in developmentally appropriate ways.

As psychiatrists and health-care practitioners are well aware, physical clumsiness is often linked to learning disorders.

As well, insufficient attention is paid to the kinds of activities that are appropriate to the child's development. For instance, a child needs to work with fine-motor skills before the gross-motor skills are in place. Weikart's research indicates that the ability to keep a steady beat—simply clapping hands rhythmically—figures prominently in cognitive development. Children who cannot keep a steady beat have great difficulty reading. This basic sense of timing is learned through early experiences of being rocked or sung to or from listening to rhymes and stories—all experiences dependent upon intimate contact with an adult. By pressing abstract thinking upon children prematurely, we may be ignoring many such subtle links between physical coordination and intellectual and emotional development.

One fine-motor activity that is intimately connected with computer use is keyboarding, a skill that children are encouraged to learn at an ever earlier age. But this activity is developmentally inappropriate for young children because they do not possess sufficient tactile dexterity to carry out complex actions with their fingers while looking at the computer screen. (Back when typewriters were in use, children did not learn to type until they were thirteen or fourteen years old. Most people take months to learn how to touch-type and do not remember how hard it was not to glance continually at the keyboard while memorizing the position of the keys.)

Learning to type is difficult as it involves a separation of the most natural eye and hand combination such as that which occurs in handwriting. In the primary school years children are still struggling with the basics of handwriting, copying words letter-by-letter or syllable-by-syllable. Expecting children to acquire sophisticated skills before they have become proficient in the basics may well cause them problems in the future because sufficient time and attention have not been devoted to activities that would allow them to build up gradually their small-muscle coordination.

Of course, many computer programs for young children do not require fluent typing skills. But even where children have the motor skills needed to operate a program, they also need to be able to direct and hold their eyes on the details of what they are looking at on the screen. One behavioral optometrist reckons that "15 to 40 percent of primary children have not achieved a level in this skill needed for everyday classroom tasks."[36]

Activities such as learning to sew, modeling with clay, baking, catching a ball, knitting, marble games, or playing a recorder are much better ways to teach fine-motor skills, especially eye-hand coordination. They are far more appropriate from a developmental point of view because they give a child more physical freedom and a sense of accomplishment. They are also much gentler on the eyes.

In *Mindstorms*, Papert describes how he used his body to think about gears. "I could feel how gears turn by imagining my body turning. This made it possible for me to draw on my 'body knowledge' to think about gear systems."[37] Without adequate experience of bodily movement, however, it is unlikely that he could have imagined the way gears move. Papert learned about abstract thinking by first using the concreteness of his body. Ironically, in computerizing the classroom in the name of greater learning opportunities, a situation that Papert did much to bring about, this lesson has been ignored. In concentrating on the development of children's minds, we have all but forgotten their bodies.

Although the computer is touted by many as a complex multimedia machine, it relies mainly on only one sense— the visual. Bill Gates has said that computers can do a better job of supporting varied thinking than lectures and textbooks. He calls the computer "thought support" and suggests that students can more readily grasp complex processes while manipulating information using several media.[38] He would do well to acknowledge that, for children, the greatest aid to "thought support" is, in fact, the human body.

## CHAPTER 4

# Online to Success?
# Computer-Based Instruction and
# Academic Achievement

> *We must guard against the belief that computerizing always represents progress. Convenience, speed, and accuracy are not necessarily tied to validity and importance.*
> —D. LaMont Johnson and Cleborne D. Maddux[1]

**P**arents naturally want the best possible education for their children. Just as the parents of baby boomers purchased home encyclopedias in record numbers, today's parents are buying computers and software to give their children what they believe to be a head start in their education. But whereas parents in the past might have waited until their children could read before purchasing home encyclopedias, today's parents are buying computers and software (known as lap ware) for their preschoolers, including babies as young as eight months old. Hoping to provide children with an advantage before formal schooling begins, parents are turning their toddlers into a generation of cybertots.

Like the encyclopedia salesmen, software marketing companies are targeting families with young children, and the market for home computers and learning software is growing even faster than the school market. In 1995, approximately 30 percent of U.S. homes had a personal computer. By 1999, this figure had risen to more than 50 percent. Parents want their children to have this magical tool whose use has become synonymous with academic success and marketable skills. They fear that without this vital piece of technology, their children will be left behind, ending up intellectually undernourished and almost certainly unemployed.

Public perception of the computer as a passport to success has been heightened by the industry's relentless advertising. Advertisements designed to humanize the technology give computers friendly personalities and a desire to please. "You won't believe the things I do for this family," says an AST computer, which then describes how it helps "Junior," "Ms. Social Success," Mom, and Dad.[2]

In another glossy magazine, a child cozied up with a computer is pronounced "the head of the class"—a favorite slogan in Apple's promotion of its technology. Apple and Microsoft also use television regularly to advertise the virtues and advantages of home computing, although the scenarios presented are sometimes less than convincing. One Apple commercial shows a father and his young son apparently bonding while looking at the computer screen. At one point, the father smiles proudly and caresses the back of his son's head. Oblivious to his father's touch, the child is totally absorbed in the screen.

Behind the comforting assurance that computers are part of a close-knit family life is another, more urgent theme—children need computers because those who have them will outperform those who do not. At least, this is the assumption behind a number of computer hardware and software advertisements. Take, for example, a double-page advertisement for Microsoft's *Encarta* multimedia encyclopedia that appeared several years ago. "Forget Goldilocks and the Three Bears, tell us about Sartre," the headline reads. The ad continues: "'C'mon, dad, tell us about Sartre and existentialism and his belief in the inescapable responsibility of all individuals for their own decisions and his relationship with Simone de Beauvoir,' we pleaded as he tucked us in for the night." The ad shows the faces of two little girls who cannot be more than six years old.

Even less convincing is a Sears Brand Central ad showing a little girl standing behind a computer with her arms stretched above her head. "She may be only 5 but she's light-years ahead. By the time she reaches first grade, she'll have *traveled* to Jupiter and back." The computer monitor shows two planets in false proximity to each other. What help "traveling" to Jupiter will be to a first grader is left unexplained.

The message conveyed by this advertising onslaught is that children with computers will outperform those without them. But do computers really enhance learning? Does consistent and convincing evidence exist to support this view?

Educators have been conducting research into the link between computers and improved academic performance for more than thirty years. In the past two decades, thousands of studies have been conducted in classrooms across the United States in an attempt to examine the effectiveness of computer-based instruction.

The evidence that emerges is inconclusive at best. Reviews of research published between 1985 and 1998 show mixed and sometimes contradictory results.[3] For example, researchers at the Center for Research on Learning and Teaching at the University of Michigan analyzed the results of 254 controlled evaluation studies and concluded that computer-based instruction "usually produces positive effects on students." Specifically, their analysis showed that the average student in a class receiving computer-based instruction would outperform 62 percent of students in a class not using computers.[4] On the other hand, a research team from Florida A&M University and Florida State University found a number of reviews that showed no significant difference in performance between students who were using computers and those who were not.[5]

Results of several individual large-scale projects also do little to provide support for computer-based instruction. For example, the Minnesota Technology Demonstration Project, undertaken in the mid-1980s, involved more than 20 percent of the state's school districts. Researchers who studied computer-using fourth, fifth, and sixth graders over a two-year period discovered that, on average, these students did not perform as well in math, reading, and language arts as students taught by traditional methods.[6]

Educators and parents must realize, too, that where the results were positive, not all students benefited equally. Generally, boys appeared to perform better than girls, and low-achieving students showed more improvement than average students.

Studies looking at the effects of integrated learning systems (ILSs) show similar, unconvincing, or at best, problematic results. In an ILS, a central management system links individual computers that are placed either in a computer lab or in the library, or distributed among classrooms throughout the school. The system delivers courses as part of a school's standard curriculum. The subjects most commonly taught by this method are math, reading, and language arts. Students may spend thirty minutes a week or more working on practice drills presented on their computer screens, which are really just electronic workbooks. Newer applications have graphics and sound.

A frequently cited advantage of ILSs is that students work at their own pace. The system determines the level each student has reached in each subject and presents the lesson accordingly. The computer provides immediate feedback to the student and records the work. By monitoring the results, teachers are able to assess where their students are having difficulty and provide the necessary assistance.

At best, however, these systems have been only moderately successful in raising students' academic achievement. In some cases their effectiveness has simply been exaggerated. In an extensive review of ILS evaluation reports, Henry Jay Becker of the University of California at Irvine suggests that some studies (including the most widely cited) substantially overreport the effectiveness of ILSs.[7] As well, only lower- and higher-achieving students appeared to benefit from using this technology. Students in the middle range (the majority) performed better when taught by their teachers.

Becker also cautions that evaluating the results of ILS programs is difficult because of the quality of the research. In a majority of studies, for example, poor evaluation design (which includes failure to compare students' performance with that of a control group receiving traditional instruction) is compounded by inadequate data collection, poor data analysis, inadequate description of how the program operated and the conditions in which it was used, or a combination of these.

One reason why ILSs do not achieve more impressive results is that they promote individualized problem solving at the expense of interaction with peers. Childhood learning is primarily a social activity, however, and children learn as much, if not more, through talking with their teachers and other students as they do by solving problems on their own. Where an ILS is in place, children have fewer opportunities for discussion not only with other children, but also with their teachers. Given that self-paced instruction is possible with an ILS, each child could conceivably work at a different rate on a different program. This means that little context would exist in which children could discuss their classroom work, and they would have fewer opportunities to share problem-solving strategies. Such systems make it difficult for teachers to focus class lessons and discussions.

Critic Douglas Noble views the growth in the use of ILS programs as a potential catastrophe. He believes that increased use of such systems "will almost certainly lead to more reliance on standardized testing to measure achievement," something for which an ILS is ideally suited. There will thus be a tendency "to reduce education to skills and facts pre-programmed into the computer, leaving little role for reflection, imagination, discovery, and creativity." This creates a kind of educational straitjacket in which "children are viewed as 'things' that are taught to perform specified tasks rather than as human beings to be cultivated."[8] The fact that ILS programs appear to be effective only if used intensively seems to bear out his concerns.[9]

With a growing pressure for accountability, the computer seems, at first glance, an ideal means of objectively measuring student achievement. It appears to be the perfect equalizer—one which does not play favorites. Yet not only does computer technology work better for some students than for others, but it also cannot accommodate the wide variety of learning styles evident in any classroom.

Even where the use of computers appears to improve academic performance, we must approach the results with caution. First, most research studies take place over a relatively short period, often no more than three months. It is difficult to determine whether gains made in such a short time indicate a long-term trend or whether they merely reflect students' increased interest and motivation as a result of the attention lavished on them by the researchers and the novelty of using computers. When the novelty wears off, students' interest and performance may well return to previous levels.[10]

In addition, the type of work that students do on computers is still mainly drill and practice and is not likely to interest them once the initial thrill of using a computer has dissipated. In spite of games and appealing graphics, once using a computer becomes routine, students find that they have no real control over what they are doing, and learning becomes dull and repetitive.

A Tennessee study discovered that students' attitudes toward computers changed the more they used them. Over a three-year period, students' enjoyment of the technology declined steadily, confirming that the novelty of using any technology plays a significant role in learning. In addition, the older students were generally less enthusiastic about computers than younger students, and the girls' responses were consistently more negative than the boys'.[11]

The novelty effect is one reason why so many people believe that computers can motivate students and thereby improve their academic performance—motivation is a critical factor in determining how well children perform in school. The intensity with which children play video games makes many parents think that such enthusiasm will spill over into math, language, or science activities.

There is no proof, however, that such enthusiasm translates to other areas of learning. In a study involving six schools and 803 first and second graders, researchers at the Tokyo Institute of Technology studied the effectiveness of using computers to enhance creativity and motivation in primary school children. They found that the children who used computers appeared to have a more positive attitude toward the technology—a finding consistent with a number of North American studies. Computer use did not, however, encourage greater creativity or motivate the children to study more. What *did* motivate them were creative experiences such as reading books and saying rhymes.[12]

In addition to the novelty effect, there is another reason for having reservations about the results of research studies; this concerns the role of teachers in implementing these studies. Students in experimental groups (those using computers) and those in control groups (not using computers) are often taught by different teachers, so that it is impossible to determine whether the teacher made the difference rather than the technology itself.[13] If teachers enjoy working with computers and believe in their value as a learning tool, their enthusiasm is more likely to transfer to their students, at least in the short term.

Although some teachers get excited about using new computer-based materials and approaches, other ways of giving them fresh challenges certainly exist. Some schools, for instance, have discovered that when teachers attend workshops in the creative arts, their motivation and enthusiasm improve significantly. Computer technology is not the only way to reinvigorate a tired curriculum and listless students.

So why has there not been more public debate about the limitations of computer-based instruction? This is due, in part, to the selective nature of the information that is reported. Positive results receive more attention and are more likely to be published than negative ones. Companies that produce and market educational computer programs conduct and publicize the results of their own studies, which tend to place their products in a favorable light. Discussion of research studies that are critical of computer-based instruction has only recently made its way into the mainstream media. The belief that computer technology will positively influence our childen's education is so widely held that few have questioned it.

Separating advertising copy from journalism is often difficult. Don Tapscott, author of *Growing Up Digital: The Rise of the Net Generation*, wrote:

> interactive software makes learning more fun for many children.... Early research indicates that the technology holds great promise—children appear to learn the three Rs more quickly and are more motivated to explore new subjects.[14]

A recent television commercial for Patriot computers shows a pretty blonde teacher in an elementary school classroom demonstrating the latest software while proclaiming computers

> make learning fun as our kids perfect their reading, writing, and math skills. They can delve into the worlds of science, history, and geography, using interactive technology.... Ask yourself this: Do you want the best for your children?

Critical writing on the subject of computer technology began to emerge only in the past few years. One notable exception to the trend of media bias came from the *San Jose Mercury News*, a daily newspaper based in the heart of Silicon Valley. In 1995, the paper, led by journalist Christopher Schmitt, examined the link between academic achievement and computer technology to discover whether schools that had significant relationships with technology outperformed those that used computers to a lesser extent. In other words, was computer technology a significant factor in improving students' academic achievement?[15]

The study examined the results of a 1994 statewide test, the California Learning Assessment Study (CLAS), in reading, writing, and mathematics. Taking each school's average in these subject areas, researchers tried to find a link between schools with high technology use and those with high averages.

The *Mercury News* did not find in favor of the technology:

> In general, the analysis showed no strong link between the presence of technology—or the use of technology in teaching—and superior achievement. The only exception was found in schools serving low-income students, where there was a stronger association between achievement and technology investment.[16]

The significance of the *Mercury News* study, however, lies not just in its results, but also in the type of test that produced them. Despite being controversial (it has since been discontinued for political reasons), the CLAS was regarded as an improvement over other standardized tests in that it attempted to measure the quality of students' thinking and their achievement across the curriculum, rather than their ability merely to memorize facts, fill in the blanks, or select the correct answers to multiple-choice questions. By using the CLAS, the *Mercury News* study had at its core a much broader assessment of students' abilities than is normally used in studies that evaluate the effects of computer-based instruction.

More recent research in this field suggests that too much computer use in class can actually hurt students' academic performance. A study[17] undertaken by the New Jersey–based Educational Testing Service (ETS), which examined data from the 1996 National Assessment of Educational Progress (NAEP) in mathematics, found that frequent computer use in school tended to have a negative effect on the math scores of fourth and eighth graders. Students did not benefit from using computers more often, but from using them in particular ways.

For example, eighth-grade students who learned higher-order thinking skills through computer simulations—which allow students to examine the concept of velocity, for instance—had higher math scores than students who used drill-and-practice programs, which focus on lower-order thinking skills. Children can only benefit from such high-er-level uses of technology, however, when they are developmentally ready to do so, and when their teachers are adequately trained.

Among fourth-grade students, frequent computer use at home had a negative impact on math scores. The opposite was true for eighth-grade students. This may be because older students were not playing video games or using low-level software at home; instead, they were using computers for word processing and research.

Black and low-income students had less access to home computers than white students and those from higher-income families. But the real inequality lay not with computer access, but with how well trained the teachers were in technology and how computers were used in class. Most troubling, said the study's author, Harold Wenglinsky, was the fact that black (and poor) children tend to use computers to learn basic arithmetic more often than white (and wealthier) children and that the programs they use are mainly for low-level exercises such as drill-and-practice programs. Their teachers are also less likely to have received training in the use of technology.

Inexperienced teachers who rely on computers in the elementary school years may be unwittingly abandoning their students because the makers of many software packages stress the fact that these will "free the teacher" to work with other students. This means that when students are occupied with the technology, they often receive little or no attention from their teacher.

Educational researchers Larry Miller and J. Dale Burnett have cast some light on this issue, suggesting that sometimes inexperienced teachers simply "set it and forget it," meaning that they set up students at a computer and then leave them to work alone. Not only do students sometimes miss out on enriching group activities such as story reading or discussion because they are preoccupied with the computer, but they also miss out on interaction with their teachers. "This observation was especially interesting," say Miller and Burnett,

> because it was different from their normal behavior where interactions with students were frequent. For example, when students engaged in seat work, these teachers would move from child to child, asking questions, clarifying problems, reteaching when necessary, and offering encouragement.

One teacher simply said, "The computer program is looking after their needs, and, besides, I get a printout of their performance."[18]

The ETS study concludes that middle school students in grades seven and eight are more likely to benefit from using computer technology than children in elementary schools. This makes sense because regardless of how sophisticated the software program, it is simply no substitute for a teacher when a child needs answers to complex questions. As children grow older, they are more able to work independently and, because they now possess some basic skills, may derive greater benefits from using the computer for more sophisticated learning. Significantly, the ETS study found that private school students used computers less frequently than public school students in the fourth grade, but more frequently in the eighth grade.

It is difficult, if not impossible, to measure accurately the impact of computers on learning. This is not only because it is virtually impossible to separate the role of the technology versus that of the teacher, but also because of the nature of the achievement tests themselves.

There are, in fact, well-documented limitations of the standardized tests that are generally used to assess the effects of computer-based instruction. The rationale of standardized tests is that they measure students' ability to perform well in school. But, to a large extent, the scores *determine* how well they will perform in school. What a test does is measure how well students are likely to do on subsequent tests of a similar nature. High test scores are not related to the depth or scope of students' learning, but merely to their test-taking abilities.

The origins of standardized testing go back to Sir Francis Galton, a cousin of Charles Darwin and creator of the infamous bell curve. In

1869, Galton published *Hereditary Genius*, a book in which he hypothesized that one could measure the degree to which people differed from one another in intelligence. He devised a way of representing the distribution of intelligence among a given population by constructing a curve, based on a purely imaginary scale, which showed that 50 percent of individuals would fall within the middle (normal) range, and the remainder would be divided equally among those of lesser or greater intelligence. The resulting curve was in the shape of a bell.

Galton assumed, then, that intelligence could be measured on a linear scale and that such measurement would result in a bell-curve distribution. These assumptions were based on no scientific proof whatsoever.

It is important to understand that standardized tests are designed to produce scores that conform to the bell curve. In other words, their level of difficulty is calibrated to ensure that half the students score above the norm and half below. Rather than assessing students fairly on skills and knowledge they might reasonably be expected to possess, the tests are constructed to create, as Herbert Kohl put it, "a hierarchy of success or failure."[19] This is done in the name of an untested hypothesis that is supported by a completely arbitrary measurement of intelligence, a concept that, in many respects, still defies definition.

A standardized test provides a very narrow measure of a person's capabilities. Harvard University psychologist Howard Gardner has suggested that everyone possesses a number of intelligences, which contribute in varying degrees to each person's potential. In his book *Frames of Mind: The Theory of Multiple Intelligences*, Gardner differentiated among seven kinds of intelligence: logical–mathematical, linguistic, musical, spatial, bodily–kinesthetic, interpersonal, and intrapersonal.

For example, writers are more likely to be strong in linguistic intelligence, athletes in bodily–kinesthetic intelligence, and visual artists and chess players in spatial intelligence. The traditional straight-A student demonstrates a high degree of logical–mathematical intelligence—the type of intelligence measured predominantly by standardized tests. By focusing on one type of intelligence, such tests ignore other forms of intelligence that can promote success later in life and, as a result, often fail to predict how well a child will do at the postsecondary school level or in the workplace. The fact that high test scores cannot necessarily be equated with later achievement lends support to the view that intelligence is multifaceted and cannot be measured by means of a simple test with "right" and "wrong" answers. Although current modes of intelligence testing appear to offer numerical precision, they are often conceptually flawed.

Just as disturbing is the fact that generations of researchers have discovered that standardized testing results in a narrowing of the curriculum. Where these tests are administered, teachers, and indeed whole school districts, begin to alter their curriculum in order to ensure that their students score high on the tests. But the teach-to-the-test approach has proven unwise. In such a situations, students soon learn to be good test takers, but perhaps little else. As many critics have suggested, improved test scores do not necessarily mean that students are learning more. They may, in fact, be learning less. As teacher and writer William Hynes has said, "What produces a good exam-taker is the opposite of what produces a citizen of literate habits."[20]

In addition, most tests do not measure students' ability to analyze and solve problems and apply their skills and knowledge in other contexts. Indeed, without direct teacher involvement and evaluation, thinking skills are difficult both to teach and measure.

Software developers often claim that computer use in classrooms gives teachers more opportunities to be involved with their students on an individual basis, but direct teacher involvement can be better achieved by reducing class sizes rather than by putting children in front of computers. Smaller class sizes have a positive impact on children's academic performance. This is especially true of young children.

The 1984–1990 Student/Teacher Achievement Ratio (STAR) Project study out of Tennessee provides striking evidence. The study, involving more than 7,000 children, found that smaller class sizes allowed students more contact with their teacher and resulted in strong academic and social gains. Students also achieved consistently higher scores in their statewide tests. In fact, these gains continued throughout high school. Teachers reported a greater awareness of their students' family lives and had fewer discipline problems. Because teachers were able to give children more individual attention, they could identify children who had learning disabilities or who were having trouble with reading or arithmetic earlier, and these children received remedial instruction. And with fewer students in the classroom, teachers suffered less fatigue.

The cost to Tennessee, a traditionally poor state, was $1 billion. But the parents, teachers, and school administration believe the money is well spent. In 1988, elementary class sizes were cut virtually in half, and in 1989 the state legislated a fifteen-student cap on class sizes. Now seventeen other states have begun to follow Tennessee's lead. California, for example, launched a program to trim class sizes in the first through fourth grades, and in spite of difficulties in obtaining certified teachers and sufficient classroom space, teachers report high levels of satisfaction with the program. Perhaps if more school districts cut class sizes (and certainly this is a direction that early-childhood educators have urged for decades), school districts would have less reason to spend money on technology and more reason to focus on the relationship between student and teacher. Reducing class size also has another advantage: all students benefit equally.[21]

Although the initial costs of reducing class sizes are high, school districts can find cost savings in other areas. Children who fail a grade in elementary school must repeat the grade, which costs the school system as well as the child. When class sizes are kept small, teachers can more quickly identify learning problems that are often undiagnosed in larger classes. When the system fails to identify a child with special needs when he or she is young, these problems become more difficult—and often more expensive—to fix later.

One of the biggest problems with educational software that is designed to improve test scores is that it takes learning out of context. But children need a meaningful context for learning so that they can make connections between abstract knowledge and concrete experience. When children use educational software to enhance their factual knowledge, they are expected to answer questions or solve problems with no other point of reference.

We find scant evidence that using such software results in smarter or more enthusiastic students. For example, a California study of fifth and sixth graders compared those who played *Where in the World Is*

*Carmen Sandiego?* with students who drew maps and played noncomputer games involving the same geography facts. It found no significant differences between the groups in either their ability to recall facts or their attitudes toward the study of geography.[22]

*Where in the World Is Carmen Sandiego?* is by far the best-selling educational software in North America. The game first appeared in the mid-1980s and has been followed by six sequels, three of which are also among the top five best-sellers. These programs use a detective game to teach geography and history. According to one review, teachers like the *Carmen* games because they send students scurrying to look up facts in reference books. (In the original versions of *Carmen Sandiego*, these consisted of *Fodor's USA Travel Guide* and *The World Almanac and Book of Facts*; later versions enable students to conduct searches on CD–ROM.) "The software," writes a *Home PC* reviewer,

> gives children a context for the geographical and historical information they uncover, so they tend to understand and retain it.... The idea is to keep children from being passive learners.[23]

Thoughtful teachers, however, might have reservations about using a format that arbitrarily jumps all over the place, preferring, instead, an approach that allows children to explore a single topic from various angles and gives them time to absorb and fit together the details of what they are learning. While playing one of the *Carmen* sequels, *Where in Time Is Carmen Sandiego?*, we discovered that the game propelled us around the world on a whirlwind tour that never stopped long enough in any one place to show what was really going on. For example, during the game the following facts appeared on the screen, in this order:

- The founders of the unified Russian State were ruthless in the pursuit of their goals. Ivan the Terrible was notorious for the cruelty of his methods.
- Commercial dynasties such as the Medici family of Florence controlled much of the wealth and power in Renaissance Italy.
- Francisco Pizarro, a Spanish conquistador, sailed to Peru in the mid-1500s. There he ambushed the Incan ruler and forced him to pay a ransom of a room full of gold.

- Holland in the fifteenth and sixteenth centuries was first ruled by France and then by Spain. The Eighty Years' War ended Spanish rule and ushered in Dutch independence.

Such information is skimpy and sometimes misleading. On the last two items, minimal research revealed the following: Pizarro in fact made two voyages to Peru, the first in 1526 and the second, his voyage of conquest, in 1531, and the unnamed Incan ruler was Atahualpa; and the Eighty Years' War in fact ended in 1648, in the mid-seventeenth century. This kind of whistle-stop info-tour is of questionable educational value because the purpose of looking up information is to solve clues to Carmen's whereabouts rather than learn more about the times and places involved. Players cannot even do this at their leisure because they are given a limited amount of time (which can be varied according to a player's ability) to solve the mystery. The only context, and the only real point of the exercise, is to find out where Carmen is as quickly as possible.

The problem with games such as *Carmen Sandiego* is that they provide no framework into which students can fit the facts they learn. Instead, people and places pop up as isolated phenomena that are discarded as soon as they have served their purposes. To discover, for example, that "If that's the Eiffel Tower, Carmen must have gone to Paris" does little to teach children about the geography of France. Children are much more likely to develop an understanding of geography if they are first taught to find their way around their own neighborhood, and then create their own maps of where they have walked and what they have seen.

While visiting an inner-city school in Boston, I noticed that during a geography lesson the teacher took several minutes to draw out of the students the name of the river (the Charles River) that flows through their city. Every student in the fourth grade would have known this fact, along with many other observations about the river, if they had simply been taken on a field trip to walk along its banks.

Our schools spend vast sums of money on the integration of technology, the effects of which are often counterproductive. Computer drills might help, in some cases, to raise students' standardized test scores, but such measures are a narrow form of assessment. Test scores, whether delivered electronically or not, do not even begin to hint at the potential in each child.

## CHAPTER 5

# The Young Reader and the Screen

*The ability to read is of such singular importance to a child's life in school that his experience in learning it more often than not seals the fate, once and for all, of his academic career.*
—Bruno Bettelheim and Karen Zelan[1]

**W**hen people think about children learning to read, certain images spring to mind—a parent reading a child a bedtime story, a teacher pointing to the letters of the alphabet on the blackboard, or a child curled up in a favorite chair immersed in a storybook. These days, however, young readers are more likely to be engaged in a very different kind of reading. When children visit their school libraries, chances are they will spend some of their time in front of a computer screen. There is a wide range of computer software designed to help children learn to read, along with a growing list of storybook and reference CD–ROMs for children, and these are widely used in homes as well as schools. But how much can computers help children become fluent and attentive readers? Are their effects necessarily beneficial?

As spending on computer technology increases, school districts often have to reduce the funds available to purchase books. To some, this reallocation of resources is justified: it signals the fact that one technology is giving way to another. According to this view, the way in which we acquire and communicate information depends less on the static technology of print and more on a dynamic interaction with image. That old cliché "a picture is worth a thousand words" has been given a new twist.

Yet the ability to read unadorned text is as essential as ever. We are witnessing an exponential increase in the amount of data available, much of it printed on a screen rather than on a piece of paper. Literacy remains of fundamental importance. It will be almost impossible for those who are not literate to keep up with the changes we are experiencing. As one U.S. educator warned, "Children who cannot read fluently today will simply not have access to the responsible jobs of the future."[2]

With this much at stake, we should be open to any approach that will yield improved results. But will such improvements result from the use of computer technology? In the initial stages of learning to read the answer seems to be "no."

The basis of literacy is oral language—words spoken by real people in real situations—and the path to literacy begins long before children actually learn to read and write. The formal instruction children receive in school is, in many ways, the culmination of a process that began to unfold practically at birth. Reading and writing are not isolated functions; they are inextricably linked with the acquisition of oral language. The relationship between speech and literacy has been described as follows:

> Without a mastery of speech, we would lack the internal voice that automatically accompanies us as we read and that we instinctively use to clarify meaning and interpret nuances of tone. Similarly, writing involves an internal dialogue that helps us to sort out our ideas as we set them down on the page.[3]

The first step toward literacy, then, is taken when a child starts to learn oral language. Because nearly all parents talk to their babies from day one, if not before, learning begins long before the child is aware of language itself. Children learn to speak because speech is all around them; they realize instinctively that speaking is both useful and desirable.

Speech is not just a matter of communication; it also helps us clarify our thinking. When children learn to speak, they do not just acquire a means of expressing their thoughts and feelings; they also find a way to sort out in their minds what they want to say. As their knowledge of oral language develops, this ability becomes more sophisticated and enables children to think about the situations and experiences they encounter in their daily lives. In doing so, children also develop the powers of reflection that are necessary to their ability to read and write.

When young children are learning to speak, much of what their parents say to them is concerned with the nature of language itself. Many parents, for example, encourage their children to take an interest in language by reciting nursery rhymes and by playing word games with them. One of the virtues of word games and nursery rhymes is that they make children more aware of the existence of words as individual units of language.[4] Rhymes are especially effective in this respect because children have a natural affinity for them and delight in matching words that end with the same sound. In this way, they learn that words are separate bits of speech that can be changed by replacing one sound with another. Several studies have indicated that children generally find it easier to learn to read words through the use of rhymes and that their ability to do so is seldom affected by the nature of the vowels involved.[5] This is a significant finding in view of the fact that vowels often cause children the most difficulty when they begin to read.

Even after the early years, when children are developing their reading and writing skills, oral language continues to play an immensely important role. By listening and trying to absorb what they hear, children develop memory and concentration. Without good auditory skills, children have a hard time learning to read and spell accurately. Their reading comprehension and writing ability also suffer because they are often unable to remember something they read long enough to understand what it says, or to keep the sound of a sentence in their heads when they want to write it down. The Waldorf schools place great emphasis on students' ability to reproduce orally, in their own words, what they listened to in previous lessons before they put anything down on paper. In this way, the children assimilate what they have learned and make it their own. This process mirrors the way in which children learn to speak—by hearing others talk, then trying out words and phrases for themselves.

We should keep in mind the central role that oral language plays in children's learning now that so much information about the world comes to us in the form of images on a screen. Many teachers and parents introduce young children to computers in the belief that technology will enrich and accelerate the children's learning. But if computer time becomes a substitute for talking and listening time, they are doing these children a disservice. Voices from the screen are no substitute for a parent's speech because they are not connected with a human presence that directs the children's attention to what is going on around them and responds to their reactions. Parents generally point to what they are talking about and tend not to refer to things that are not there. By focusing on the child's experience of its immediate surroundings, they reinforce the child's mastery of language as a useful, meaningful accomplishment. Voices from the screen do not perform this critical function because they refer only to images of things, many of which the child has had no experience of. What the child hears, as one researcher put it, is "words without content."[6]

When it comes to written language, children learn about print in much the same way as they learn about speech—as a part of their environment. But unlike speech, learning to read does not come naturally. As child psychologist Margaret Donaldson has written,

> all normal children learn to use and understand speech in the first few years of their lives without specific instruction but...very few learn to read and write with equal success within the same period of time.[7]

Of course, some children *do* learn to read by themselves at an early age before they have received formal instruction, but most do not, and even those who do start reading early have learned to speak sooner. Although most children in our society are surrounded by print in much the same way as they are surrounded by speech, they will not automatically make the connection between printed words and their meanings unless they are led to understand the nature of print and the purpose it serves.

Frank Smith, an authority on reading, points out that

the first requirement for children who will become readers must be the recognition that written language exists, that there are aspects of the visual environment worth paying attention to in a particular way.[8]

Children come across print in a wide variety of forms. Besides books, newspapers, and magazines, flyers, signs, calendars, and posters all carry text. Children also come in contact with letters and cards, shopping lists, recipes, address books, messages left on the refrigerator, utility bills, and so on. By exposing their children to such materials, parents can draw attention to the existence of print and demonstrate its uses.

When this happens, children acquire a good deal of knowledge about written language by the time they start to read. In observing how a class of first graders learned to read, one researcher discovered that

all were aware of the alphabetic nature of English print. They knew that the print in books and on other objects in the environment communicated written language messages. They knew how to handle books—which way was up, how and when to turn pages, and which aspects of print were significant for reading and which were not. They knew that print was read from left to right most of the time…. They used pencils to write, observed the writing of others, and knew that what they had written could be read.[9]

Knowing what books are for and how they are used has been shown to have a strong positive effect on how well children do in their early years at school. And, of course, achievement at school is closely tied to the ability to read and write.

Some years ago, a friend of mine was relaxing in his study one day after lunch when his four-year-old granddaughter came in dragging a volume of the Encyclopedia Britannica that was almost as big as she was. She plopped herself down by his chair with the book in front of her.

"Grampa," she said, "whaddya want to know?"

"Well," he replied after a moment's consideration, "what about elephants?"

"Elephants," she said. "Okay." She opened the book at the beginning and ran her finger down the page as if scanning the table of contents. "Elephants," she repeated as her finger stopped at what she judged an appropriate place. "Here we are." Then she opened the book somewhere near the middle and began to tell her grandfather what she knew about elephants. She could not read a word, but, as a former educator, her grandfather realized that she would have no difficulty learning. The episode demonstrated that she already knew what books were for, had a good idea of how one set about finding specific information in them, and was interested in doing so.

Children discover what books are for by seeing adults use them. My friend's granddaughter had no doubt recognized that books contain useful information by having seen other members of the family refer to them. These days, however, people increasingly consult CD–ROMs and electronic data bases rather than reference books. Computers, too, are rapidly becoming a means of introducing children to the written word.

For a young child, a computer screen merely presents another surface that displays print, and there is no harm in children discovering this. We should, however, be concerned about the effect computers may have on a child's understanding of written language.

Reading printed text is not the same as reading text from a computer screen. In a recent speech, Bill Gates, chairman of Microsoft, admitted that "reading off the screen is still vastly inferior to reading off of paper.…When it comes to something over four or five pages, I print it out and I like to have it to carry around with me and annotate."[10] Printed text, in other words, can be used in ways on-screen print cannot.

The limitations of the screen as a medium for reading might lead a child to form a limited idea of what reading entails. Watching an adult access texts on a computer, the child could gain the impression that print is something to be searched, with maximum speed and efficiency, for specific information. This is a perfectly valid use of print—a newspaper reader scans a story in much the same way—but it presents reading as having a purely functional value. It does nothing to convey the intellectual, emotional, and imaginative dimensions of reading for pleasure and enlightenment.

The possibility also exists that, by being conditioned to expect something more exciting than text on the computer, children will tend to devalue text itself, focusing instead on the pictorial or animated aspects of the screen. Researchers have already found some evidence that this happens when children look at electronic books, which combine the traditions of storytelling with the interactive attractions of multimedia. Far from encouraging childen to read, the visual excitement of much "edutainment" software can actually impede reading development.

Even if children do read what they see on the screen, they might not be able to absorb its contents due to the way the text is presented. This is because electronic print lacks the structure and permanence of print on paper. If we pick up a book, we know at a glance how long it is, and by turning to the table of contents, we can see how the author approaches the subject and, often, the author's point of view. Flipping through the pages and stopping when our eye catches something of interest gives us an idea of whether the book lives up to our initial expectations. In other words, we get a sense of the work as a whole. Moreover, the contents of a book remain the same no matter how often we turn to it, so that each time we refer to a book, we reinforce our understanding of its structure.

On screen, however, things are very different. A CD–ROM cannot be physically handled and explored the way a book can. True, we can move easily from one part of its contents to another, but the linear nature of numbered pages gives way to a more dynamic, but potentially far more confusing presentation. Instead of turning pages, which have a fixed position, the on-screen reader is confronted with a series of screen-sized packages of print, the order of which can be changed at will. And unlike the contents of a book, which remain physically present in their entirety, print on the screen comes and goes with the click of a mouse. When scrolled up or down, the text flows past, rushing quickly into and out of sight.

Because of these fundamental differences, readers respond to electronic and printed texts in different ways. Derrick de Kerckhove, director of the McLuhan Centre for Media Studies at the University of Toronto, thinks that it is essential for children to start with fixed text before they experience "movable text." The reason for this is that fixed text lets the mind move at its own pace; it allows time for reflection and stimulates the imagination. With electronic movable text, on the other hand, the mind stands still while the text flashes past. Unless the user already understands the concept of "fixed-text technology" (that is, the structures and uses of printed materials), the result can be confusing. As de Kerckhove puts it, "Mobile data will turn your mind to static."

The negative qualities of electronic print are easily overlooked in the rush to provide children with the latest offerings in reading software. After all, the argument goes, the computer environment, with its sights, sounds, and interactive possibilities, is so much richer than that of a book. But as with any kind of learning, it is the quality, not the quantity, of stimulation that counts. The current tendency to believe that more technology means better results must not be allowed to obscure the value of a simple, low-tech activity that plays a vital role in the development of children's literacy—reading stories to children.

Experts agree that reading to children is particularly important in preparing them to be readers. For example, the authors of *Becoming a Nation of Readers*, the report of the U.S. Commission on Reading, noted that "the single most important activity for building the knowledge required for eventual success in reading is reading aloud to children." Marilyn Jager Adams, whose book *Beginning to Read* contains an exhaustive survey of research on how children learn to read, writes that "the most important activity for building the knowledge and skills eventually required for reading is that of reading aloud to children."[11]

More than perhaps any other activity, reading stories to children makes them aware of the possibilities of written language. They not only discover that written language is different from speech, but also learn that it can be organized in particular ways. For example, stories have a formal structure—a beginning, a middle, and an end. Reading stories to children helps them develop listening comprehension and an ability to follow and remember sequences of events and details of description. It is also valuable beyond the stage at which children are able to read on their own because their comprehension of oral language will be ahead of their reading ability for some time to come. By listening to stories that they would find too difficult to read on their own, children have opportunities to enrich their vocabulary and develop an understanding of more complex narrative structures.

Perhaps most of important of all, reading to children opens their imagination to worlds that lie beyond their own observations and experiences. The images that children create in their minds are among their most powerful and emotionally satisfying responses to story reading. These images, unique to each child, are the means by which children make stories their own. This ability develops even further when children become readers themselves.

The introduction through computer technology of new forms of storybook reading may undermine these crucial benefits. Intended as a supplement to or substitute for the human reader, electronic books on CD–ROM enable children to look at and listen to text that appears on screen accompanied by colorful illustrations, which are often enlivened by animation. One of the best-known examples of these electronic books, which are appearing in increasing numbers, are the titles in the Living Books series from Random House/Broderbund, found in many school libraries.

Children have always been active participants when stories are read to them. They ask questions about the story, make comments on characters or events, and sometimes direct the reader to repeat a passage they especially enjoy. Electronic books try to take this involvement with the story a stage further by enabling children to access features of the program that provide information about the story's content, help with unfamiliar words, or activate additional elements of the animation and sound track. It is the last of these features that constitutes the main attraction, and here the drawbacks of the high-tech approach become apparent. "More technology" may be equated with "more fun," but the danger is that the multimedia dimension of electronic books will lead to less attention being paid to the story itself and will therefore do less to develop listening and reading skills than the traditional activity of reading aloud. Children whose parents do not have time to read to them would be better off listening to stories on cassette. Apart from the fact that the sound quality on a cassette player is generally superior to that of most home computers, the children would also have to listen carefully to the story to understand it.

The trouble with the multimedia features of electronic books is that the story itself takes second place to a variety of visual diversions. The small amount of text that appears at the top of the screen is visually overwhelmed by the colorful scene that comes with it, and animation and sound effects provide additional distractions. Moreover, by selecting the "play" option, which most children do, the reader can activate a number of "hot spots" on each page with a click of the mouse, which makes a person or object perform some kind of action accompanied by dialogue, sound effects, or both.

Although one must admire the ingenuity, and often the whimsical sense of humor, that has gone into these special effects (one of our favorites is in "Arthur's Teacher Trouble," in the Living Books series, in which some of the cookies on a baking tray grow legs and walk around munching happily on the others), they often have nothing at all to do with the story itself and may have a negative effect on the child's understanding of what reading is all about. With the special effects providing what one might call the "real entertainment," engaging with the text becomes trivial. Finger on mouse, the reader (or viewer) criss-crosses the screen to make sure that none of the hot spots has been overlooked. As a result, children are quite likely to lose track of the story altogether.

Yet animation is promoted as an important selling point of electronic books, the idea being that children will find a multimedia presentation more stimulating than text alone, and thus will be tempted to return to the stories again and again. Repeated use, however, may have little to do with reading. Researchers in one recent study that observed a class of third graders noted that the rereading of electronic books invariably entailed playing with the animation and little else. One student boasted that he knew "everything on the page that would move, sing, or speak."[12] Some teachers, on the other hand, have found electronic books to be "too busy" for their students. Many children, we were told, react in a very passive way, just staring at the pictures and paying little attention to the accompanying text. If these are common responses, electronic books will not do much to help children become fluent, thoughtful readers.

Research on reading primers has already indicated that too many pictures can delay or interfere with learning to read, especially when the text has little or no intrinsic interest for children.[13] The visual images of electronic books cause a similar form of interference. The animated sequences perform in ways that make the accompanying text largely irrelevant. Good illustrations work *with* the text rather than *against* it. Pictures are a means of extending the reader's imagination. Their function is not just to let the reader see what things look like, but also to tell the story in another way. They do this by giving a heightened sense of certain aspects of the story, which adds to the impression made on the reader.

Celia Lottridge is a storyteller and children's book author. Her award-winning book *The Name of the Tree*, a retelling of an African folk tale, starts with a full-page illustration of the sun shining over the parched land while a line of animals files by in search of food. One small boy who saw this picture said it hurt his eyes to look at it "because the sun is so hot." Although the book was produced primarily for children, the illustrations are not meant to distract readers but, rather, to enhance their appreciation of the story. As Lottridge says, "We underestimate children's ability to relate to subtle and imaginative art." There is nothing subtle, however, about the visual appeal of electronic books. Software designers seem unable to resist the temptation to upstage the text, invariably emphasizing flashy multimedia effects over educational goals.

Interactive fiction (sometimes referred to as hypertext stories) takes the hands-on approach of electronic books a stage further by allowing the reader to manipulate the text itself. By selecting from a number of options at various stages in the story, the reader can exercise some control over what happens next. The reader thus becomes an "active" partner with the author in determining how the story will unfold. In fact, in the words of one researcher, "One of the most striking ways that computers distinguish themselves as storytellers is by blurring the boundary between teller and audience."[14]

But is this a good thing for young readers? Hypertext stories sacrifice a good deal for direct reader participation. Our ability to identify with fictional worlds is what makes fiction so satisfying to read. Writers of children's books create worlds that are authentic and consistent on

their own terms, places the reader can inhabit without being constantly reminded of their artificiality. But when we can choose the way a
story develops, our involvement as readers undergoes a fundamental
change. We begin to indulge in a game of "Let's see what happens
if...," and thus we become more interested in what we can do to the
story than in what the story is all about.

If a story is to have meaning, the reader needs to find out and
understand what it is all about. As they become familiar with a story,
children gain a sense of the *shape* of things. Once they know how the
actions and events unfold and fit together, they come to realize that life
does not happen in unconnected bits—they learn, for example, that
problems develop, reach a climax, and are finally resolved. Realizing that
human experiences have certain patterns is an extremely important step
for young children who are still trying to make sense of the world
around them. Good stories help children make that step; it is a part of
their enduring popularity.

This appeal is as much emotional as intellectual. The fact that a
conventional (as opposed to a hypertext) story is always the same no
matter how many times it is revisited provides reassurance, and this
emotional connection with the story can be a spur to further learning.
When a child of two or three, on a visit to a children's bookstore, asked
for a copy of a story he already knew, his mother suggested they get
something different, a book he had not been read before. The child
protested: "But sometimes I need it," he said, "and sometimes I don't
have it."[15] The story was familiar to him—something he could count
on when the rest of the world didn't make sense.

For children, stories are not just a form of entertainment; they are
alternative *realities*. "Stories," writes Frank Smith, "do not *represent*
experiences for children; they *are* experiences as immediate and
compelling as actual events."[16] Children therefore need stories that
make sense to them, and to help them unravel the meaning of what
they listen to or see on the page they need an understanding guide.
Another *person* must be involved. The guidance might come from a
parent or from an older child acting as a reading buddy, a practice widespread in U.S. schools. Computer technology does not offer any real
alternative. Sending children off to "read" an electronic book on their

own is a grossly inadequate substitute because the kind of assistance provided by the voice of an electronic book is extremely crude compared to what an older reader would offer. Reading stories to and with children opens up a dimension of childhood that cannot be explored in any other way.

Reading stories is only one side of the learning-to-read equation— the side that stresses a whole-language approach in which children learn to read by searching for meaning. On the other side is the viewpoint that emphasizes the need for basic skills to "decode" the signs of written language into the sounds of speech, a process that is taught by phonics.

There is a good deal of evidence that children who have had difficulty learning to read have made good progress after phonics instruction. With phonics, children learn the sounds associated with letters, then learn to combine these sounds to read (that is, sound out) complete words. Perhaps more important, phonics instruction also teaches children that they need to pay attention to each letter in a word in order to identify it correctly and that there are certain spelling patterns that make word recognition easier.

A child who cannot recognize individual letters or words is not going to be a fluent reader. As well, many children start school with little or no ability to identify written words, let alone read continuous text. Some may have very little idea of what reading is all about. Many educators see the use of phonics as necessary to helping these children get started.

In many ways, computers are tailor-made for phonics instruction. They combine sound and visuals so that children do not just see the words but also hear them. They provide instant feedback as to whether an answer is right or wrong, and exercises can be played again and again. Phonics-based software programs have been and continue to be widely used both in homes and schools. Perhaps the most popular is *Reader Rabbit*, which first came out in 1984 and has since sold more than 2 million copies.

Although some teachers have reported that children both enjoy and benefit from *Reader Rabbit* and similar on-screen phonics games, educators are far from certain that such programs provide an effective means of learning basic reading skills. For one thing, they offer a limit-ed range of activities and lack the variety and flexibility of teacher-directed exercises so that, at best, they play only a supporting role. Another factor to consider is that a drill program cannot distinguish among types of errors. All it knows is that a wrong answer has been given, and it responds in the same way, regardless of why the answer is wrong. But children need to know why an answer is wrong if they are to learn from their mistakes.

Research, in fact, indicates that learning-to-read software programs are no more effective than other materials in helping children to become fluent readers. A number of studies have found that using computers has little effect on young children's ability to learn basic skills such as matching letters, recognizing letters and words, and spelling simple words.[17] A recent survey of reading programs concluded that few computer-based programs "have consistently proven to be effective, and few have produced substantial achievement gains in students' reading performance." Moreover, these programs are generally more expensive than programs that do not involve the use of computer technology.[18]

Not all of the survey findings were negative. For example, *Fast ForWord*, a training program that helps at-risk children improve their understanding of oral language, has, in a majority of studies, produced favorable results. The program presents a series of exercises in a game-like format, which gives children practice in recognizing word sounds in isolation, in groups, in words, and finally in sentences. Computer technology enables the speech sounds to be reproduced at different speeds, so that children can start with sounds that are slowed down and emphasized and work their way up to natural speech. *Fast ForWord* is designed, however, as an intensive, short-term intervention for children who are having problems with oral language comprehension, and the skills gained will not necessarily ensure later reading success.

Prereading skills are also the focus of *DaisyQuest*, another program that has achieved positive results. This program, for children in kinder-garten and earlier, teaches skills in phonological awareness—the aware-ness that words are comprised of individual sounds. These skills include rhyming; identifying sounds at the beginning, in the middle, and at the end of words; and breaking up words into sounds and putting sounds together to form words (thus: bat = b/a/t and b/a/t = bat). However, John Schacter, the author of the survey, notes that phonological awareness is only one factor in predicting future reading ability and that, by itself, *DaisyQuest* will not necessarily lead to an overall improvement in reading.

With regard to more comprehensive reading programs, the track record is less impressive. Research on *SuccessMaker* and *Tomorrow's Promise Reading*, which are both components of an integrated learning system, show mixed results. And for IBM's *Writing to Read (WTR)*, which is designed to help kindergarten and first-grade students develop reading and writing skills, the survey found only small to moderate gains in the reading ability of kindergarteners and none at all in that of first graders.

*WTR* is the most widely evaluated early reading software. Children using this program work in rotation at five "stations," each providing a different activity, two of which involve computer use.[19] As the name of the program indicates, it emphasizes encouraging children to begin writing before they can read and spell. The program was eventually mandated by several U.S. governors for all the elementary schools in their states, despite, as one commentator put it, "devastating research results" concerning its lack of effectiveness.[20]

A number of studies have found that *WTR* has little or no effect on children's reading and writing.[21] In addition, educators typically use *WTR* to supplement existing language arts programs. Thus, children in *WTR* groups tend to receive more language arts instruction than other children, and this, rather than the effectiveness of the program, could account for any positive results. According to one research review, "many of the benefits attributed to *WTR* can, in fact, be explained by increased instructional time devoted to writing activities in the classroom rather than the technological innovation of the program."[22]

We should bear in mind that these results were obtained at considerable cost in terms of both personnel and resources. Using *WTR* in a lab usually requires that at least three adults be present while the children are working on the program.[23] In addition to staffing considerations, there is the cost of the equipment that, for a lab designed for twenty-four to thirty students, might include nine PCs and at least one printer, as well as tape recorders, cassettes, and the program software.[24]

But perhaps the most serious stumbling block is the nature of the program itself. *WTR* is designed to operate in a controlled environment. One study noted that some teachers resisted the rigid routines on which *WTR* is based. They did not like being told that

> they had to follow a preset routine, where some kind of sound goes off every fifteen minutes to signal to the children to move from one station to the next.[25]

Far from providing the flexibility that would allow children to learn in the way that suits them best, the program possesses the rigidness of so much computer-based instruction. This means that children do what the computer tells them, when it tells them to do it. One researcher observed that

> whether they were listening to tapes, using the software, or working in the workbooks, students had few choices about what, where, or how they could learn.

The children could not choose the stories on the tapes and were not encouraged to bring in others of their own. They also spent a good deal of time waiting, either because their classmates were not ready to begin or because they had finished at a workstation ahead of time. The greatest frustration occurred when children were at the writing station. If they had difficulty in getting started, they would sometimes end up with "only three or four minutes of actual writing time." On the other hand, time was still a problem when the children began writing immediately because, in this case, their frustration "resulted from being interrupted when they were deeply involved with their stories."[26]

No doubt the developers of *WTR*, like those of other computer-based learning programs, designed their program to be implemented on its own terms, leaving little room for teachers to exercise their own judgment and creativity. But Jeanne Chall, author of *Learning to Read: The Great Debate*, who visited more than 300 schools in the course of her research, concluded that children's interest in reading is not determined by the method of instruction or the materials they use. Instead, "it was *what the teacher did* with the method, the materials, and the children rather than the method itself that seemed to make the difference."[27]

Bruno Bettelheim and Karen Zelan remind us in their book *On Learning to Read: The Child's Fascination with Reading* that "for most children, learning to read is not an entertainment but hard work, a difficult task requiring serious application."[28] Children are unlikely to apply themselves seriously to this task unless there is a commensurate reward. The reward of learning to read is being able to read. How the prospect of this reward is presented is of crucial importance.

Drills to develop basic skills may have their place, and software programs may make such drills more palatable for some children, but they must be seen as just one means of helping children toward the only goal that counts—that of being able to read on their own. In this latter context, computer technology could have unfortunate effects. The multimedia attractions of electronic books and CD–ROM encyclopedias may well lead children to equate reading with visual entertainment, so that, in Jane Healy's words, they "keep looking around for meaning instead of creating it inside their own heads."[29] At the same time, as they begin to discover the vast amount of print that can be accessed by computer, children may develop a purely functional approach to reading, one that is limited to finding facts and processing information.

Reading is much more than this. Children need to have stories presented in a way that appeals to their imagination and opens doors to new worlds they can create inside their minds. The most effective way of doing this is to read books to and with them. One might call this a low-tech approach, but there is nothing unsophisticated about the imaginative, intellectual, and emotional development it fosters.

## CHAPTER 6

# The Young Writer
# and the Screen

*Writing draws us deeper and deeper into ourselves. . . . We will begin to see the rich garden we have inside us and use that for writing.*

—Natalie Goldberg[1]

Imagine you are observing a class of fourth graders engaged in a writing assignment. The class is in a school that is well equipped with computer technology, and as you begin your observation, a number of students are settling in at the keyboard of their machines. You focus your attention on one student in particular, and this is what you see: First he changes the fonts, then he changes format size, after which he changes the text style to bold, introduces lines, changes font again, changes text size, changes text color to red, then to black, then green, and then changes the font and font size.[2] Clearly, little writing is being done. What, you may wonder, is going on?

There is no doubt that the computer benefits the process of writing. Professional writers were quick to trade in their old electric typewriters for word processors because of the amount of labor saved in revising their work. Avoiding this kind of repetition is a boon to anyone.

As well, many professional writers who are enthusiastic about computers discovered that the word processor changed the way they write.

The ease with which they can enter and revise text on the computer screen makes it a more flexible medium of expression than typing or handwriting. They believe that this flexibility allows them to explore ideas more freely than ever before.

We should not assume, however, that children will find word processing equally liberating. Professional writers bring a formidable array of writing skills and a depth of subject knowledge, to their craft; children generally do not. Since children are still learning the basics of writing, they may not be able to take advantage of the flexibility offered by on-screen composition. The question we must ask, therefore, is: Does the use of word processors really help young students develop their writing skills as many educators seem to believe?

Writing is at the heart of so much of children's learning in school. Good writing skills are critical for academic success. Because of this, it is crucial to look closely at what happens when elementary school children are encouraged to use word processors as they learn to write.

What made word processing so attractive to teachers and parents was that it promised to make writing easier for young children and to encourage greater creativity in the process. It would thus help teachers overcome a problem they often encountered with their students—a reluctance to engage in writing because of the physical tedium of correcting mistakes and recopying—while helping students express themselves more effectively. This would create a kind of virtuous circle in which the more students wrote, the better they would write, which, in turn, would lead them to write even more.

Writing is difficult, even for those with experience. It is full of false starts and dead ends. Getting started is hard; getting stuck is easy. A computer screen can appear to be a more forgiving medium than a blank sheet of paper because a writer does not have to live with his or her mistakes. Children can change on-screen text almost instantly, whereas they must cross out or erase what they have handwritten. Many claim that, as a result, children are more likely to take risks and try out their ideas on the screen, and will revise more often and more thoroughly than they would when writing by hand.

At the same time, the computer screen is a much more visible medium than a sheet of paper. The text can be easily read by more than one person as the writing takes place, making students' writing more accessible to comment and criticism. This encourages teachers to engage students in discussions about what they are writing, and students are able to work together and critique one another's work as they are producing or revising their texts.[3]

The overall effect of the computer screen is that it makes writing a process that can be talked about *and observed* simultaneously. As one researcher puts it, "What was once the hidden process of mentally rearranging information becomes visible in our word processors."[4] As a result, it is argued, children become more aware of what goes on in their minds when they are writing—more conscious of what is required to produce a written text—and this realization plays a vital part in the development of their writing skills.

This combination of factors, many educators believe, makes writing with a word processor a very different experience from writing by hand. Students have more freedom to determine the order in which they write various parts of their text—there is no need to start at the beginning and work straight through to the end. Students can put thoughts or observations on the screen as they occur, then fit them in with the rest of the text later. Because writing on-screen encourages discussion and collaboration with other children, young writers come to see that, in many ways, writing is not so different from speaking, and this realization can help them come to grips with an activity that is still relatively new to them. Finally, a word processor creates a different view of the nature of writing. Instead of approaching their writing as something that is fixed and unchangeable once written, students see that it can be easily revised. This knowledge gives them more confidence and a greater sense of control.

This view of writing coincides with what is normally referred to as the "process approach," which sees writing as consisting of several stages. Prewriting activities involve thinking about what one wants to write about, researching facts and developing ideas about the topic, and deciding how these facts and ideas should be organized. The writing that follows is only a first or working draft, one that students will revise several times after rereading it and incorporating comments and suggestions from other students and their teacher.

With so many advantages claimed for word processing, one might expect that the use of computers has led to dramatic improvements in students' writing. The results, however, are decidedly mixed.

A sample of research shows results that are divided almost equally among positive, negative, and insignificant effects.[5] In some cases, the writing appeared to improve as a result of computer use. It was generally of a higher standard and contained fewer grammatical and spelling errors. (Notably, the greatest improvement appears to have been among students who received remedial writing instruction.) In other cases, the writing produced by hand was better. One particularly telling comment concerned third-grade students whose handwritten work "appeared better organized, was longer, and seemed to better express what the child was thinking." In contrast, the writing they did on computers "appeared stilted, was brief to the point of insignificance, and had only one point of superiority—neatness."[6]

Why such inconsistent results? An obvious answer is that individual students respond to computers in different ways, depending, among other things, on their temperament and their style of thinking and learning.

Many students clearly enjoy working with computers, and there is some evidence that computer use can create a more positive attitude toward writing.[7] Positive attitudes may, in fact, have less to do with writing than with computer use.[8] Nevertheless, a willingness to write could improve students' performance, at least in the short term.

A major attraction of writing with a computer is that when students see their work printed out, it appears to be more "finished" than if they had written it by hand. Although this does not necessarily have any bearing on the quality of the work produced, it could explain why students who write with computers obtain greater satisfaction from their work, as well as higher marks. The professional appearance of a computer printout can make it easier to overlook shortcomings that would not be ignored in handwritten work. One ten-year-old boy said he liked the computer because it "makes my writing look better than it is."[9] Some teachers fall into this trap. Many admit that they have a tendency to give higher marks to papers that are computer typed than those that are handwritten, even if the quality of the writing is similar.

On the other hand, some students find that using a computer inhibits their ability to write because they lack the necessary keyboarding skills and knowledge of software commands. Writing with a computer is obviously harder than writing by hand if you cannot type and are unfamiliar with the word processing program you are using. Many students do not find it easy to reach this basic level of computer competence. Until they do, students focus primarily on how to get the technology to work. The computer, far from making writing easier, creates new problems, and the child's enjoyment of the process most likely will suffer.

Pushing young children to learn keyboarding skills may be more trouble than it is worth. Karen Silver, a parent of four, recently described how, when her son Stephen was forced to learn keyboarding in the first grade (at an age she now thinks is far too young), his enjoyment of writing, reading, and school in general began to suffer. One day in early January, five months after the keyboarding program had started, his teacher sent home a note, alerting his parents to what the teacher suggested was becoming a serious problem: "It took Stephen forty-five minutes today to key in nine words on the computer. During the same length of time, about half of the class had completed about three full verses of the poem they were all learning." Like many children across the country, Stephen had to attend forty-five-minute keyboarding classes twice a week. His teacher was attempting to teach the class the necessary skills that in many states are now mandated. Stephen's mother wasn't worried about her son's keyboarding skills; instead, she was concerned that all the joy would be taken out of her son's love for poetry. "I can't imagine anything more inappropriate," she said sadly. "My wiggly little son shouldn't be forced to sit in front of a computer for forty-five minutes at a time. He should be hearing poetry from somebody who is able to express it in meaningful ways."

Karen was concerned that Stephen's difficulty with keyboarding would affect his attitude not only toward literature and writing but also toward school in general. "When he came home and threw a book across the room because he didn't want to read, we knew it was time to do something." His teacher made it clear that he had to learn to keyboard because it was a curriculum requirement. Karen and her husband decided that pushing their son to learn a skill he simply was not ready for was doing more harm than good. In order to preserve his love for reading and writing, they took him out of their local public school and enrolled him in a Waldorf school, where keyboarding is not taught until high school. A year later, by then in the second grade, Stephen was happily reading poetry and writing out his stories by hand "in very beautiful cursive writing," said his mother.

A common assumption is that if children do not learn to keyboard early, they will acquire bad habits that will be hard to correct later on. There is, however, little evidence that this actually happens, and some researchers consider that a hunt-and-peck approach, using one or two fingers, does not inhibit the later development of proper keyboarding skills any more than printing letters interferes with the introduction of cursive writing.[10] On the other hand, children do seem to need time to learn to type before they can use computers productively for writing. This was the case in a two-year study involving five- to ten-year-olds, where "regardless of the tasks that teachers assigned during the learning period, children focused their attention on mastering the word processing system and on developing keyboard familiarity, rather than on the content of their writing."[11]

This problem is not confined to young children. One study of seventh and ninth graders found that, although they had had considerable typing and word processing practice, they still found using the computer difficult and, as a result, wrote less on the computer than they did with pencil and paper. According to another study, students in the eighth grade managed a typing speed of only about eight words per minute, and tenth-grade students with little computer experience tended to write a good deal more when writing by hand than when they used word processing.[12]

Some students prefer handwriting, although they may be in the fifth or sixth grade before they are able to articulate their preference. One such student, George, a fifth grader at a Boston public school I visited, said:

> I don't like the computer. I like writing in pencil. When I first started writing I got a bump. [He held up his middle finger.] Then I started writing, writing,

writing. Now I'm used to it, and it doesn't hurt any more. I like writing a lot. I can't do that much by hand because [the teacher] tells us to do it on computer. But I can do some of it by hand. The only thing I like about [the computer] is that it's got games. Other than that I don't like anything about it.

George's handwriting was very small but quite legible, and, from my observation, he was clearly a fluent writer comfortable with his chosen medium. He had not been put off by the initial discomfort caused by the bump on his finger. He had known that using a pencil was right for him, and he persevered. At his school, however, students were required to use the computer for forty-five-minute periods four times a week.

Not all children want to use word processors, and allowing them to write by hand if they want to seems reasonable. Some young writers do better on the computer, and some do worse; therefore, we can reasonably conclude that students' personal preferences play a large part in the outcome.

The way in which teachers introduce word processing to their students also has an effect. Approaches to computer use for writing vary widely. Some teachers emphasize the computer as a motivating tool that will encourage students to write (and write better) even if they were previously reluctant to do so. Others use word processing primarily as a means of producing a "more correct" text.

A three-year study conducted by researchers from the Centre for the Study of Computers in Education at York University in Ontario provides an interesting example of how computer use can motivate students to write. The study compared the work done by students in two elementary schools in the same school district. At one of these schools, students made extensive use of computers for their writing assignments; at the other school they seldom did so. The study assessed the effects of computer use on the development of students' writing skills as they progressed from third grade to fifth grade.[13]

At the first school, in an effort to encourage their students to write on the computer, teachers allowed them to choose what they wanted to write about (much of the writing they did consisted of fictional narratives) and let them get started. They made limited use of prewriting activities such as brainstorming and students often started writing as soon as they had selected a topic. Teachers placed less emphasis on correct spelling and grammar, at least in the drafting stage. Two of the teachers, in particular, stressed the importance of getting ideas down "on paper" (that is, onto the computer screen) before worrying about editing their work. The students seem to have had little help from their teachers in making revisions.

As a result of the freedom they were allowed, the students using computers seemed to be less inhibited about writing and pursued it with genuine interest as they developed their stories. Moreover, their teachers encouraged their growing involvement with their compositions by giving them extended due dates, often as much as two months—hence the unusual length of their stories. By fifth grade, students with average writing ability were producing more than 2,000 words, and in some cases the texts were considerably longer.[14]

But length is not everything, and if the work of three students featured in the study is representative, the quality of much of the writing produced using computers may have suffered from too much emphasis on quantity. Two of the stories, written by students who were rated low and average, respectively, show much youthful energy and spontaneity, but little understanding of the conventions of written language. The story written by the low-rated student is essentially a series of action sequences with a strong comic-book flavor. Much of the writing reads rather like a monologue a child would create while playing with action figures. The average-rated student tended to write in a kind of headlong rush—the manner of a breathless child whose words come tumbling out so quickly that one has difficulty keeping up with what he or she is saying. Only in the story written by the high-rated student do we encounter writing that has a sense of self-assurance (the writer was skillful in evoking the protagonist's feelings of uncertainty and fear and included some nice descriptive detail), but even here the story would have been better had it been shorter.[15]

The report unfortunately does not provide examples of the writing produced by hand at the other school, so it is impossible to make a comparison. It is worth noting, however, that not until fifth grade did the students using computers draw ahead. In the previous two years, the handwritten work generally received higher scores. These results raise the possibility that students need a certain level of maturity and writing ability before they can benefit significantly from the use of a word processor. Another study involving eleven-year-olds supports this theory.[16]

Any approach that makes students enthusiastic about writing is worth pursuing. The more writing students do, the better their writing will become. Richard Sterling, president of the National Writing Project, states, "If writing occurred in every classroom every day, student achievement would, in my view, reach new heights for all."[17] At a time when, according to the 1998 National Assessment of Educational Progress, three-fourths of U.S. students are not proficient writers, there is certainly room for improvement. But encouraging students to write as much as they can is only part of the answer. Young writers must also learn how to focus and organize their thoughts and observations so that what they have to say is presented in an appropriate form. One of the greatest challenges students face is quite simply developing the ability to think clearly about what they are writing. Part of good writing is knowing when one has said enough, something that many word-processing writers fail to understand.

Expecting that students will become competent writers simply by using a computer is unrealistic. No amount of technology can replace a teacher's guidance. Students need teachers to show them how to develop and revise their written work. As one word-processing software writer points out:

> It is teachers who have to help students learn how to start an assignment, frame an argument, and select which revision processes are most productive, and then teach students how to use the new technology to make the most of it as a creative medium. THE WORD PROCESSOR WON'T DO ANY OF THAT.[18]

So what will the word processor do? Unlike a sheet of paper, which just lies there waiting to be written on, a computer screen offers all sorts of possibilities for action depending on the software being used. The danger is that young writers will be seduced into exploring these possibilities rather than concentrating on the real task at hand—learning to develop and express their thoughts in a clear, coherent way.

One of the hardest things about writing, especially for students, is getting started. Children often do not know what they want to write about or how to approach their chosen topic. No problem—several writing software programs provide help by suggesting ideas; some will even compose sentences from randomly-selected words or phrases. For example, as one enthusiastic newspaper article explained:

> The top level of the *Creative Writer* "house" is the "ideas" attic. If you get stumped for a getting-started idea, you can pull the lever of a slot machine that will put three random parts of a sentence together. It delivers nonsense sentences such as "the likeable ornithologist blasted into reverse close to the magic garden." Sometimes these contain the germ of a good story.[19]

Similarly, the writing component of Logo enables children to make random groupings of categories of words that may eventually result in "meaningful" or "poetic" statements. Students are directed to create vocabulary lists for each part of speech—article, noun, verb, adjective, adverb, pronoun, and so forth. Words from each list are then selected at random and strung together in a specified order.

Although this no doubt affords a certain amount of fun, it also encourages a scattershot approach to writing. Such an approach is incompatible with the idea that good writing requires disciplined thought in order to achieve clarity and coherence. It also overlooks the value of using children's own observations and sensory experiences as a basis for their writing—for example, having them listen to the wind or the rain and then describe the sound it makes. Simple activities such as this are good at stimulating children's imagination as they encourage students to look within themselves (rather than at a computer screen) for ideas.

Even if the suggestions of the software do spark ideas, there is no evidence that this kind of exercise is more effective than other prewriting activities. For example, one study found that primary school children wrote better narrative compositions if they took part in drawing and drama sessions before they started writing. Because drawing and drama are both creative activities, they are particularly effective in helping children test and sort out their ideas before they begin to write.[20]

Moreover, drawing and drama are meaningful activities. The

random-selection approach ignores the fact that creative writing is drawn from thoughts and feelings that are rooted in the experiences and imagination of the writer. Theodore Roszak questions whether Logo's poetic programming inspires writing with any validity as an expression of human thought and feeling.

> Aren't poems *about* something? Don't they have a *meaning* that comes out of somebody's life? When the children make up poems, their own minds would not seem to be doing anything at all like the poem-program. They mean to *say* something, and that something preexists the words as a whole thought. They are not shuffling parts of speech through arbitrary patterns.[21]

While I was volunteering to help with a writing unit in my younger daughter's second-grade class, I assigned the students a journal project. I asked them to write the stories of their seven-year-old lives. What they produced was remarkably fresh. With little prompting, one boy wrote about the open-heart surgery he had as an infant; another child about visiting her grandparents in Greece; a few children described their sorrow over their parents' divorces; and others wrote about the joy of acquiring a pet or learning to skate. Each story was different and, although the children needed help with spelling, grammar, and the general structure of their work, every child created something original that had particular meaning for them.

In addition to prompting children to play around with random words as a preliminary to writing, word processing also encourages them to play around with how the words will look on the screen. They can easily change the type size, font, and line spacing, and can even vary the color of the text. For mature writers, these are options that are selected according to need. For children, on the other hand, these options can become a fixation.

This is certainly the impression given by the three-year Ontario study mentioned earlier. According to the authors of this study:

> After lengthy observations with a number of students it became apparent that student creative activity was often being subverted by the students' obsession with formatting their texts. By allowing students greater freedom to produce

a stylish product, the computer seemed to be diverting them away from sustained creative effort.[22]

The teacher was apparently unaware that this kind of compulsive reformatting occurred so frequently, perhaps because, from a distance, the students appeared to be working busily. This behavior was not unique to this particular class. In another fourth-grade class taking part in the same study, students seldom produced an extended piece of writing without making repeated changes to the format of their text.

Other researchers confirm these observations. A group of eighth-grade students was monitored by screen-recording software, which provided a running account of everything they did while writing on the computer. An analysis of their actions found that the menu-bar option most frequently used during the drafting session was the "format" label, which made layout features available.[23]

Some teachers who have observed this kind of compulsive formatting believe that it undermines the usefulness of computers as writing machines. At the Louis Riel Elementary/Middle School in Calgary, Alberta, language arts teacher John Portway now insists that his seventh- and ninth-grade students use pencil and paper, instead of computers, to draft their stories. He thinks the students become lost in playing with the headlines, fonts, and other formatting features, which distract them from writing. Portway concedes that computers are good for teaching formatting and for getting students to write to a specific length, but overall, he says, "I would swear that [the computer] is more detrimental than beneficial for creative writing. It's not that the technology is inherently bad, it's just that it is very distracting."

Portway, also a published writer, believes that computers have had a negative effect on the way students approach their writing. "The process of writing is lost," he says. "It becomes a visual medium. The kids go in without a working draft, it goes down, and it doesn't change. It looks good, so the students think it *is* good." Portway found that his students made only superficial revisions on computers. When he switched them from composing on-screen to writing drafts by hand, they were more prepared to edit and change their work and also produced more text.

The ease with which text can be entered, erased, and reentered is another aspect of on-screen writing that can, paradoxically, be a disadvantage for inexperienced writers. It means that they do not feel so committed to their initial choice of words because changing them requires little effort. As a result, they may draft less carefully than when writing by hand. A number of high school students in one study pointed out that, "because of the tedium involved in rewriting handwritten text, they had to be clear about what they wanted to say before handwriting, whereas on the word processor they 'wouldn't really bother.'"[24] Generally they planned *less* when using the word processor, a response that seemed to indicate a diminished respect for the discipline that writing requires.

Word processing also does not seem to help students revise more effectively than when they write by hand. The underlying assumption is that the more students review and revise what they have written, the better their writing will be. Because on-screen revising is easier, the argument goes, using computers will enable students to revise more, thereby improving their work more than when writing by hand. But the quality of the writing that results from revision depends on the nature of the changes that are made. On-screen revisions do not seem to help students improve their writing in terms of the logic of its structure or clarity of expression.[25] In the study that monitored keyboard actions, the eighth-grade students had ample time to revise their texts, yet they attempted no in-depth revisions. Of the three students whose work was featured in the report, the first two neither elaborated on their ideas nor added any descriptive detail to what they had written. The third student, described as a "graphics experimenter," managed to produce only five sentences in his first draft, and his final version was not so much a revision as an extension of what he had previously written.[26]

Using revision time simply to add more to the end of the existing text is, in fact, another common tactic among students using computers. One researcher, who observed this approach among seventh- and ninth-grade students, linked it with the fact that, when students revised on the computer, they no longer had to copy by hand what they had written. Students often say that copying is one of the things they like least about writing, and many educators condemn it as a waste of time; but this researcher concluded that recopying "is not the meaningless process it appears to be" because it "slows the writer down" when reviewing the text and "leads the writer to focus on each word." The students in this study appeared not to have done this and, evidently, did not focus on the overall content and organization of their writing as many of the additions they made "related to ideas that could have been developed more fully in the body of the text."[27]

The use of word processors can also lead to teachers correcting their students' work instead of the students themselves. While visiting a large elementary school during "literacy week" where students' writing—mostly stories made into "books" and colorfully illustrated by hand—was on display, I noticed that most of the work produced by first, second, and third graders was done on a word processor. It was also remarkably free of grammar and spelling errors. When I asked the principal why this work was so perfect, he told me that the teacher input the corrections before the work was printed out. This may produce a better-looking, "more correct" product, but I couldn't help wondering where the students' work left off and the teacher's began. As a parent, I would much rather see my children's work written by hand, with all its mistakes, than receive a perfectly produced version which I know has been corrected by the teacher. As any writer knows, correcting mistakes once they have been pointed out is an extremely important part of the process of learning to write.

Writing by hand may present physical challenges for young children, but it allows them to concentrate more on the writing and less on the technology they are using. When children write with computers, they are bound to direct some of their attention to the capabilities of the software. Writing with a pencil, a familiar and much simpler tool, leaves them freer to concentrate on what they want to say.

Pencil and paper have another advantage over word processors in that the writer can review several pages at the same time. With a computer, unless the composition is short enough to be viewed in its entirety on a single screen, it is not possible to see the complete text all at once. As one eleventh-grade student complained, "You don't have your full story in front of you."[28] Yet at both the drafting and editing stages, the writer (or editor) needs to be able to view the text as a whole in order to see how its parts fit together. Here, too, word processing makes additional demands on students' attention—because of the physical limitations of the screen they must either hold more of their composition in their minds or continually scroll up and down to remind themselves of what they have written. The answer to this problem is for students to print out what they have written and revise the "hard copy" after a careful reading. Unfortunately, this stage is often skipped because on-screen revision appears to be more efficient.

Writing requires focused attention and anything that diverts attention from the process is going to affect the quality of the work produced. Of course, some aspects of writing can, with mastery of the keyboard and of program commands, be performed more quickly and easily on a computer than by hand. Correcting spelling errors with a spell checker is an obvious example. But without a teacher's careful intervention, computer technology tends to undermine the development of many of the skills needed to produce good writing—in particular, the ability to think clearly, to choose words carefully, and to organize one's writing into a coherent whole.

As adults, we have become so used to the advantages of word processing that we tend to assume that children will benefit in a similar way. In doing so, we forget that children can easily be distracted when using complex adult tools, and we overlook the complex stages involved in learning to write clearly. We cannot dispense with the technology of paper and pencil—the skills associated with learning to write by hand are not adequately developed in other ways. We must focus on learning to take advantage of both kinds of technology, but each in its own time.

# CHAPTER 7

# The Information Maze

*Infomania retards rather than accelerates wisdom.*
—Michael Heim[1]

In May 1998, at a hearing in the Texas state capitol to propose replacing public school textbooks with laptop computers and CD–ROMs, a software vendor poured water onto a laptop computer and then "invited a portly legislator to jump on the machine." The vendor, in a display of what one participant called "pure Texas hucksterism," was not trying to destroy the technology. Instead, he was demonstrating the machine's durability, hoping to convince the legislators, presenters, education officials, and reporters who were present that the technology was tough enough to withstand handling by the state's public school children.[2]

If this software vendor and the then-chairman of the Texas State School Board of Education, Dr. Jack Christie, had had their way, the entire state school system would have replaced textbooks with laptops and CD–ROMs. Christie, like many other educators, politicians, and parents, believes that linking children to the Internet via computers is perhaps the most important goal in education today. Christie wanted to spend the state's annual textbook budget to lease computers for the state's 4 million children. He also hoped that, eventually, such a switch would save money because Texas is facing a $1.2 billion outlay for textbooks over a six-year period.

Although Texas has since dropped its plan to replace textbooks with laptops, some schools in Ohio and South Carolina are already implementing a version of this plan. Many politicians and vendors from the computer and software industries have already jumped on the bandwagon. Former House Speaker New Gingrich said, "One of the goals should be to replace all textbooks with a PC. I would hope that within five years [students] would have no more textbooks." Bill Gates has compared the rapid development of the Internet to the California Gold Rush of 1849. (One might remember, however, that many prospectors came up empty handed.)

Even at more conservative schools, libraries are buying fewer books and magazines, replacing them with subscriptions to electronic databases on the Internet or, at the very least, with CD–ROMs. Unlimited information on any subject, we are told, is now just a touch away. At the Saturn Elementary School in Ohio, for instance, children do most of their reading and writing on computers and use databases instead of newspapers to get their daily dose of current affairs.

Electronic databases promise a new and better way of acquiring information. No more leisurely browsing through library stacks or card catalogs. No more dusty volumes on crowded, poorly-lit shelves. No more bottlenecks because access is limited to the number of copies of a particular book. A few deft strokes on the keyboard will pull up precisely the right piece of information or point the way to the best authority on any topic.

Along with this seductive promise of instant, universal access is the notion that it is mere child's play to gain access to this vast body of information. Many believe that computer technology allows children to learn on their own and that it will lead to a new era of child-centered education with the computer as an all-knowing tutor free from the shortcomings of human teachers. No longer will a child's question go unanswered by a busy teacher or her curiosity be thwarted by the limitations of the local library. With a world of knowledge accessible from her desk, she will be able to find answers to any question she could possibly ask.

Proponents of computer use in elementary schools believe it will create an environment that will nourish independent, motivated learners. As one elementary school principal explained, "Knowledge is doubling every fifteen months, and we want our students to be exposed to the most up-to-date information. Classrooms are information-poor; the computer makes them information-rich."

That, at least, is the theory. However, if we look at what goes on in schools when students use electronic databases and consider the quality of these materials, a different picture emerges.

Surfing the Internet is fraught with diversions and difficulties for the learner. For one thing, there is just too much to see. Picking one's way through the Internet is like walking through a giant shopping mall—there are a lot of interesting things to dazzle the eyes and pique the interest, but how does one find what one is looking for? The possibilities for distraction are endless. Children who have access to a vast and ever-growing body of information are more likely to be briefly dazzled, then confused by all the choices that confront them.

The Internet also offers many activities that have little or nothing to do with learning in any formal sense, and such diversions are magnets for student users. Students may have difficulty resisting the lure of the Backstreet Boys or the latest Sarah McLaughlan video while researching a frog habitat. They may have trouble paying strict attention to the history of the Great Depression when the latest release from Spice Girls or Smashing Pumpkins is just a few clicks away. Montreal education consultant Remi Dussault visited more than forty schools and observed about 1,000 students to find out just what students were really doing when they were working on the Internet during school hours. What he discovered probably would not surprise most teachers, or even most conscientious parents. Although students were supposed to use the Internet to work on school projects, most students, he discovered, simply engaged in surfing. "In the course of an hour," said Dussault, "they will visit between fifteen and twenty Web sites, and they are unable to deal with the information they find there. They get lost, look at the images more than the text, and learn very little." In his opinion, "the reputation of the Internet is overblown. Moreover, the material on the Internet is not always reliable. Students don't know how to verify the information they find there."[3]

Without teacher guidance and supervision, computers are used, more often than not, in trivial ways. The technology, by itself, will not inspire children to learn. To say this is not to blame the students. It is unrealistic to expect children to start using computers as academic research tools on their own initiative, especially when they are distracted by the latest Madonna video. (To paraphrase Neil Postman, if you want children to learn more, you do not need a new kind of software—what you need is another species of child.) And it isn't just the screen in front of them that can cause problems. "As soon as a child sits down," said Naomi Morse, head of the children's department at a public library in Maryland, "and sees that the person on the computer beside them is watching a cartoon, or playing a game, or sending e-mail, he or she becomes distracted."

It is also unrealistic for educators to expect children to find their way, unaided, among the mountains of information a computer can provide. "Sometimes students have no idea at all where to begin the search," Morse told me recently. "Students do not receive adequate instruction in elementary and middle schools, and the problem extends right into junior high school and senior high school."

In fact, using the Internet is anything but child's play. Whereas any child can easily go to the library and browse through a section of books on, for example, old-growth forests or the history of earthquakes, browsing on the Internet is a far more complicated undertaking. "It's difficult for a seasoned adult to find information from the Internet," Morse noted. "Children need to be walked through the process from the beginning."

A child whose reading skills are minimal can still take a book from a library shelf. If she cannot judge the book by its cover, she need only open it to see the contents. But little can be gleaned about a Web site without extensive on-screen reading. Children can assess the relevance of a reference book far more quickly and easily, and there are no on-screen graphics to distract them.

Using a card catalog or a computerized catalog system is a relatively easy way of finding out what books a library has and where they are to be found. Readers are also able to locate books on similar or related subjects because they are grouped together on the shelves. If a student is looking for information on the ancient city of Troy, researching figures such as Helen, Paris, Ajax, or Nike, for instance, she will probably encounter other books on Greek or Roman mythology. Most likely, these will be classics written by well-known scholars. Her chances of success are not nearly as high on the Internet. She will stumble across all kinds of irrelevant information, from chat rooms, to travel services, to advertising. In this instance, the older technology of print offers a greater chance of success even though the volume of information available via computer is potentially far greater.

When using an Internet search engine, a certain amount of technical knowledge is required to get into the system. Different databases and search engines have different methods of accessing information. They also have different focuses and functions—some are good for current affairs; others for finding out about business, science, or technolog; others for music; and a few for historical or literary research. To find out which one to use for research requires both guidance and experience.

The success of a search also depends on students having a basic grasp of the topic they are researching. Suppose, for example, a student in rural Iowa is using the Internet to find out how his congressional representative voted on a farm aid bill. He is familiar with the Yahoo search engine and knows how to access its Web site. Because Yahoo works in a hierarchical way, with broad subject areas that are broken down into successively more specific items, clicking on "Government " would start the search, but the student would then have to click "U.S. Government," then "Federal," then "Congress," then "House," then "Representative," then the name of the representative to reach the representative's Web site. A faster way would be to type in "House of Representatives," or the name of the representative if the student knows it. To find the representative's position on the specific bill, the student would have to search the site by topic. This kind of search presumes a student understands the basic structure of government. It also presumes that the student understands not only what a *position* or a *representative* is, but also that he knows the difference between a *congressman* and a *senator* and grasps the law-making function of Congress. After finding the information, the student must also be able to decide if his representative made a sound decision. Without a basic understanding of the economics of farming, as well as a well-developed critical faculty, however, the information found would be of little value.

Although the technical aspect of the search itself can be time-consuming and confusing, learning to evaluate the quality of the information found is far more difficult. For this reason, children need a lot of training and careful, ongoing assistance when using the Internet. For example, while searching the Internet for material on right whales with my nine-year-old daughter, we came up with three hits on one search engine. The best Web site was the Florida Marine Research Institute. Although my daughter is well aware that some sources are better than others, she would have had a difficult time understanding the concept of a marine research institute without a discussion about both the institute and the reasons why the material we found was likely to be accurate. Although the material was correct, we found much more detailed information in three books and a National Geographic video, which we discovered at our local library.

Students, especially young ones, cannot be left to navigate the Internet on their own. Guidance is necessary, and parents, teachers, and especially teacher-librarians are the ones who have to provide it. As well as helping students find their way around, they must continually track down pools of information that are both useful and accurate. Examples are Web sites for environmental organizations, science associations, or human rights groups. This process is called "bookmarking." Teachers must bookmark sites (often in conjunction with librarians) because so much of what a child can find on the Internet is overly complex. Given that Web sites are constantly being constructed and abandoned, keeping up with the changes is an ongoing job.

In fact, far from allowing students to be independent learners, working on the Internet takes a great deal of one-on-one tutoring. When a classroom gains access to the Internet, the teacher must spend much of her time supervising her students' forays into cyberspace. Not to do so would most likely lead to misguided or inappropriate use. This, according to librarians such as Morse and others, is best done either one-on-one or in small groups of no more than five students.

Children who are given unlimited access to information—whatever its form—without ongoing guidance are often unable to distinguish among the important, the trivial, the inadequate, and the simply erroneous. "Students don't quite believe that something that looks good and rolls out of the computer might not be accurate or even have an available author," said Morse, adding that teaching students to write a bibliography using source material found on the Internet is a very complicated undertaking for adults, let alone for children.

While working on a project about Hannibal, my elder daughter came across a site that looked promising after wading through numerous unrelated hits. The site, however, was filled with factual errors as well as bad grammar and even worse spelling. One reference had Hannibal fighting the Romans at the Tigris (which is in Iraq) instead of the Trebia (which is in Italy). Without a good general knowledge of geography and history (which her father was able to provide), she could easily have absorbed a lot of inaccurate information.

Even with careful supervision, unwelcome surprises may be in store. A fifth-grade teacher described how two random Internet links on the classroom computer landed her and her class in the middle of a Nazi bulletin board. On another occasion, one of her children, who was searching the Internet for information on chickadees, followed the links to a sex chat-room. Many parents have also expressed concern about the possibility of their children encountering online pedophiles.

The fact that information is available on the Internet is no guarantee that it is accurate or unbiased. Information that appears in print may not be accurate or unbiased either, but at least with print, certain well-established procedures are generally in place to ensure that the material has been vetted—by publishers' readers, by editors, and sometimes by fact checkers—and to inform readers of the author's identity, credentials, and point of view. Web sites generally dispense with these formalities. The information they contain could have come from anywhere and been put together by anyone. Because few recognized forums, such as book reviews, exist for discussing their contents, Internet users themselves must determine the value of a particular site. This is a lot to expect of young children.

When information is disconnected from books, children may have difficulty understanding how material is acquired and where it comes from. "The speed of retrieving information from the computer and the polished, finished look of what is retrieved," said Morse, "goes against the rhythm and natural process of amassing information. Everything is so fast and so finished." She noted that children have a much easier time understanding where something comes from if they can relate it to a book—something concrete that they can hold in their hands. If they can say, "I found this in the blue book," or "I took that information from the big book with the killer whale on the cover," the process of researching will make more sense to them.

There are similar problems with CD–ROMs. Teachers rarely have time to screen and evaluate such material and published reviews are generally uncritical. Previewing a CD–ROM is a much more difficult and time-consuming undertaking than skimming a book, both because of the way information is presented and because of the amount of material a CD–ROM contains. Consequently, educators purchase material on the basis of packaging and advertising. Yet a careful, critical review is even more necessary for CD–ROMs than for books because the haste with which new CD–ROMs are placed on the market has led to uneven quality. For example, a topic much in vogue at the moment is dinosaurs. When dinosaur specialist John W. Merck, Jr. undertook a thorough review of four student-targeted CD–ROMs for the magazine *The Sciences*, he found the quality ranged from "terrible to pretty good." The content of one CD–ROM even failed to give an adequate definition of the term *dinosaur*, made fundamental errors, and presented "a welter of shallow, inaccurate and misleading information."[4]

One writer of CD–ROM text confirms the poor quality of much CD–ROM material. In a provocative essay published in *Harper's* magazine, "Virtual Grub Street, Sorrows of a Multimedia Hack," Paul Roberts wrote with despair about the quality of writing contained on CD–ROMs. The writers of this material, he noted, are not experts, but merely

> filters, whose task is to absorb and compress great gobs of information into small, easily digestible, on-screen chunks. Brevity and blandness; these are the elements of the next literary style. Of roughly one thousand "essays" I've "written" for CD–ROM companies here in Seattle over the last year and a

half, fewer than forty ran longer than two hundred words—about the length of the paragraph you're reading now–and most were much, much shorter.... Nowadays, whole months go by when I do nothing but crank out info-nuggets on whatever topics the multimedia companies believe will sell: dead composers, large African mammals, sports stars of yore. It is, without question, hack writing.[5]

Roberts points out that, typically, the budget for writing is much smaller than that for the video or audio components, a fact that reflects how little importance manufacturers assign to the text.

Unfortunately, the multimedia attractions of CD–ROMs can distract users from the factual information presented. This certainly seems to be the case with CD–ROM encyclopedias. Until recently, the *Encyclopedia Britannica* and the *Book of Knowledge* were considered the best encyclopedias for use in schools. But the advent of encyclopedias on CD–ROM has created a situation where slick marketing and glitzy graphics—which consume vast quantities of space and memory and are produced at the expense of the text—can make inferior encyclopedias look good. Few schools, for example, wanted to own the Funk and Wagnall's encyclopedia it before it was animated.

The CD–ROM version of the *Encyclopedia Britannica* sells for $400, but some electronic encyclopedias cost as little as $80. This looks like a good deal. But the relentless pressure to upgrade software brings other costs, not the least of which is the need to upgrade hardware every few years because older machines may not be able to handle the latest software. Buying new machines carries additional costs such as installation and training. And, if a library has only one computer on which to run the electronic reference material, only one child can use the encyclopedia at a time, resulting in long line-ups at the computer. With a printed edition of an encyclopedia, almost the entire class can use it at the same time because each set has several volumes. Few schools can afford to purchase all the computers and CD–ROM licensing fees necessary for an entire class. Finally, the strength of the *Encyclopedia Britannica* lies in its high-quality essays written by distinguished scholars. Using it as a resource requires more sustained reading than other sources would.

With so much new information on the market, it is more important than ever for school librarians to filter materials. Librarians, like teachers, have a bigger job than ever before, sifting through an increasing volume of material to ensure that what gets into the library or classroom is appropriate and has educational value. Eighteen states now evaluate software and online instructional materials according to an *Education Week* survey. Florida, California, North Carolina, and Ohio publish formal evaluations that are available to the public. Yet trying out—let alone evaluating—new software is still a difficult undertaking. "It's not like a textbook, where you can thumb through it," said Bridget R. Foster, the director of the California Instructional Technology Clearinghouse, which evaluates electronic learning resources. "You have to sit down and load it onto your computer and figure out how to use it before you can even begin to evaluate the content."[6]

Dwindling book collections and decreased budgets for the librarians who must buy and review them have caused myriad problems that are only beginning to surface. Out-of-date books are becoming a big problem in libraries all across the country. "On the pages of library books in schools across the Washington area, communists still rule the Soviet Union, apartheid reigns in South Africa, and Golda Meir is prime minister of Israel," the *Washington Post* recently noted.[7] "A room full of old books is not a library," said Michael Gorman, dean of library sciences at California State, Fresno.

Although average annual spending on school libraries has increased to approximately $12,185 per school in 1999, up from about $11,000 in the previous school year, with the soaring increase in the cost of textbooks (the average price is $16) this money does not go far. As well, the amount of money spent per pupil varies widely. The Baltimore City school district in Maryland spent 92 cents per pupil in 1998, whereas Worcester County spent $19.34 in the same period. In Virginia, spending on books ranged from $21 per student in Arlington down to $10 per student in Prince William County. In Montgomery County, the budget for library materials fell from $19.26 per pupil in 1997 to $5.89 per pupil in 1998.[8] California, notes Gorman, is fiftieth out of fifty states in provision for libraries, a fact he attributes to the declining reading, writing, and research skills of incoming college students.

"We are now spending tens of thousands of dollars teaching remedial English to incoming students," Gorman told me recently, "because sustained reading is not part of their educational experience. Many students are not in the habit of reading—they are the product of poor school libraries."

The time-tested way of building library collections was to read the review journals and then the recommended books themselves. With fewer qualified school librarians, fewer opportunities exist for this kind of personal selection. As a result, school libraries rely increasingly on material collected for them by others—usually large, market-savvy book distributors who send out prepackaged selections of printed material with return postage paid. When schools are forced to rely on wholesalers to do their buying for them, the materials that arrive are increasingly homogenous and of dubious quality.

Often when a school spends money on electronic resources, little is left for books. Celebration School, in spite of its impressive electronic resources, has a woefully understocked library. The school currently has about 20,000 titles in its collection—too few books for a school serving grades kindergarten through twelve, and whose library also serves as the community library. When I visited the school in October 1999, the Women's Club was raising money to buy new books.

Inadequately stocked libraries cause other problems. Although people such as Jack Christie believe that electronic libraries make books redundant, this is simply not true. If teachers tried to use the Internet to replace a language arts text, for example, they would soon discover that even if they could find the material, copyright issues would prohibit them from downloading and copying the novels, poems, and plays their students need. Imagine trying to download a class set of Mark Twain's *Tom Sawyer* or *Huckleberry Finn*, a Toni Morrison novel, poems by William Carlos Williams or Emily Dickinson, or plays by Shakespeare or David Mamet.

The need for books and good school libraries remains as critical as ever. In those schools that have dispensed with textbooks in the classrooms—often because of electronic resources—the need for books in the library *increases*. At the Peakview School in Denver, Colorado, for instance, the library budget was small compared with expenditures on technology. "We don't have textbooks," the school librarian told me when I visited the school, "so the number of books per child in the library should go up from the standard twenty per student to forty or fifty." The librarian was forced to rely on interlibrary loans to compensate for the shortage. In fact, there is no way to get the necessary range of high-quality material without buying a wide selection of science, history, language, and geography books. And even if all the resources in libraries were available through the Internet, few would want to spend time reading from the screen.

The biggest dilemma now facing children's librarians is the fact that staff have less time for the kind of brief but meaningful interviews that were once a significant part of the job. Whereas in the past a librarian would question a child about her interests and reading level, and then steer her toward a good book, today's librarian usually does not have the time to do so. Thus, even when good books enter the library, they may not be read because no one has brought them to the attention of children or their parents. This means that when the time comes to cull the collection, books with low circulation rates may be disposed of prematurely.

These are not isolated problems. Pressures on library services are widespread. When the California State Library commissioned a study to evaluate public library reference material, it found that, although the demand for library service was very high, the human resources needed to meet this demand were inadequate. Between 1978 and 1993, when the California study was commissioned, the number of queries for information increased dramatically, but staff cuts resulted in reduced library hours and more requests handled per staff member. This meant that librarians spent less time on each question. In some libraries, staff cuts meant that *fewer* requests for information were handled, which led to a decline in service that the staff described as "reduced goodness (completeness, authoritativeness, soundness) of answers."[9] Indeed, what good is an abundance of information if the staff is not in place to help children benefit from it?

The California study also cites the loss of school librarians and the inadequate amount of library instruction in the schools as a reason for the increased burden on library resources. Today's students have greater difficulty finding their way around the public library, not only because it is more complex, but also because students receive less library instruction in school than they did in the past.

The irony of all this is that the new information technologies were supposed to make everything easier while providing library users with access to a vastly expanded range of information. By allowing the librarian's role to be largely superseded by online services, many library systems have left their users baffled by all the choices open to them. Where, they wonder, should they begin? The obvious answer is that they should consult a librarian—if they can find one available.

According to Thomas Childers, director of the Library and Information Science program at Drexel University in Philadelphia, "the 'new' public library is so complex that effective self-help is virtually impossible without more bibliographic instruction or better tools, such as good electronic gateways." Childers, a consultant to the California State Library and author of the California library study, says that most people have no idea of how to build the right search strategy or how to evaluate what they find. Although electronic information systems sometimes make finding information faster, library users generally cannot be relied upon to find the best sources for themselves. Librarians are critical to the quality of a search.

Particularly worrisome for children are the brutal cuts to library services and the steadily diminishing number of school librarians or teacher-librarians. Increasingly, lower salaried library clerks or computer technicians are replacing trained librarians. One teacher-librarian I spoke with told me he had to leave the elementary school where he worked because the school had redefined his position as a computer "technologist." Although offered the new position, he preferred to stay in his chosen field and had to move on.

This unfortunate trend stems from a view of libraries that values the technical knowledge required to keep the system going above an understanding of the sources of information the system makes accessible. Replacing librarians with technical staff might mean that students learn to replace the paper in a printer or to initialize a disk, but it is doubtful whether they will acquire the skills they need to navigate the sea of information that awaits them.

Even if students receive the kind of guidance they need, technology use encourages certain tendencies that conflict with educational goals. First, the ease with which computers can copy and print material has created more opportunities for plagiarism (and laziness) than ever before. Librarians and teachers frequently report incidents of students who copied entire articles or sections of information and turned them in as their own. A teacher told me about a student who copied a 35-page biography of Shakespeare from an electronic database. The librarian was alerted because of the amount of time the printer was printing and the amount of paper used.

It is also not uncommon, say teachers, for students to list books in their bibliographies that they have never looked at—the students add them to their essays simply because they were on a Web site. Michael Gorman sees "an epidemic of plagiarism" at the college level, and it is a subject much discussed among professors. Gorman told me about one student who had torn the pages out of a library book and attached them to an essay. "Students are so uneducated in the world of learning," he explained, "that they don't realize that it's a bad thing."

Plagiarism has always existed, but in the past, students were at least required to write or type the text they were using, which ensured that they read what they had taken (though their use of the material remained plagiarism nonetheless). With a computer, they can easily skip this step. As one librarian said, "Sometimes people think that because they are working on a computer they don't have to read. Often students hand things in without reading the material they have copied." For example, a second-grade teacher related a story about a girl who had been assigned a research project on the planet Venus. The child had managed to find a CD–ROM and had obviously keyed in the word "Venus." Perhaps because she had not read what she downloaded, however, the child handed in a perfectly printed report, complete with a graphic on the *Venus de Milo*. Although school district meetings and school seminars are now devoted to ways in which it can be addressed, teachers predict that this problem will continue to grow.

If students have not read the material they use, they certainly will not have made notes. Yet note taking is a vitally important skill. The most important part of research, says Paul Kraft, "is to get students to describe what they have read in their own words." Kraft, who is the media specialist (head librarian) at Florida's Celebration School, spends a lot of time working with students to assist them in their search. "I don't want them to just copy the information," he told me. "I want them to take notes, and I also get them to type in the bibliographic data."

Only by writing things in our own words do we make them part of our working knowledge. If we do not take notes, we reduce the likelihood that what we have read will be fixed in our minds. Note taking forces us to read carefully and to reflect on the text because only in this way can we determine what our notes should contain. "Too often," says Kraft, "kids will jot something down from the Internet and not credit where they caught it. A big problem on the Internet is forgetting to cite where material came from." Because Celebration School is dedicated to project-based learning, Kraft and two other teacher-librarians spend a lot of time teaching students about finding and citing accurate sources—and how to evaluate critically what they encounter.

Another problem is that information obtained from a database search is often devoid of context. For young children, contexts are essential if they are to arrange what they learn in any meaningful way. Books, with their clearly defined scope and linear organization, are good at helping children fit new information into a broader framework; computer databases are not.

In presenting information, the computer screen tends to break it up into separate little chunks or "mind bites." Often, what we see on the screen are little boxes of text or illustrations, each under a particular heading, which are not necessarily related to each other in any formal way. Some may be useful for the task at hand, others may not. In the latter case, we quickly move on. Thus, like birds feeding on a lawn, we hop from one box to another, keeping a sharp eye out for tidbits that appeal to us.

Hyperlinks, which are used to connect tangentially related texts within many databases and CD-ROMs, encourage this kind of learning. Using hypertext, we can branch off into related topics and pursue associations beyond the context in which our research originated. For example, a piece on fashion that mentions cotton could lead to the topics of how and where cotton is grown, suitable climate conditions, the need for pest control, the economics of production, and so forth, and each of these topics could lead to others. By enabling us to do this, however, hypertext tends to undermine our sense of context even further because we soon leave behind the topic with which we began.

Students need discipline to stay on topic when researching hypermedia, but they have difficulty deciding what the topic really is. There are so many tempting side roads along the way that might lead to new and unexpected discoveries. As one researcher pointed out, "Placing an inquisitive, undisciplined young learner in a rich hypermedia environment may be similar to giving a remote control unit to a student in front of a television with 80 channels of action programming."[10]

For those who are enamored of the new information technologies, the goal of contemporary education is not to master any particular body of knowledge, nor is it to examine the classics of literature or study the details of the world around us. What lies behind current beliefs about education in the information age is the notion that children should be exposed to, and become used to handling, an increasingly varied range of information from a vast body of growing data. Yet, given the exposure children already have to different media—from the total environments of shopping malls, to television, to computers—it could be argued that they are already drowning in a sea of information.

As it is, with the resources currently devoted to computerizing education and the increasing role the private sector plays in shaping curriculum, it is hard to escape the conclusion that navigating the information superhighway has become *the* primary goal of contemporary education. Children, just like their adult counterparts, are cast alternately in the role of data processors and information consumers.

# CHAPTER 8

# Caught in the Web: Children's Advertising on the Internet

*In many ways the Internet in the school is like a Trojan horse, and I don't think many parents realize the extent of the commercialism that is coming into the classrooms.*

—Katherine Montgomery[1]

*There has been a shift in American business culture—our children are now seen as an economic resource to be mined or exploited, like bauxite.*

—Gary Ruskin[2]

As the number of Internet users grows exponentially, more and more children are drawn into this new electronic environment. According to Jupiter Communications, a company that tracks Internet trends, in 1998, 8.6 million children between the ages of five and twelve were online. By 2002, that number is expected to swell to 21.9 million, and more than 90 percent of these children will have Internet access in school.

Although many parents and teachers view the Internet as an educational resource for their children, corporate advertisers have something quite different in mind. A growing number of companies are devoting significant resources to turn the Internet into a potent marketing tool that will allow advertisers unprecedented access to children both in the classroom and at home. When students in Peoria, Kansas City, or Los Angeles turn on their computers each morning, the first image they see might be an advertisement for Pepsi or Nike, the figure of Ronald McDonald, or a Pizza Hut logo.

The use of the Internet to mount massive advertising campaigns

127

aimed at children has brought a new dimension to the infiltration of corporate values and objectives into the classroom. Computer companies have long known the advantages of supporting computer use in schools by donating equipment and software to schools—it helps to build a customer base of loyal users. Now they are joined by a rash of other companies who have realized the potential of the Internet as a means of pitching their consumer goods directly to students. Increasingly, there is a price to be paid for visiting, say, the Smithsonian, PBS Kids Pages, or the World Book in its electronic version—users must first be willing to run a marketing gauntlet. In an even more disturbing twist, some schools are receiving "free" computers in return for giving advertisers uninterrupted time with students during the school day.

At a marketing conference held in New York in 1995, a representative of one of the world's largest advertisers said of the Internet: "There is nothing else that exists like it for advertisers to build relationships with kids." Erica Gruen, former director of Saatchi & Saatchi Interactive, made this remark during a discussion about how best to tap into one of the most lucrative markets for advertisers—the children's market. Catching children early, advertisers know, is the best way to instill brand loyalty in everything from high-tech consumer goods—computers and computer games—to soft drinks, candy bars, fast food, and clothing. Children are no longer just the consumers of tomorrow but a prize market from infancy on. As Gary Ruskin, director of Commercial Alert, a group that opposes the excesses of commercialism, advertising, and marketing, told me recently, "There has been a shift in American business culture—our business executives see children as a market to be exploited like bauxite." To illustrate his point, in a recent article he wrote for *Mothering*, he quotes General Mills executive Wayne Chilicki: "When it comes to targeting kid consumers, we at General Mills follow the Proctor & Gamble model of 'cradle to grave.' We believe in getting them early and having them for life."[3]

The children's market represents a gold mine for advertisers and marketers. In 1996, U.S. children age fourteen and younger spent $20 billion, money they received as gifts, allowances, and pay for part-time jobs. Teenagers spent an additional $67 billion. Together, the two groups influenced their parents' annual spending to the tune of an additional

$200 billion.[4] According to the International Mass Retail Association, children aged eight to seventeen each spend roughly $3,600 on consumer products every year. That's $3.6 billion for every 1 million children.

It is no wonder that, in advertising parlance, the market for children online is known as the "lucrative cybertot category." By 1995, Saatchi & Saatchi had already established special teams to gather information about the online habits of children in order to develop sophisticated techniques for marketing to children in cyberspace, an area that, until recently, remained unregulated. This multibillion-dollar company hired cultural anthropologists and psychologists to study "kids' culture" and to determine how children process and respond to information online. Speaking at the conference in New York, Gruen said that the online world corresponds to "four themes of childhood...attachment/ separation, attainment of power, social interaction, and mastery/ learning."[5] Each area corresponds with an important stage in child development. Children need to feel secure but, at the same time, they want independence and need to explore the world on their own. They also want to bond with people and characters who are familiar to them. Children like to demonstrate that they have control over their lives and playing on the computer gives them a sense of power. Social interaction on the Internet frees them from adult supervision and allows them to form independent relationships. Finally, children who have mastered basic computer skills will apply their understanding to an exploration of Web sites. Child psychology is, in effect, harnessed to sell products. What is perhaps more telling is that advertisers at the conference spoke of how much pleasure children got from using computers and how this "flow state," a state characterized by sensations of pleasure and absorption, could be used as a perfect vehicle for advertising. As Ruskin writes:

> Thousands of the brightest minds in the country devote their great talent, and use sophisticated psychological techniques, to influence your children to purchase products—or rather, to want products—regardless of whether or not they are good for your kids. These minds do not work to solve the nation's real problems; they work to create new problems for you.[6]

The advertiser's first objective, getting children in front of computer screens, has been achieved without much difficulty. In fact, it was largely handed to them. In most cases, adults are happy when children spend time on the Internet.

With their target audience within reach, advertisers are hard at work looking for the best ways to present their products to young and highly impressionable minds. Currently, their options are extensive. Because much of children's time on the Internet is unsupervised, in school as well as at home, they get little help dealing with the commercial messages that are presented in increasingly subtle and seductive ways.

Young children are especially susceptible to the lures of advertising. Bonding with role models is a natural part of their social and emotional development. Such emotional ties lend particular force to the advertising messages children see on-screen because of their belief in the "friendship" and "goodwill" of the messenger. If Ronald McDonald and the Power Rangers tell them how good eating hamburgers and playing with plastic toys is, these are what they will urge their parents to buy. Wonderland's Wading Pool, billed as "The perfect place for two- to three-year-olds to get their feet wet in the World Wide Web," gives toddlers the opportunity to play Click-a-Part Choo Choo. This computer game, according to Sony Wonder, was "inspired" by John Denver's CD for children, which the company also distributes. This Web site advertises itself as "a safe place to play and grow." For children who are fond of Dr. Seuss books, an animated Cat in the Hat awaits visitors at the Seussville Web site along with links to books, toys, and CDs.

Mattel's Web site features a disco-dancing Brandy doll (named after the young singer–actress) and links children with dozens of Barbies. The site describes Brandy in glowing terms: "Singing sensation, model and star of the hit TV show 'Moesha,' Brandy's dreams have all come true before she's 21 years old! She has two multiplatinum albums—*Brandy* and *Never Say Never*, a popular TV sitcom, and featured roles in TV movies, a remake of Rodgers and Hammerstein's *Cinderella*, *Double Platinum*, and the motion picture, *I Still Know What You Did Last Summer*." Although the site notes, "This Web site contains product information and advertising material," such statements are not likely to influence a child who is surfing the Internet alone. Disclaimer or not, parents are likely to be pestered by their kids not only to buy the Brandy and Barbie products, but also to see her movies. Any child who is young enough to play with a doll, however, is far too young to be exposed to the teen horror flick *I Still Know What You Did Last Summer*. This movie is the sequel to *I Know What You Did Last Summer*, and both are tales of teenagers who are stalked and brutally murdered.

Most children younger than age seven do not possess the ability to distinguish between what is real and what is imaginary. Many young children regard the characters from storybooks, comic books, television programs, and commercials as no less real a part of their social and emotional landscapes as family members and friends.

The deep emotional bonds children form with these imaginary characters stay with them in some form into adulthood. In previous generations, the characters of childhood came to life in stories told or read by parents or other family members. These stories generally had some moral purpose beyond their value as entertainment. They showed what happens to people who are good and kind or selfish and uncaring, brave or cowardly, clever or stupid, persevering or lazy. They dealt with the most basic of human motivations and the most powerful of human emotions. But with the coming of television, and now even more so with the Internet, children's fantasy lives have been invaded by a host of one-dimensional disposable creatures whose sole purpose is to capitalize on these emotional bonds for the purpose of turning children into lifelong consumers. Some of the traditional fantasy figures of childhood have also been co-opted. Thus, the fantasy lives of children are permeated not only by the iconography of advertising but also by icons that the advertising industry has appropriated for itself.

The Internet provides a particularly favorable environment for children's advertising. Unlike watching television, playing with a computer gives a child a sense of having control over his or her environment. Sitting by oneself close to the screen—tapping out commands on the keyboard, seeing one's name appear in a "personal" message—creates an intimate atmosphere and gives the child an impression of close contact. In such circumstances, children think they can make friends with Sailor Moon, Ronald McDonald, the Power Rangers, or Barbie, creatures they believe are real. These are the "people" who will make their wishes come true. In fact, they are also the ones who are trying to influence what these wishes will be.

According to Media Metrix, an Internet-traffic measuring service, in one month, more than 30,000 children between the ages of two and eleven visited Nickelodeon, while thousands more visited the Pokemon, Lego, Broderbund, Gamesharks, and Yahooligans Web sites. Although parents may want to believe that time spent on the computer is educational, indications are that children are now being exposed to more advertising on the Internet than anything else.

The interactive nature of the medium and the sense of trust and security that it establishes have consequences that extend beyond the creation of a desire for consumer goods. By playing on children's need for attention and understanding, Web site advertising can easily persuade children to give out very personal information about themselves and their families—information that will enable advertisers to microtarget them.

Equally indefensible is the practice of collecting information without the user's knowledge. The electronic gathering of information online is done through "cookies," which is technical jargon for a way of secretly keeping track of a visitor's movements through the Internet to develop extremely precise marketing data. Jeremy Hoey, a Vancouver writer for *Adbusters*, kept a running tally of how many "cookies" were blocked after he installed a "cookie blocker" on his computer. In the first week, it blocked 212 banner ads (ad space, often animated, at the top of a Web page) and 325 cookies. In the approximately five hours he surfed the Internet, his program blocked approximately 42 ads and 65 cookies per hour. "It serves," Hoey wrote, "as a sobering reminder of the extent to which we are inundated with marketing messages each day without fully realizing it."[7]

The Center for Media Education (CME), a Washington, D.C.-based children's advocacy group, has for years been documenting the numerous sophisticated techniques that advertisers use to target children online. In a report entitled *The Web of Deception*, the Center concludes that the boundaries between Web site content and advertising are often so blurred that, in many cases, they are being eliminated altogether.[8] In cyberspace, for example, there is nothing to prevent the alcohol and tobacco industries from targeting children as future consumers and doing so in a way that masks their real intentions. Cuervo Tequila, has a cartoon character called J. C. Roadhog, a "cyber-rodent" who inhabits the virtual community of the "Republic for Cuervo Gold." As part of an online game, the character races through a desert littered with empty tequila bottles displaying the company logo. Visitors are urge to "defect" and join the Republic, a land of "untamed spirits." To advertise its product online, Budweiser beer has a radio network, "KBUD," hosted by a DJ, which brings children a stream of interviews with rock stars, music, and reviews of albums, along with promotions for beer. Its online promoter is a character called Budbrew J. Budfrog, whose biography announces that he "drives a German luxury car, has memorized the entire Oxford English Dictionary, and likes to hang out on the beach with a hot babe, a cold Bud, and a folio edition of the *Kama Sutra* in its original Sanskrit." Another brewer, Amstel, has a "virtual bar" and a friendly barkeep named Hank, who dispenses advice on relationships and beer.

Innocent searches for information on the Web can easily lead children into Web sites for tobacco and alcohol. A study that searched key words children might commonly look for turned up several alcohol and tobacco links for topics such as "games," "entertainment," "music," "contests," and "Halloween." The Budweiser Budfrog character even popped up during a search for "frogs."[9]

In 1997, CME examined the information-collection practices of thirty-eight Web sites specifically targeted at children and noted that 90 percent of these Web sites actively collected personally identifiable information. Forty percent of the sites used cookies. Only one site in five asked children to "check with your parents before releasing information," and not one site asked for verifiable parental consent before collecting this information. One-fourth of the sites sent an e-mail message to children after their initial visit. In addition to this, several sites used product spokes-characters (such as the Power Rangers) to solicit information. Forty percent of sites gave away free merchandise, ranging from screen savers to sweepstakes prizes, to encourage children to give out personal information.[10]

Once this information is obtained, consumers have no way of knowing how it will be used. There is nothing to stop a company that collects information on the Internet from selling it to other users. This should be a matter of considerable concern because such users may have other than legitimate motives. For instance, *Money* magazine described an incident several years ago where a television reporter who posed as the wife of a man on trial for the abduction and murder of a twelve-year-old was able to obtain a list of the names, sex, addresses, and phone numbers of 5,500 California children from a company called Metromail. She simply used an alias, a mailing address, and a disconnected cellular phone number. This information cost the reporter only $277. Metromail says that it no longer sells mailing lists of children, but as reporter Anne Reilly Dowd discovered, other companies do. A firm in Tucson, Arizona, will sell children's names for 8.5 cents each and a copy of the material the advertiser plans to send to them. The company will give out as many as 8 million children's names designated by gender, age, and city.[11]

In 1997, the Federal Trade Commission (FTC) ruled that certain practices were deceptive and unfair. It specifically cited KidsCom (an entertainment corporation) for soliciting personal information in a deceptive manner and for failing to "fully and accurately disclose the purpose for which it collected the information and the uses made of information." (KidsCom released the information to other companies for marketing purposes.) However, the FTC did not take action because KidsCom modified its conduct. KidsCom now sends parents an e-mail when children register at its site, and it will not release personally identifiable information to other parties without parental approval, either by return facsimile or by mail.[12]

The Children's On-Line Privacy Protection Act (COPPA), passed in 1998, was designed to prevent such abuses in this area and is the first law to protect privacy on the Internet. The act stipulates that children younger than age thirteen must have parental consent before companies can collect, use, or disclose personal information about their young customers. "The law should curtail some of the most egregious data collection practices," according to Kathryn Montgomery, president of CME. "But it's not going to correct everything." Although

Montgomery and her organization believe computers can be used in positive ways in the classroom, she realizes that they come with significant drawbacks. She told me recently that,

> In many ways the Internet in the school is like a Trojan horse, and I don't think many parents realize the extent of the commercialism that is coming into the classrooms. We will need to continually monitor the development of this new and powerful medium.

"The problem that I have with COPPA," says Michael Brody, a Washington, D.C.-based child psychiatrist and a CME board member, "is that it has to be enforced." With tens of thousands of sites operating and new ones springing up every day, it is impossible to police them all. "The amount of advertising is astronomical and the toy Web sites are just incredible…advertising on the Internet exploits children's lack of judgment."

While representing the American Academy of Child and Adolescent Psychiatry at an FTC workshop on privacy protection, Dr. Brody was shocked at how little discussion took place regarding child development theory. We must remember, he says, that children are not little adults; their cognitive development takes place in stages.[13] For Internet advertisers to use well-known characters such as Batman and the Power Rangers as spokes-characters to sell consumer products to children—something that is not allowed on television—seems particularly exploitive because these characters are among children's most trusted role models. Brody emphasizes that role models are exceedingly important to children. "They help with impulse control, the ability to learn, and how to socialize." But what lessons will children learn when their role models tell them to buy, buy, buy? This question seems to be largely ignored by those who favor increased use of the Internet among children, perhaps because young people appear to be so adept at handling this medium. Brody finds this shortsightedness especially troubling. "It takes a whole village to raise a child," he insists. "It takes only one corporation to exploit one."

As for blocking commercial advertising, politicians are opting for a technological solution, hoping that a V-chip will be developed to block commercials as well as pornography. However, the blocking technology is simply one more thing that teachers and parents have to worry about. They must buy it, install it, and monitor the children who are using it. Although several software packages promise to block "cookies" and advertising banners and keep children from straying into Web sites parents and teachers do not want them to see, the software is far from foolproof. While playing on the Internet at a friend's house one day, my twelve-year-old daughter and her friend were easily able to remove the Net-minder that my neighbor—a knowledgeable and technically proficient librarian—had painstakingly installed.

Websense, a San Diego-based software company that specializes in filtering software, studied the Net-surfing habits of 501 teenagers aged thirteen to seventeen. It discovered that 58 percent of them were visiting sites during school time that contained sexual content, violence, hate material, or "music that might offend people."[14]

Commercial interests are already widespread in U.S. schools. Hershey Food Corporation distributes the Chocolate Dream Machine, a video and curriculum guide to nutrition which features Hershey products; Nike provides sports teams with new athletic shoes; soft drink companies donate score boards with company logos to high schools; students receive free stick-on tattoos and textbook covers that display corporate logos such as Calvin Klein's "CK"; producers of Tootsie Roll candies give kindergarten through third-grade teachers an arithmetic program called, "Tootsie Roll: the Sweet Taste of Success," which has students count Tootsie Rolls; Campbell Soup company offers teachers posters and lesson plans for using Prego Traditional spaghetti sauce; and General Mills gives "Gushers: Wonders of the Earth," a science kit about volcanoes that depicts the company's fruit gushers candy.[15]

About 12,000 U.S. schools now subscribe to Channel One's commercialized newscasts. Now owned by Primedia, Inc., Channel One loans television sets to public schools in exchange for the school's agreement to give the company access to its students for twelve minutes every day. Marketers provide a ten-minute "news" program, generally aired during homeroom, along with two minutes of commercials. In spite of being banned in New York State and being opposed by almost every major education group in the country, including individuals ranging from Ralph Nader to Phyllis Schlafly, 8 million students are exposed to Channel One advertisements for "Pepsi, Mountain Dew, Snickers, M&M's, Twix, Bubble Yum bubble gum,  Extra bubble gum, and Fruit Loops."[16]

Marketers, it seems, are one step ahead. Take the company ZapMe!, for instance, a San Ramon, California, firm that generates revenue by granting advertisers unprecedented access to students age thirteen and older. The company typically provides schools with fifteen computers, a server, high-speed Internet service, and Microsoft software, including built-in word processing and spreadsheet programs. (Schools, however, are responsible for insuring the equipment.) In exchange, schools must sign an agreement promising to allow the company to monitor students' Internet browsing habits. The company then breaks down the data by age, gender, and ZIP code. The agreement also states that schools must ensure that the computers are used on average four hours per computer terminal per school day. Corporate sponsors such as Microsoft, Compaq, Dell, and Toshiba provide equipment and technical support.

Gathering such information is, of course, a boon to advertisers and marketers. As a ZapMe! brochure states:

> Children in grades K–12 are arguably the toughest audience for marketers to reach, and quite possibly the most valuable… The pinpoint targeting of such an elusive audience is made possible via the most revolutionary educational medium in the world, The ZapMe! Knowledge Network.

ZapMe! provides computers with a custom-built Web browsers and maintains a network of about 10,000 Web sites. According to the company, more than 100 schools in twelve states have signed up and more than 8,000 schools have applied for a ZapMe! lab. By collecting age- and gender-specific material, the company can develop a precise profile of the student population, which will allow advertisers to micro-target their audience. As Elizabeth Bell writes in the *San Francisco Chronicle*:

If a 15-year-old girl from Concord logs onto ZapMe, the computer would ask her age and gender and would then select an ad designed for a typical teenage girl, such as sportswear modeled by Monica Seles. A boy who logs on might see Michael Jordan making a pitch for shoes or sweats.[17]

Students whose schools sign on with this program can expect an extra daily dose of advertising while they do their schoolwork. ZapMe! sells advertising that runs as a rotating advertisement built right into the company's Web browser. Advertisements are constantly displayed in the lower left corner of the screen.

While demonstrating the system for the Associated Press, Frank Vigil, president of ZapMe!, clicked on the banner advertising Schick razors. The screen was soon filled with an attractive blonde woman who marched through the streets as people rushed to protect her freshly shaved legs.[18] While using this system students can easily click on banner ads that take them into Web sites or full-blown commercials. System users will have an identifiable profiles and advertisers will receive very valuable information.

Not everyone, however, is enthusiastic about this in-school advertising blitz. Paul Kraft, the media specialist at Florida's Celebration School, told me recently, "This is very distasteful to me, and our school would not consider participating." Kraft said that Celebration School also turned down participation in Channel One precisely because of the advertising. "We are," he insisted, "committed against advertising." Celebration School's state-of-the-art technology gives it direct Internet access without dial-up, without modems, and without advertisements on its Web browsers.

U.S. Representative George Miller is working on a bill that would require a parent's written permission before a student could participate in market research at school. Many parents may not, in fact, be aware that their children are viewing advertising as part of their curriculum. The legislation also calls for a thorough study on commercialism in public schools.

"Students should go to school to learn, not to provide companies an edge in the hotly contested youth market," said Congressman Miller, a senior member of the House Education and the Workforce Committee, in a statement to the media,

> but increasing numbers of companies are targeting school as the best place to learn the purchasing preferences of young people. Unfortunately, there is no requirement that schools seek parental consent before this occurs. Parents have a right to know how their children are spending their days at school. If parents do not want their children to be objects of market research firms while in school, they should have the right to say no. My bill gives parents that right.

Children already spend more time learning about life through the media than they do in any other way. By the time most North American children graduate from high school, they will have watched some 22,000 hours of television, of which up to one-fifth could consist of commercials.[19] In a 1998 study, "The Hidden Cost of Channel One," Max Sawicky of the Economic Policy Institute and Professor Molnar of the University of Wisconsin–Milwaukee, concluded that Channel One's cost to taxpayers in lost class time is $1.8 billion per year. Another study by William Hoynes of Vassar College in Poughkeepsie, New York, concluded that the content of Channel One's news programming was shallow. In schools that permit Channel One to operate, students spend the equivalent of one full week each year watching the program, including almost one full day watching advertising.

By bringing computers into the classroom, educators create the potential for children to receive even bigger doses of advertising than they are already getting at home by watching television. Although television remains a strong influence in the lives of children, the Internet, with its sense of intimacy and interactive attractions, could become an even more potent force. Indeed, the Internet's potential for good has been seriously undermined by its slide into commercialism. As commercial opportunities increase, the Internet becomes more like television—more a mass merchandising tool than anything else.

But the greatest danger from advertising may lie not so much in the seductive promotion of corporate agendas as in the more subtle effects on children's imagination. As Stephen Kline writes in *Out of the Garden: Toys and Children's Culture in the Age of TV Marketing*:

> Although there has been constant criticism of the tediously violent stories that television feeds to children, one factor has tended to be overlooked: that the rise in character marketing has all but eliminated images of real children playing in the normal course of their lives—in dramas or narratives about and for the young.[20]

A lack of such images is leading to a gradual deterioration in the imaginative lives of children.[19]

Adults often underestimate how deeply advertisements effect children, especially when they come with the approval of the teacher. If Pepsi, Nike, Calvin Klein, and Pizza Hut ads are beamed at students while they work in schools, they are apt to associate these products with education. Even if students are not actually watching the screen, the constant repetition of advertising images embeds them deeply in the unconscious. Will our children go through life needing to reach for a Tootsie Roll whenever they are assigned a math problem? Will they feel a desire to put on a pair of Calvin Klein jeans or fragrance whenever they have to research or write an essay? Will they forever feel the need to reach for a Pepsi when working on a science project?

"Schools," says Joan Almon, U.S. coordinator of the Alliance for Childhood,

> should be sanctuaries for children. They should be as far removed from the commercial marketplace as possible. It's one thing for children to study the marketplace at school, but it's another thing entirely for them to be the unconscious and unwilling subject of an onslaught of advertising.

Almon's organization is part of a growing international movement of doctors, teachers, scientists, parents, and others concerned about the decline in health and well-being of children.

> Advertising presupposes that you aren't being very conscious and that you are taking things in on an unconscious level—the very opposite of what educa-

tion is designed to do. Children look to the teacher as being a moral force or as being the representative of a moral life,

Almon said in a recent interview.

> When you talk to youngsters you realize they know what is right and what is wrong, and they have a deep sense of being let down because teachers allow them to be subjected to the force of this commercialism. And you know it's penetrating into children. I have known children to pull down the collar of another child and make fun of them for not wearing the right label. These things are going very deeply into the psyche of children. Probably deeper than the manufacturers intend to go.

Television has already staked out a claim on children's imaginations, and now the Internet is moving in on the territory. These invaders, with the odds stacked heavily in their favor, can do much to undermine children's sense of self. Young egos are in the early stages of development and are highly susceptible to outside influences. As children spend less and less time with their busy parents, they are increasingly at the mercy of role models that come from television and the Internet. "Increasingly," says Michael Brody,

> I see parents who give toys as compensation or they give media [television, CD players, computers] as compensation to assuage their guilt for not being around. Kids then assume media figures as parents. Children today need more human connections.

If children cannot imagine futures for themselves other than those that are provided for them by the entertainment and advertising industries, what resources do they have to solve their personal problems, let alone the vast difficulties facing the planet?

That such a dangerously influential force as advertising should be allowed to intrude on young children's learning is a sad reflection on the current state of education. Advertising is not just a distraction; it is altering forever the mental terrain of children with an infusion of fast food, plastic toys, and other consumer goodies. And unfortunately it is coming with the tacit approval of a great many teachers, parents, and policy makers. We would do well to consider the mental environment in which our children learn as seriously as we consider the state of the physical environment in which they live.

# CHAPTER 9

# The Physical Effects of Computer Use

*What could possibly be harmful about striking a key at the computer? Nothing—unless you do it several thousand times a day.*

—Deborah Quilter and Emil Pascarelli[1]

**W**atch any group of children sitting in front of computer screens and you will see a variety of positions. Some kids slump forward, their faces almost grazing the screen, others kneel or sit on the very edge of the chair, while a few twist around in their seats, watching the screens from an angle. I've observed children where they had no room to put the drafts of their essays, so they propped them against the computer screens or held them on their laps. Some students must put the keyboards on their laps, too, because there is no room for them in front of the monitors. Chairs in some classrooms are so high for young children that their feet dangle inches from the floor. We tend to think of computers primarily as an extension of our intellectual capabilities which allow us to access vast amounts of information at the touch of a finger. As a result, we ignore what is happening to children physically as they sit and gaze at the screens in front of them.

Computers do have physical effects on those who use them and these effects can be serious and long lasting, if not permanent. Moreover, they contribute to a wide range of disorders—from muscle, joint, and tendon damage to headaches and eyestrain. Toxic emissions and electromagnetic fields produced by computers and video display terminals (VDTs) are also potential health hazards.

However flexible they may be as a means of accessing and manipulating information, for the user, computers are a kind of straitjacket into which the body must adapt itself. The eyes stare at an unvarying focal length, drifting back and forth across the screen. Fingers move rapidly across the keyboard or are poised, waiting to strike. The head sits atop the spine balanced, in the words of one physician, like a bowling ball. Built for motion, the human body does not respond well to sitting nearly immobile for hours at a time.

The most prevalent injuries suffered by computer users are musculoskeletal ailments that fall within the broad category of repetitive strain injury (RSI). The tendons, tendon sheaths, muscles, ligaments, joints, and nerves of the hand, arm, neck, and shoulder can all be strained by repetitive movements such as those involved in keyboarding or clicking a mouse (mousing). Caused by a combination of bad posture, improper technique, badly designed workstations, and simply working for too long without a break, these types of injuries have reached epidemic proportions in today's computerized workplaces. Most at risk are those who spend a good portion of their day keyboarding in front of a VDT. Secretaries, journalists, and data-entry clerks are particularly prone to these disorders.

Because RSIs result from cumulative trauma to the body, years might pass before their symptoms become apparent. Studies by the U.S. National Institute for Occupational Safety and Health (NIOSH) show that RSIs often begin with "occasional" discomfort in the back, neck, and shoulders. According to the NIOSH reports, more than 75 percent of VDT users occasionally experience these symptoms, and more recent studies indicate that 20 percent of users experience daily discomfort. British researchers recently suggested that mousing and keyboarding contribute to sensory nerve damage in the hands and wrists. Jane Greening of University College in London and neurophysiologist Dr. Bruce Lynn say that people with RSI have reduced vibration sensitivity in the hand area, especially in the median nerve—the major nerve in the hand.[2] Overuse of the hand and arm can cause the joints in the hands to swell and ache so badly that sufferers wake up at night.

As children spend more time using computers, both at home and at school, the possibility that they, too, will experience these ailments increases. In fact, there is evidence that this is already happening. "Anecdotally, physicians and rehabilitation therapists say that the average RSI patient is [getting] younger and younger," says Deborah Quilter, author of *The Repetitive Strain Injury Recovery Book*.[3] Richard Pilkington agrees. An occupational health and safety consultant, Pilkington says that he is seeing increasingly younger patients with injuries consistent with computer-related RSI.[4] Most are boys, some as young as seven. The most common complaints are headaches and neck aches. Pilkington believes these injuries are caused by poor posture at the computer. Children who use computers often display worse posture than adults—lounging, lying on the floor (while playing computer games), hunching over the keyboard, or leaning on their elbows. These postures all place added strain on the arms, neck, wrists, and spine.

Dr. Mark Gilbert, a Harvard-trained specialist in chronic work-related injuries, prefers to use the term *work-related musculoskeletal disorder* (WMSD). He has found a similar trend in certain sectors of the population. Musicians are a case in point. "Ten to twenty years ago," he told me, "the musicians would get WMSD later in their thirties, forties, and fifties. Now it's showing up in their teens." Gilbert speculates that, by spending time on a computer as well as playing a musical instrument such as an electronic keyboard or piano, young musicians are overtaxing muscles in their hands, neck, shoulders, and arms. Having treated hundreds of patients at his Toronto clinic, some of them very difficult cases, Gilbert strongly believes that children should be educated about the importance of taking safety precautions, including rest breaks, stretching, and aerobic activity, when using computers.

Although we still have much to learn about these injuries, we do know that they are painful and disabling. A growing number of university students also suffer from these kinds of injuries. According to the *Boston Globe*, a twenty-one-year-old Harvard University student had such a bad case of RSI that he was forced to turn down a summer internship at the *Washington Post*. Sewell Chan was in his senior year when he began to feel a tingling in his forearms whenever he typed, took notes, or edited the school paper. Eventually, the pain became so intense "his wrists throbbed with pain whenever he tried to type."[5] Often the most motivated and ambitious students and workers develop these injuries because their drive and concentration keeps them working at the computer for hours at a time without taking a break.

Dr. David Diamond of the MIT medical center in Boston said recently that RSIs are a growing problem among students. Half of the students who responded to a general health survey said they were having some discomfort associated with computer use. Based on that survey, Diamond estimates that about half of the students at MIT suffer from mild RSI. A specialist in both internal medicine and occupational and environmental medicine, Diamond sees about 150 to 200 students each year with mild to severe RSI. Currently, the medical center educates students, staff, and faculty about the need to prevent such injuries. Pamphlets, Web sites, posters, and talks are all part of the campaign to inform students about prevention. RSIs are on the rise at other universities across the country, as well. "Mostly these are preventable injuries," Diamond notes, "if you recognize early on that there is a problem and you make changes in the work activity accordingly. Don't just treat the symptom," he urges, "treat the cause."

RSIs are also alarmingly widespread in the workforce, indicating that not nearly enough prevention occurs among adults, let alone in our schools. Approximately 2.5 million workers are affected annually in the United States. According to the American Occupational Health and Safety Association, RSIs cost U.S. businesses $20 billion in 1993 alone. According to the *Workers' Compensation Monitor*, the average claim for RSI cost $11,479 in 1997.

Only in the past few years have we begun to understand the importance of creating ergonomically correct workplaces. A well-designed computerized workplace should have adjustable tables and chairs to minimize strain on the body, as well as good lighting. Some companies make keyboards that split in the middle which, they claim, allow the operator to maintain a more natural position. So far, however, there has been little interest in designing a computer keyboard, VDT, chair, or table for the health and safety of children. Given that more than 90 percent of the 50 million children in the United States now have access to computers at home or in schools, we have reason to be concerned.

Women in the workplace are frequent victims of RSI, not only because of the high number of female secretaries, administrative assistants, and data-entry clerks, but also because office furniture has been designed primarily for men. Children fare even worse. Computer workstations are simply not made to fit the size and shape of a child's body. Elementary school classrooms outfitted with computers, or even a library where children conduct research, typically have the computers placed on ordinary desks with unadjustable chairs. Given the greater variation in size among children (especially in multiage settings) than among adult office workers, this equipment is patently unsuitable. A desk that is too high, for example, forces the elevation of the shoulders and causes muscle fatigue and pain across the shoulders and base of the neck, which often leads to headaches. Many children are introduced to computers at such an early age that they have no hope of achieving correct posture at the computer screen.

While visiting a computer lab with my daughter and her second-grade class, I watched as the children received a crash course in the use of various software programs. Although the chairs swiveled and were adjustable, they had clearly been made for adults. My daughter, who is tall for her age, was seated in a chair at the same height as a boy who was about four or five inches shorter. Students' legs dangled because the furniture was too big for them. No one took the time to discuss correct hand or body posture, the potential for eye strain, or the need for the children to take regular breaks to refocus their eyes and to stretch their muscles. The equipment was completely out of proportion for virtually this entire group of seven-year-olds. Consequently, all of these children spent the morning with their heads tilted upward at the screens in a posture designed to put strain on the spine and give them sore necks. A school I visited in New York City had workstations so out of proportion to the children using them that several kneeled on their chairs in order to look up at the screen. Even at Florida's Celebration School, a school specifically designed to house the latest computer technology, all of the computer keyboards were placed on flat desks level with the computer screen. None of the tables or chairs in the elementary school rooms was adjustable.

Although this issue has barely been addressed in the United States, the Swedish Institute for Working Life has begun to examine the working conditions for children who use computers in schools. A survey designed in Sweden is now being distributed in Japan by the National Institute for Health, in Italy by the Institute of Occupational Health, and in the United States by Nova Solutions, Inc. Japanese researchers at Waseda University in Saitama have already reported a huge mismatch between the size of the children's bodies and the dimensions of the computers.

Researchers at Cornell University in Ithaca, New York, have noted the same problem with children in the United States. While studying the computer workstations of children in grades three through five at six New York and Michigan elementary schools, they found that all six schools had computer-equipped classrooms in which students' posture put them at high risk for developing musculoskletal disorders. In all cases, the keyboard, monitor, and mouse were placed on a standard desktop—the situation in most schools across the country.[6]

Most workstations are too high for elementary school students; this is particularly a problem for younger children. In the Cornell study, 39 percent of the children used equipment that put them at postural risk and none of them were within "an acceptable postural comfort range. Although children do not currently spend prolonged periods of time keyboarding," the researchers concluded, "developing musculoskeletal structures could be especially vulnerable to trauma. Moreover, trends suggest that children are using computers at increasingly earlier ages and for longer durations of time."[7] Although another Cornell University study found that the posture of sixth and eighth graders improved when using adjustable workstations,[8] researchers in Japan suggest that regardless how much an adult workstation is adjusted, it remains a makeshift measure for most children. They conclude that it is essential to design workstations of various sizes to suit children's growing bodies.

Although we may think that children do not spend enough time at the keyboard to warrant concern, specialists in this field have suggested that anyone who spends more than two hours a day at a computer may be at risk for RSI. Emil Pascarelli, an RSI specialist in New York City, and Deborah Quilter are coauthors of a book entitled *Repetitive Strain*

*Injury: A Computer User's Guide.* They maintain that two to four hours a day at a computer is enough time to put someone into a risk category. The medical profession offers a wide range of opinions about the best ways to treat such injuries—everything from hand splints, which must be worn to bed, to surgery. But health-care professionals who deal with RSI agree that the best treatment is prevention.

Like adults, children need to limit their computer time and take frequent breaks when using computer equipment, but the strong attraction exerted by the software children favor (video games in particular) makes their doing so unlikely unless a parent or teacher monitors their time. Many children, in fact, spend far longer at VDTs than either their parents or teachers realize.

Few parents are aware that children can sustain injuries at the computer, so they tend not to worry about how much time their children spend with it. Even when confronted with an injury that has been caused by computer use, parents and children often attribute the pain to other sources, such as a sports injury. "Children can be suffering from wrist, elbow, or shoulder strain and the parent won't know," says Pilkington. In the past few years, he has seen an increase in computer-related ailments in children and he attributes them to improper posture as well as to the sheer amount of time children spend in front of VDTs.

High on the list is an injury children refer to as "Sega thumb," which comes from playing video games. Because the thumb is a weak joint to begin with, heavy action with a game controller, which drives the thumb continuously and rapidly forward, overtaxes the joint. The result is a painful condition much like skier's thumb—the kind of injury skiers get from jabbing their ski poles into the snow and jarring their thumbs. Computer games tend to utilize only one hand, placing tremendous strain on the index finger or thumb and the wrist. Pilkington says this is a routine injury in his practice.

The mouse poses another problem for children. Many adults suffer from RSIs as a result of continuous use because of the continual pressure placed on the index finger. Because the mouse is designed for adult hands, children are at an even greater disadvantage. The mouse is dangerous, says Deborah Quilter, because it can overtax the index finger as well as cause arm and neck strain.

The long-term effects of computers on a child's developing body are not understood fully. Moreover, because RSIs are cumulative and can take years to appear in adults, researchers believe that the full extent of the damage to children will not be evident for many years to come, so that, in the meantime, the gravity of the problem will be overlooked. Children suffering from RSIs might not get appropriate treatment, thereby making them vulnerable to long-term injuries.

Another major concern about children's use of computers is the extent to which the eyes are affected by staring for long periods at a video screen. Good vision is essential for academic success. Children who cannot see properly, either to focus on the blackboard or to do close work such as reading or writing, will naturally make more mistakes and, therefore, find learning a frustrating experience. In the workplace, adult eyestrain results in loss of productivity. Children react differently, often by avoiding the task at hand. A child experiencing eyestrain related to VDT use may begin to avoid all academic work linked to that activity. The teacher may also fail to realize that the problem is related to the tools, not the child.

The American Optometry Association recommends that to be effective, eye exams for schoolchildren should test how well their eyes actually perform in classroom conditions. This means checking near and far vision, how quickly the eyes can switch focus from near to far, and how well both eyes work together as a team. If children use a computer, then an eye exam should take this into account.

The effects on the eyes of VDT use is an area that has been studied in some depth, but the research to date has been conducted on adults. We simply do not know what the long-term effects of heavy computer use will be on children's eyesight, but we may logically assume they will be no less serious than they are for adults. Until the full effects of VDT use on a child's developing visual system are understood, it is imperative that adults limit the amount of time children spend on computers and make safety a priority during those early years.

As far as the effects on adults are concerned, a 1998 Louis Harris poll shows that computer eyestrain or "computer vision syndrome" is the number one job-related complaint in the United States. As early as 1991, U.S. optometrists were treating more than 7 million patients with

VDT-related vision complaints, according to Dr James Sheedy, chief of the VDT eye clinic at the University of California at Berkeley. At Dr. Sheedy's clinic, 80 percent of the patients reported eyestrain and 50 percent reported blurred vision and headaches.

Spending too much time in front of a VDT causes intermittent blurring and general eye fatigue because looking at the screen forces the eyes to work continuously at one focal length. Toronto optometrist Barbara Caffery has seen an increase in the number of adults and children who need eyeglasses as a result of computer use. "What we used to ignore, we now end up giving a prescription for glasses for, because [the client focuses] on one focal distance for such long periods of time." Any close work such as reading or sewing can also cause eyestrain, but unlike a book, the computer screen emits light and reflects glare, which puts additional stress on the eyes.[9]

Staring for hours at a computer screen can also produce a "charley horse" of the eyes. Sheedy says that because the computer tires the eyes' ocular focusing mechanism (their ability to shift focus between varying distances), the eyes don't readjust to distance viewing after being in this position for a long time. This happens, according to Sheedy, even when a person is wearing eyeglasses or contact lenses. The result, as several studies have shown, can be a rapid onset of transient myopia (temporary nearsightedness).[10]

Researchers have no way of knowing which children are predisposed toward myopia, but adults whose vision is less than 20/20 are more likely to develop both myopization and other eyestrain symptoms after working with a VDT. "The significance of these individual differences is very important for children," writes researcher Shirley Palmer of Ohio State University in Columbus. "Some children could rapidly develop myopization as a result of VDT work, while others might not be much affected."[11]

Because transient myopia is temporary, we may be tempted to think that it is not serious. However, a Japanese study reports that after a ninety-minute stint at a VDT, the eye can take up to an hour or more to recover its full ability to see at other focal lengths. This finding indicates that students who spend significant amounts of time at VDTs may have difficulty readjusting their eyes to other visual tasks, and thus be unable to concentrate on other activities immediately afterward.

Another common complaint reported by VDT users is dry, itchy eyes. This occurs for two reasons. First, the normal blink rate is reduced by as much as 80 percent when reading from a VDT. Second, compared with printed material, VDTs are positioned relatively high, which causes us to open our eyes wider and expose a larger portion of the eye's surface. Together, these factors reduce substantially the eye's tear film or surface moisture, which causes irritation. Contact lens wearers are particularly susceptible. Although children have a better tear film than adults, they also suffer discomfort.

Northern California pediatric optometrist, Pia Hoenig, notes that children *are* feeling the effects of sore eyes from computer use. In an interview with *Education Digest*, she said:

> Computer vision syndrome has always been looked upon as an adult-world issue, but we're seeing children as young as three or four experiencing some of the same symptoms. Children, in fact, have a stronger response to stimuli than adults, and a more active visual system. This and other factors, like poor ergonomics and an inability for many children to adequately voice their discomfort, actually make them more susceptible to development of these symptoms.[12]

The fact that many children can read text on-screen without significant loss of comprehension is seen by some as a vindication of the merits of computer-based learning. As a result of this enthusiasm, the possible physical effects of such learning are overlooked. A study testing the assumption that reading text on-screen is more difficult than on the printed page found no clear disadvantages related to reading text on-screen, except that 20 to 30 percent of children who were using computers "said it hurt their eyes." It is curious that this startling observation drew no comment from the research team.[13]

Even under the best workplace conditions, VDT users still suffer from eyestrain. In classrooms, where computers are often inadequately lit and poorly positioned, the chances of eyestrain are much greater. Eyestrain often occurs in tandem with muscle pains because, as Sheedy says, "the eyes lead the body." When, as is often the case, eye defects in children go undetected, the risk of VDT-related eyestrain and other injuries increases. Children who need glasses but do not wear them and who thus have difficulty seeing the screen, will compensate by squinting or by craning their necks to get a better view. Such postural contortions can result in neck strain and headaches, and contribute to overall poor posture that is hard to correct.

VDT operators who are aware of the risks of eyestrain know to assume a correct posture, take frequent breaks, do eye exercises, and use proper lights. Such essential health and safety precautions are rarely taken in school. Poor lighting conditions still plague many schoolchildren and may be getting worse. Schools routinely put computers into brightly lit classrooms, which causes glare from computer screens and working surfaces and subjects children to too much light or the wrong kind of light—two causes of blurred vision and eyestrain.

Although little research has been conducted in this area, a study undertaken for the Alberta Department of Education indicates that children's health and cognitive development can be correlated with the kind of light their bodies ingest. The study found that full-spectrum lighting—illumination approaching daylight in its color quality—appears to enable children to improve their scholastic achievement and their health. Children who experienced full-spectrum lighting grew faster and had better attendance than children who were exposed to the pinky-orange glow of high-energy sodium-vapor lights. The latter were absent more often, got lower marks, and showed signs of slower physical development. Dr. Warren E. Hathaway, author of the study, cited it as evidence that lighting systems are not neutral with respect to their effects on people.[14]

If school boards and teachers are going to set up classrooms with computers in mind, they should be aware that the correct lighting for computer work (which entails, for instance, blocking out natural sunlight to avoid glare) may not promote the health, or the academic achievement, of the children.

Another health concern is the correlation of epileptic seizures in children with the playing of video games. According to a Seattle study, epileptic reactions in children occur more often than previously thought, although the total frequency is still unknown. The study reported on video game-related seizures in thirty-five patients between the ages of one and thirty-six. This group was comprised of mostly teenage boys. Although strobe lights and even sunlight shining through leaves are known to trigger epileptic seizures, many of the patients in this study were not light sensitive. The researchers concluded that the video games triggered the seizures. Of the thirty-five patients studied, twenty-seven had never suffered a seizure before being exposed to computers. The youngest patient, a one-year-old girl, was standing next to her brother while he was playing a game. Although scientists do not think video games actually cause epilepsy, they do believe the games can trigger seizures.[15] In Holland, marketers of such games are now required to include a warning about seizures.

Skin problems also appear to be associated with VDT use. Studies have generally shown consistent correlations between VDT use and increased reports of various problems including rashes, dryness, itching, and burning. Though it is unclear why VDT use should have this effect, increased stress is probably a factor. Higher stress levels often accompany computerized work, and stress can produce skin problems in many people. Another possibility is that the static electric charges of the VDT screen might cause ambient, potentially toxic air particles to be deposited on the face of the user. It is also possible that the toxic chemicals given off by new computers cause dermatological problems.

Toxic emissions bring a new dimension to the health hazards of a computerized environment because they affect not only those who are actually using computers, but also anyone who is regularly in the same room with them. The U.S. Environmental Protection Agency (EPA) has identified a series of chemicals that are found in the off-gassing from hardware construction materials and internal components.[16] Such emissions are highest when equipment is new, and the EPA estimates it can take from 144 to 360 hours for them to dissipate completely. "The implications of these emissions can be particularly significant in an indoor environment containing several new pieces of electronic equipment, e.g., a computer room in a school."[17]

Exposure to such chemicals has been shown to cause ear, nose, and throat irritation, as well as skin problems among office workers,[18] and the effects on children are likely to be just as harmful. Edward Lowan, an environmental consultant to Ontario school boards, believes children, especially those with allergies, may be affected by the gases given off by new computers. He cites figures showing that traces of 300 chemicals have been found in the vapors given off by new computers. The result may be that some children generally do not feel well, whereas others get sick frequently and miss days at school. Because most people are unaware that off-gassing of potentially harmful chemicals is taking place, children's symptoms and sicknesses, whether skin rashes or ear, nose, or throat irritations, are attributed to unknown causes and are not diagnosed properly by parents or family physicians.

Toxic emissions are, however, a temporary hazard. The effect of electromagnetic radiation (or electromagnetic fields—EMFs for short), on the other hand, is a permanent concern. This is a particularly significant issue for schoolchildren because of the association between childhood leukemia and exposure to EMFs from power lines.[19]

EMFs of differing strengths are emitted by all everyday electrical sources—televisions, computers, radios, dishwashers, electric hair dryers, house wiring, power lines, and so forth. VDTs are probably the most constant source of exposure for children. For many, this exposure begins in kindergarten and continues throughout their working lives. Many children already spend large amounts of time sitting in front of VDTs by playing video games or doing schoolwork. Although children are often told by their parents to sit well back from the television, they are frequently found sitting closer to their computer screens than the recommended minimum of twelve inches.

Children are not only exposed to EMFs from the front of the screen. Field strength from the back and sides of a VDT is typically two to three times higher than in front. Yet in schools, terminals are often placed close together, so children are also exposed to the fields emanating from the back or sides of the computers around them.

Cathode-ray tubes are found not only in television sets, but also in VDTs and the display screens of virtually all desktop computers and computer network terminals. The tubes emit radiation across the frequency band, from X-rays to extremely low frequency EMFs. But cathode-ray tubes are not the only source of EMF radiation. All components including the tube, the main processor, and the drives, operate on an alternating current that generates fields and charges of various frequencies and intensities.

Citizens' groups in both the United States and Canada have lobbied for a basic standard for individual EMF exposure. The current Swedish standard, known as MPRII, sets an allowable EMF emission level at 2.5 milliGauss (mG) at 30 cm (1 foot) from the source. The TCO standard (a standard developed by Sweden's white collar union) is even more stringent—2.0 mG at 30 cm (1 foot). Computer manufacturers are usually unwilling to give out information on their computers' EMF emission levels, although many will say that they meet the Swedish standard. However, because computer parts can be manufactured at different sites, different units of the same make and model can register different emission levels. When our PTA requested that the electric company measure the EMFs from computer terminals (as well as power lines) at my daughter's school, it discovered great variance among machines of the same make and model.

Many scientists consider the 2 mG level to be safe, but there is no hard scientific data upon which to base this estimate, partly because it is impossible to find a control population that has never been exposed to artificial EMFs. Any standard for now remains an arbitrary one.

Although many studies have sought to correlate biological effects with EMF field strength, some research suggests that more significant factors may be the shape of the pulsed wave form, the frequency, and whether the field is continuous or intermittent. Researchers Indira Nair of Carnegie Mellon University in Pittsburgh and Jun Zhang of the Oak Ridge National Laboratory in Tennessee noted that, whereas the EMF strength from a VDT is similar to or lower than that from other sources such as hair dryers or toasters, it has different attributes.[20] Notably, EMF strength tends to fluctuate suddenly. They argue that this fluctuation could have significant health effects. Consequently, lowering field strengths may not be as useful as was once believed.

For example, researchers are increasingly suspicious that EMFs can disrupt the production of melatonin. Produced by the pineal gland, this hormone is linked to the visual system. Melatonin appears to include among its functions the inhibition of tumors by "mopping up" free radicals, thereby preventing damage to DNA.[21] The work of Russel

Reiter, a neuroendocrinologist at the University of Texas Health Sciences Center at San Antonio, indicates that melatonin production is suppressed by static and by extremely low frequency EMFs.[22]

Other researchers believe that electric and magnetic fields disrupt the circadian systems (or biological clocks) of humans and primates as well as other animals.[23] Whether such effects are harmful or long-lasting is not clear. Disruption of the circadian system has also been associated with physiological and psychological disorders, including altered sensitivity to drugs and toxins, interrupted sleep, and psychiatric disorders such as chronic depression.

These studies and the questions they raise underscore the complexity of the factors that affect the function of the human body. Given that the current generation of children is likely to spend more time at computer screens than any before it, it seems only prudent to teach children to keep a safe distance from VDTs, and to recommend that parents and schools purchase computers that meet the lowest possible emission standards.

These precautions may help to mitigate some of the adverse health effects of a computerized environment, but they do not address a more basic problem—the long-term effects of the sedentary habits encouraged by television watching and computer use.

We have already seen a marked decline in the physical fitness of North Americans, children included. The incidence of obesity in children in the United States between the ages of six and eleven has doubled since 1980. In 1998, the U.S. Surgeon General declared that childhood obesity had become an epidemic, with one in five children estimated to be significantly overweight. These developments are attributed to the prevalence of sedentary pursuits, such as watching television and playing video games, and the eating of high-calorie food—the latter no doubt often takes place in front of the television.[24] Researchers from the University of Memphis discovered just how sedentary children can become. When they focused on the resting metabolism of children between eight and twelve years of age, they found that the amount of energy expended was higher when the children were doing *nothing* than when they were watching television.[25]

The increase in computer use in the classroom, as well as at home, means that children are spending a much greater part of their day in a way that exposes them to a number of serious health hazards and that deprives them of physical exercise. In North America, the average child already spends twenty-six hours a week watching television and another twenty to thirty hours sitting in class. The current generation of children is the least physically active generation in history. The situation will hardly improve if the amount of time young children spend in front of computer screens increases.

Although it is possible to purchase ergonomically correct equipment for adults, no such option exists for children. The Open Charter School in Los Angeles is one of the few schools in the country that has designed computer tables to accommodate the bodies of young children. Designed by the technical teacher, each table accommodates two computers and costs about $600 to build.

A tour of classrooms generally reveals that computers are placed on desks or writing tables. One ergonomically conscious educator has developed a proposal to build workstations for elementary school children, but so far no company has agreed to manufacture it.[26] Similarly, one primary school in Toronto tried to work with a furniture company to produce a workstation of suitable dimensions for a child, but all the companies approached were reluctant to become involved.

Schools have routinely ignored other health and safety issues surrounding the use of computers. Some problems have practical solutions that can be implemented without too much difficulty. Toxic emissions through off-gassing, for example, can be avoided. Edward Lowan recommends that parents and school boards purchase secondhand computers so that off-gassing will be reduced, although with state-of-the-art technology increasingly seen as a necessity, this recommendation is unlikely to be heeded. As an alternative, Lowan suggests that computers be purchased at the end of the school year and left turned on in unused classrooms (with the windows open) for the summer, so noxious chemicals can dissipate when children are not there.

Often, however, one must go beyond the technology itself and consider the state of the environment in which the computers are placed. The problem of air contamination, for example, is compounded by the fact that the ventilation systems in many older schools fail to meet current building standards. A bank of computers running constantly can heat up any classroom, particularly one that is ventilated inadequately. Air conditioning, which is the obvious solution, is yet another expense for schools. Similarly, a combination of carpets and computers can spark a build-up of static electricity, aggravating dust problems for children with respiratory difficulties. The solution here is to replace carpeting with another form of floor covering—another considerable expense.

New applications of computer technology, such as virtual reality simulations, which have particular side effects of their own, are already on the horizon.[27] Our children will be the first generation to use computers "from the cradle to the grave." Neglecting the safety issues that confront them, especially at an early age, could mean serious problems for them later in life. Although computer-related injuries in the workplace have cost society dearly, few resources have been devoted to studying the physical effects of computer use on children. "It hasn't been studied yet," says Pilkington, "because it hasn't cost society any money yet."

# CHAPTER 10

# The Art of Learning

*Children made to live without the arts are inevitably poorer for it. This is why every young person, without exception, should be given access to the study of the arts, not to become artists, but to be better educated.*

—Charles Fowler[1]

*What happens a lot of times in education is that your imagination and vision is the last thing that you're exposed to.*

—Nan Elsasser[2]

The Gateway Boulevard Elementary School is a nondescript low-rise building encircled by a river of traffic—an inner-city school in the heart of Toronto, Canada's largest city and, according to the United Nations, the most culturally diverse place on earth. A recent addition to the old building, which includes sixteen classrooms, two lunchrooms, and a music room, has allowed the school to remove the more than eighteen portable rooms that were taking precious space from the playing field. Seventy percent of the school's 935 students speak English as a second language. Tamil, Farsi, Urdu, Hindi, Russian, Romanian, Swahili, and more than twenty-five other languages are represented among the students. Not one single-family dwelling is to be found in the school district and sometimes two or three families share the same unit. More than 100 students are considered refugees under the tenets of the U.N. convention.

Rife with social and economic problems, Gateway Boulevard Elementary School is the kind of school that gives many principals (not to mention a few parents) nightmares—a school on the edge in more ways than one. But in many other ways, it's also a school that works.

I first visited the Gateway Boulevard Elementary School on a late spring evening and made my way through a lunchroom swarm of students, teachers, and parents in various stages of costumes and make-up. At the invitation of the school principal, I brought my own two children to see the school play—that perennial favorite, *The Wizard of Oz*. I went because I had heard that this school places a strong emphasis on the arts—a kind of back-to-basics approach where the basics include drama, dance, visual arts, and music. When I met the principal, David McGee, my ten-year-old cast a dubious look. Can this wiry fellow in black a T-shirt and matching shorts, looking for all the world like Bob Fosse, really be the principal? Indeed he was, and as we discovered, a very talented director as well. It was his voice that later filled the room as that of the Great and Terrible Oz.

In the packed gymnasium, mothers and grandmothers cradled infants and fathers helped toddlers onto seats. The stage was decorated with gaudy day-glow flowers. The talent was well-rehearsed and abundant. Kindergarten students made endearing Munchkins and the eleven-year-old who played Dorothy was riveting. Additional dance numbers were added to showcase the talents of 120 student performers. Infused with cadences of Twi, Tamil, and West Indian Creole, these children were about as far from Kansas as possible, and the energy was high enough to power a generator. When the curtain came down on the last of three sold-out performances, approximately 800 parents had seen the show.

At the Gateway Boulevard Elementary School, the arts are a serious business. "And why not?" says the principal. They are an exceptional vehicle for teaching language given their attention to diction, tone, and nuance. They also enhance social skills and body awareness. After seeing the performance, I learned that one of the leads was played by a child with a serious learning disability, which was not obvious from watching the show. The child's mother told me later that the experience of performing "transformed" her formerly withdrawn daughter.

Days after the performance, I visited McGee in his office. Musical instruments, rain sticks, and masks were strewn about, and the walls were covered with children's drawings. I could not even see his desk.

He explained that the parents whose children attend his school are used to being ignored by bureaucrats and other government officials, so when they come to see him, they often arrive angry. But, he explained, "if they come into my office and the lights are low and I speak softly, we can usually talk things out." Parents, says McGee, soon realize just how much their children get from this arts-enriched program, and given that most families cannot afford private music or art lessons for their children or buy them theater tickets, the school experience is, for most students, their only exposure to the arts. He then described how another performer, a boy with behavioral problems (previously known for punching teachers as well as other children), turned into "a great kid" since getting involved in the drama program.

"The real magic of the arts," said McGee, "is that they give kids the internal discipline they need to manage their lives."

Most teachers and parents agree that good social skills depend on how well a child learns internal discipline. Children who learn to channel their energy into worthwhile activities are more likely to succeed and less likely to become social burdens.

The arts are especially effective at teaching social skills; they encourage children to take the initiative and thus develop what Yale psychologist Robert Sternberg refers to as "practical intelligence." Children who possess this practical intelligence are often socially adept; we might call them "street smart." They are skilled at adapting to new situations because they see what needs to be done and know how to go about doing it. They also have an instinct for knowing what will and will not work and are good at fitting in.

Sternberg distinguishes among three kinds of thinking: analytic, creative, and practical. He believes that we must be able to think well in one or more of these ways to be "successfully intelligent." Having successful intelligence does not necessarily mean one does well in school—as Sternberg points out, "Many people with modest test scores are nevertheless highly intelligent."[3]

Sternberg tells the story of one ten-year-old girl who had a low IQ and needed help in basic academic subjects. In fact, she was having a harder time than other children in her group. When the group was transferred full-time to a regular class, however, she was the one who outperformed the others. This was because she knew how to ask the teacher for help, how to function independently in the class, and how to get along with the other children. Her practical intelligence enabled her to make "the best possible use of the abilities she had, whereas the other children in her group, despite their higher IQs, often failed to mobilize their abilities effectively without the constant adult direction and supervision available in a special-education setting."[4]

This type of thinking shares much in common with Daniel Goleman's concept of emotional intelligence, which includes self-control, zeal, persistence, and motivation. Our emotions, in other words, can help us move forward or can hold us back, depending on how well we are able to harness them—and this applies to all aspects of our lives. Goleman, whose theories have gotten a great deal of attention in the past few years, writes:

> To the degree to which we are motivated by feelings of enthusiasm and pleasure in what we do—or even by an optimal degree of anxiety—they propel us to accomplishment. It is in this sense that emotional intelligence is a master aptitude, a capacity that profoundly affects all other abilities, either facilitating or interfering with them.[5]

The ability to delay gratification is an important aspect of emotional intelligence and something that all arts students soon learn. It is also an essential part of growing up. Learning this ability at an early age has long-term consequences for children's social and intellectual development.

Goleman refers to research by Walter Mischel at Stanford University in the 1960s, which tested four-year-olds by presenting them with a choice—they could each have a marshmallow immediately or they could wait awhile and then each would get two marshmallows. Years later, researchers revisited these children in their senior year in high school. The differences between those adolescents who, as children, had been prepared to wait for two marshmallows and those who had wanted a single marshmallow "now" were "dramatic." The former were self-assertive, were able to cope with stress and frustrations, and could persevere in the face of difficulties. The latter tended to be more easily upset, had a more negative image of themselves, and were often unable to control their temper. Those who, at age four, had waited were also doing better academically. They also had "dramatically higher scores" on their Scholastic Aptitude Tests (SATs).[6]

Overcoming initial frustration and fear is essential to being successful in the arts. In learning to draw or dance or play a musical instrument, children must achieve a measure of control over what they do, and they will not succeed if they go about this in a haphazard way. For years now, I have watched my oldest daughter become increasingly proficient on the piano. I have seen her learn to sight read and listened while she turned complex musical notations into fluent hand and finger movements, working to evoke just the correct rhythm to create the emotional tenor of a piece.

"You have to be self-motivating to practice," she said recently, "and if you actually want to learn a piece of music you have to be very disciplined. When I'm playing I tune out everything else and just focus on that one piece of music." She has also learned—as all music students do—that it can take years of concentration and practice to become truly proficient. The self-discipline and determination she has acquired from her musical experience, however, has benefited her in many other areas of her life—from learning a new language to improving her swimming stroke. Music has taught her to persevere in the face of difficulty.

By contrast, the vast majority of software available for children caters to what is perceived as a child's need for some kind of immediate result, regardless of the energy expended. Playing computer games or working through most software programs does not take much initiative or self-discipline—certainly not compared with the effort required to learn to play the recorder or cello, or to learn to draw in perspective.

Arts activities also provide valuable experience in working with others because many kinds of performance depend on a cooperative effort. When performing in a play or singing in a choir, each individual's contribution is important, but it is the performance of the group as a whole that determines the overall result. Children who participate in arts activities early in life learn skills that will serve them well throughout their lives.

For example, being able to work well together is a quality increasingly valued in the workplace as skills become more specialized and as productivity relies increasingly on coordinated teamwork. Goleman points out that when people come together as a team, they are able to pool their resources and take advantage of a group IQ that uses the talents and skills of everyone in the group—the sum of the parts is often greater than the whole. The most important element in group IQ is not so much intellectual brilliance as emotional intelligence. Social harmony is the key to optimal group performance. Studies at Bell Labs found that high emotional IQs, which allowed employees to build good relationships and establish informal networks, made the difference between outstanding researchers and those who were merely average.[7]

Clearly, helping children develop skills that will promote social harmony is a worthwhile goal, and education in the arts is an effective means of achieving it. Music has long been recognized as a means of improving harmony within the community. The Greek historian Polybius, writing in the second century BCE, believed that much of the violence during his time stemmed from the failure to teach music to the young.

Self-discipline and social harmony provide a potent antidote to the increasing violence that is occurring among children both in and out of school. Violence has been increasingly linked to the effects of electronic media.

Although boys on the way to becoming delinquent tend to have lower IQs than others of their age, their inability to control impulses is a more direct cause of errant behavior. "Impulsivity in ten-year-old boys," writes Goleman, "is almost three times as powerful a predictor of their later delinquency as is their IQ."[8] Although there has been much debate about the causes of violent, aggressive behavior in children, the physical mechanism of violence gives us clues to overcoming this kind of behavior.

Scientists who study the role of seratonin, a neurotransmitter, have found that this chemical inhibits quick motor responses, thereby enhancing relaxation and allowing for smoothly controlled and coordinated physical movement, which gives rise to calm physical responses. Elevated levels of the chemical are associated with high self-esteem and high social status, and reduced levels of seratonin are associated with low self-esteem and low social status. Low seratonin levels seem to cause irritability, which leads to impulsive, aggressive, violent, and even suicidal behavior.

"This knowledge about seratonin," according to Robert Sylwester, professor emeritus of education at the University of Oregon,

> suggests that good school arts and physical education programs can play an important role in developing the fine-motor control that allows youngsters to discover how remarkable the human body is—whether it's drawing a picture with tightly controlled movement or dancing with abandon.9

In other words, when children learn to sing in harmony, execute a dance step, or perform a tune on the recorder, their self-esteem gets a valuable boost.

Many people with high IQs flounder because they cannot motivate themselves, control their impulses, or get along well enough with other people to get into positions where they can use their latent talents. Because they are unable to manage their own feelings, they do not deal well with the feelings of others. On the other hand, people with well-developed emotional skills are at an advantage, even if they have moderate IQs. Their emotional intelligence helps them to think clearly and make good decisions, while preventing emotional outbursts from clouding their judgment.

Music, the visual arts, and drama encourage children to explore more of the world around them and to pay close attention not only to their own feelings and thoughts, but also to those of others. In European countries such as Sweden, Italy, and France, providing children with art lessons and high-quality artist materials is routine. In the United States, however, many parents still believe that arts programs are merely frills, included only if time and budget allow. Consequently, too little attention is paid to their instruction.

I remember a story a friend told me about visiting her daughter's kindergarten class to assist with an art activity. The teacher handed out paper and crayons and then instructed the children to draw apples. My friend watched, amazed, as each child used the same color—red—to create their pictures. Confronted with such a lack of imagination on the part of the teacher and her students, my friend asked incredulously, "Are there no apples out there that aren't red?"

This story not only illustrates a need for higher-quality art instruction and teacher training, but also shows that many urban children simply lack first-hand experience of the natural world. It is unlikely that any of these children ever had the opportunity to observe apples ripening in an orchard. If the teacher had brought in several types of apples and asked students to handle them before beginning the activity, the drawings would have been much more varied and original.

Teachers today, however, must also deal with the effects of television and computers. Children spend more time gazing at electronic media of one kind or another, and they tend to be overexposed to two-dimensional surfaces. "Children today suffer from visual bombardment," says visual arts consultant Kit Kleiser. "This causes images to pass before them that they can't pay attention to." Because children see so much and retain so little, they learn to pay less and less attention to what they see. As a result, many teachers report that children do not develop the ability to build from several dimensions. The most common problem teachers currently encounter in students studying the visual arts is an inability to *envision* other dimensions, a fact that does not bode well for the next generation of architects and town planners.

The visual arts are not only about observing the world, but also about being able to express those observations creatively. Art is both highly symbolic and emotionally creative. Children have a lot of individual choice in what they create. What subject will they draw or paint? What colors will they use? How much paint should they apply? To convey the feeling of rain, or the experience of watching wind lash the branches of a tree, or communicate a secret joy or sorrow, children must be given time enough to pay attention not only to the world around them, but also to the world within themselves.

As the electronic voice drowns out a child's own ability to express herself, art becomes first a matter of restoring a child's connection with the self. Sometimes art is simply a matter of giving children enough time and encouragement to stop and concentrate on the world right in front of them.

Writing on the subject of teaching art to young children, Carol Seefeldt, a professor of the Institute of Child Study at the University of Maryland, College Park, described how two first-grade teachers in Maryland approached the theme of friendship through art. One teacher told her students they were going to produce a mural entitled "Our New Friends," and asked each child to draw a picture of his or her best friend. They all produced stick figures of their friends.

The other teacher introduced songs, poems, and stories that focused on children's names, then read a story about best friends and discussed with the children what it meant to them to have a friend. What Seefeldt described next is enlightening:

One day children were asked to pair with someone they didn't know very well. The teacher helped children find partners and then asked them to take turns interviewing one another to find out ways they were alike. She gave the children a list of questions that they might ask each other, such as what their favorite food was, what made them the happiest, and what frightened them the most, and so on.

Another day the children were asked to work with someone they thought of as a friend. Helping children make their selection, the teacher gave each pair a mirror and asked them to observe their facial features. Walking around the room, she talked with children about the shape and size of their eyes and mouth, asked them to look and compare the way their eyelashes curled or were straight, and encouraged them to describe and compare the color of their eyes, hair, and skin. She asked them to feel the shape of their faces, their eyebrows, their cheeks, and their noses and compare their own features to those of their new friend.

Only after the children had observed one another, thought about their observations, and talked and written about them did the teacher hand out markers and paper and explain her goal of creating a mural of new friends for the hall. As children began to draw, they were encouraged to continually observe their friend, to look at the way their friend's hair was arranged, the shape off his face, the color of her eyes. Taking their work seriously, children continued to observe each other, talked together, and thought about how to represent their friend, using different colors and techniques.[10]

When the two murals were finally finished, the differences between them were dramatic. The mural made by the group that had been encouraged to think about and closely observe their friends was filled with detail. Each drawing was mature, individualized, colorful, and complete. The other mural, which had been executed by children who had not been encouraged to be perceptually acute, consisted of "weakly drawn stick figures, each stick figure very much like every other."[11]

Television has long had a baneful effect on children's ability to create their own images. A study that compared the effects of radio and television found that children who listen to the radio are more likely to produce more original work than those who watch television. Children between the ages of six and nine watched one story on television and listened to another story on radio. Each presentation was stopped shortly before the end of the story, and the children were asked to supply the ending. The children wrote far more imaginative and original endings when they listened to the story then when they watched it.[12] This is because when the students listened to the story they created their own images—their minds were not cluttered with someone else's.

Although the research is still sketchy and the samplings few, educational software—so often indistinguishable from computer games and not dissimilar to television—appears destined to decrease the imaginative capacities in children. The *Atlantic Monthly* has reported that using the software program *Reader Rabbit* (one of the ten most widely used computer programs in elementary schools) caused a 50 percent drop in the creativity of elementary school students. Of the forty-nine students who used this software reading program for seven months, all had difficulty answering open-ended questions, suffered diminished verbal fluency, and by the end of the study could not brainstorm with their original degree of creativity.[13]

Recent, more detailed analyses of the effects of television and computers on children indicate that far from improving academic achievement, these technologies have a deleterious effect. A 1999 study by the Kaiser Family Foundation found that children between the ages of eight and eighteen who spent more time watching television and using computers had lower grades than students who spent less time with these media. The study, *Kids & Media @ The New Millennium*, a comprehensive national analysis of children's media use, reported that:

> Overall, youngsters with poor grades report consistently more daily exposure
> to all media but print media. The largest difference in average daily exposure
> for any single medium is 24 minutes (youngsters with fair or poor grades are
> exposed to television 24 minutes more per day than those with good grades),
> and those with lower grades report 12 minutes less daily reading than those
> with good grades. The overall result is that third through twelfth graders who
> report earning school grades of mostly B's and C's or lower also report over
> an hour per day more total media exposure than their counterparts who earn
> higher grades....[14]

As the authors of the study painstakingly note, it is impossible to
determine whether high exposure to media causes poor grades, or
whether children who do not do well in school are simply intense
media users. One thing is certain, however: children who spend their
leisure time learning through the arts are not likely to see their grades—
or their physical health—decline. A growing body of research: although
some of it, such as the Mozart effect, is contested—shows a strong correlation between higher academic achievement and the arts.

According to the College Entrance Examination Board (CEEB),
the SAT administrators, children who receive arts instruction score
significantly higher on verbal and math tests than students who take no
arts courses. In 1995, students who studied the arts for more than four
years scored 53 points higher on the verbal SAT and 37 points higher
on the math SAT than did students who did *not* receive arts instruction.
The longer students studied the arts, CEEB found, the better their
score.[15]

Overall results at the Gateway Boulevard Elementary School put its
students close to the top in the province-wide math program. A visit to
the school on a hot June morning illustrated just how the arts can
enliven math. Summer's humidity can often wilt the best of intentions
but when I arrived in a first-grade classroom I found students completely absorbed by what they were doing. Children were working
together to trace their full body shapes on large pieces of paper. After
assisting each other with the tracing, these six-year-olds proceeded to

measure the arms, legs, heads, and torsos they had drawn. Such hybrid math/art activities give children a concrete understanding of measurement, along with the opportunity to experiment. "I don't think I could teach math without using the visual arts," the teacher, Sangeeta Karia, told me. "As children become more confident in their own expression, they are more able to take risks."

As part of a national program called Learning through the Arts, teachers such as Karia receive small-group instruction from practicing artists. The program allows elementary school students to have voice and instrument lessons, painting, drawing, and sculpture classes, as well as instruction in drama, scriptwriting, puppetry, and opera. Because many teachers have had little art training themselves, teachers receive hands-on arts training in special workshops taught by professional artists. These teachers then become mentors for other schools in their district. Karia is quick to note that this experience has also enriched her own life. "I enjoy being taught as well as teaching," she says.

Teachers who integrate the arts into their classrooms have found an overall improvement in their students' motivation and academic achievement. The latter, though, is more difficult to assess accurately beyond the bounds of standardized tests.

At the Music School in Providence, Rhode Island, Martin Gardiner and several colleagues looked at the effect music and visual arts instruction has on primary school children between the ages of five and seven. One group of four classes took part in a special program of visual arts and music designed to develop artistic skills. Students in two other classes followed the standard curriculum. After seven months, both groups were tested in reading and mathematics.

What Gardiner and his team did not know until after they got the test results was that the children in the special arts program were underachievers according to their kindergarten records—their initial grades were lower than those of the control group. So the children who did *not* receive the special arts training were already ahead academically when the study began. In spite of this, however, the tests indicated that the underachievers had caught up with the other children in reading and soon outperformed them in math. The children from the arts program continued to do better in math until the end of the study the following year.

Gardiner believes that the artistic experience is so pleasurable for children that it motivates them to acquire the necessary, but challenging, skills. Teachers also report that attitudes toward school and behavior improve when children participate in the arts. Gardiner further believes that musical and visual arts training "stretches" the mental capabilities of children, making them better able to absorb learning in other areas of the curriculum, including mathematics.

A growing body of research points to the power of the arts not only to enrich the academic curriculum, but also to enliven our schools. SPECTRA+ is a Hamilton and Fairfield, Ohio, program that demonstrates arts education can have a positive effect on creative thinking and academic performance. The program aimed to provide one hour of instruction per day in music, drama, dance, art, or media arts. It featured artists-in-residence and intensive arts experiences for teachers as part of their regular professional development activities. Results of the first two years of the program (as measured by a variety of tests) showed that the SPECTRA+ students did at least as well as, if not better than, students at two other schools in the same community who were in either a "traditional" curriculum or in an innovative whole-language program. The SPECTRA+ students made greater gains in creative thinking, generally did better in math, and, at one of the schools, showed greater improvement in reading. They also had higher self-esteem and, not surprisingly, they demonstrated a greater appreciation for the arts.[16] In fact, the arts provide far greater opportunities for interactive learning and critical thinking skills than anything a child will receive from a computer.

Educators have found drawing and drama, for example, to be an excellent means of preparing young children to engage in narrative writing. A study of second and third graders in a rural Rocky Mountain region found that children who took part in drama or drawing activities produced writing that was "consistently and significantly different" in quality from the writing of children who had been part of a discussion group. The authors of the study explained the difference in terms of creative interaction:

As they involve creative products in themselves, drama and drawing allow the writer to test out, evaluate, revise, and integrate ideas before writing begins. Thus, drama and drawing are more complete forms of rehearsal for writing than discussion.[17]

This study provides a small-scale example of how arts activities can be integrated successfully into core subject areas. The Different Ways of Knowing program, launched by the Galef Institute of Los Angeles, does this on a much larger scale. Designed to improve the quality of education for high-risk elementary school children, the program is based upon the premise that integrating visual and performing arts with social studies and other core curriculum subjects will improve academic achievement. A three-year study of the program as implemented in four schools—two in the Los Angeles area, one in Boston, and one in Cambridge, Massachusetts—found that it produced impressive results. After one year, children in the program improved their language skills test scores compared with the control group, and these gains were even higher after two years. Children with three years in the program took home "significantly higher" report card grades in language arts, math, reading, and social studies.[18]

As our understanding of the arts grows, researchers document more and more reasons to enrich our schools with the arts. As part of an ongoing study, Gordon Shaw of the University of California at Irvine reported that preschoolers who study the piano or similar musical keyboard achieve higher math and science scores than those who do not. In fact, they score 34 percent higher in their puzzle-solving skills.[19]

Listening to certain kinds of music (especially classical and jazz, although not atonal music) also seems to awaken or invigorate areas of the brain that are connected to memory. A Japanese study by Takashi Taniguchi of Kyoto University concluded that "sad background music helps students memorize negative facts, like the death toll of a war, whereas cheerful music helps them remember positive facts, like when electricity was invented."[20]

In his book *Strong Arts, Strong Schools*, Charles Fowler documents dozen of cases where the arts have both transformed and renewed schools. He cites the example of Sunset Park Elementary School in Wilmington, North Carolina, which is part of large network of schools where students receive one period of daily arts instruction across a range of disciplines—music, visual arts, drama, and media arts. The program began in 1993, and after only one year, the number of students suspended from school dropped from seventy the preceding year to only three.

"Because the learning environment is stimulating and personal," writes Fowler,

> violence and discipline are not a problem. My observations in schools are that drugs, crime, hostility, indifference, and insensitivity tend to run rampant in schools that deprive students of instruction in the arts. In the process of overselling science, mathematics, and technology as the panaceas of commerce, schools have denied students something precious: access to their expressive communicative beings and their participation in creating their own world. In inner-city schools that do not offer instruction in the arts, the students have little pride and less enthusiasm, and such deprivation saps their lives of vitality and potential.[21]

Violence, endemic as it is in U.S. society, is nonetheless a way for students to assert their aggressive feelings. Giving students the opportunity to express themselves, through painting, dance, drama, or music, provides students with a wide variety of activities, methods, and outlets through which to channel their energies. Given that electronic media make spectators of us all, wearing away at our individuality, violence might be curtailed simply by honoring what is unique and special about each child. Violence, after all, is one of the most unoriginal acts in human society. When drawing or painting or sculpting, there are no "right" or "wrong" answers. Art is ambiguous, and it allows children to participate in a feeling world that is highly symbolic. These expressions of individuality are too often absent from the lives of our children.

Visionary educator Howard Gardner, author of *Frames of Mind: The Theory of Multiple Intelligences*, has written that we must reform our schools so that they move beyond merely requiring memorization of facts to establishing an integrated curriculum that nourishes what he has identified as "multiple intelligences." In Gardner's theory, the well-educated child (and hence the civilized society) will have exposure to a curriculum that not only engages the logical-mathematical and linguistic intelligences (both of which are encouraged already, although often in isolation from each other), but that also extends to encompass spatial, musical, bodily-kinesthetic, interpersonal, and intrapersonal intelligences. (Interestingly, the study of dance encompasses all of these.) Learning through the arts, among other things, helps all of us to break out of our circumscribed view of intelligence, engaging the whole child by offering a rich and more challenging curriculum.

Paying lip service to the importance of the arts in education is easy—almost everyone within the educational establishment does so. Schools typically reward and encourage the child with good logical-mathematical and, to a lesser extent, linguistic abilities because this type of child will usually produce high grades and good test results. But high scores on math tests, an ability to memorize facts for science quizzes, or an ability to write grammatically correct sentences, indicate a limited range of abilities and do not even begin to hint at the full potential in each child.

If only a fraction of the time and money spent on analyzing computer technology and its effect on students had been channeled into studying the link between education and the arts, more resources would be devoted to arts education. (A Canadian program, called Learning through the Arts, is the first to compare academic achievement in schools well endowed with technology with those that offer students an arts-enriched program.)

With more money being spent on computer technology at a time when educational budgets are tight, many schools are faced with a hard choice. If their students are to have computers, what will they have to do without? In many cases, the arts programs are cut. Too many educators and parents seem willing to sacrifice arts programs because they consider that learning to use computers is more important and, most likely, do not appreciate the vital role that arts programs can play in their children's development. And yet arts programs are much less expensive to run than computer labs. "You can run an art program for the entire school," Rena Upitis, dean of education at Queen's University, Kingston, Canada, said recently, "for what it costs to buy a single computer."

Overvaluing narrowly prescribed intelligence has unfortunate consequences. First, many children are labeled below average and these children, seeing themselves fall behind their peers, lose their enthusiasm for learning. Children capable of writing an original essay or designing an imaginative science project may be passed over because they do not perform well on standardized IQ tests. These children do not test well, not because they are not bright, but because the tests are unable to evaluate their abilities.

Second, children who are good at analytic thinking and who test well may be encouraged to believe that this type of achievement on its own will lead to success later in life. In many cases, they will be disappointed. Students with extremely high IQs often go on to lead rather ordinary lives. The kind of textbook problems that "bright" students are good at solving (problems that have a "right" answer) do very little to prepare them for real-life situations that require original ideas and creative solutions.

Creativity does not show up on report cards. In fact, Sternberg claims, quite the opposite. Teachers tend to discourage creativity because creative children are more liable to disrupt well-established classroom routines or produce work that does not meet conventional expectations.

Yet creative intelligence should not be associated with the waywardness that is often assumed to accompany artistic inclinations. Although a creative imagination is essential in any artistic endeavor, it is also relevant to other kinds of activity. Besides, how do we possibly measure creative or divergent thinking?

Nurturing a love of the arts is best done when children are young because those fortunate enough to take school or community arts courses in their youth are more likely to participate in and appreciate the arts as adults. People who do not participate in the arts as children tend not to take part as adults, either.[22] Researchers from the University of Rochester in New York who analyzed data from a 1992 survey conducted by the U.S. Bureau of the Census discovered a correlation between arts education and social class. The higher people were on the socioeconomic ladder, the more arts training they had received. Schools tended to mitigate this effect, making arts education more accessible to all.[23]

When one considers the lifelong pleasure and benefits to be gained from artistic pursuits, the wiser choice seems to favor the integration of the arts, rather than computer technology, into the primary school curriculum. Politicians who are enthusiastic to close the technology gap in schools should stop to consider that students who are deprived of the arts are missing out on much more than students who lack Internet access. Using a computer is, after all, something that most reasonably intelligent adults can learn in a fairly short time. Not learning this skill in childhood hardly seems a serious disadvantage.

Conversely, participating in an arts program at a young age offers major advantages. Learning to play a recorder, compose a poem, perform a dance step, or act out a play is much easier to do when one is young. If arts are not included in the curriculum, many children may never have the opportunity to acquire these abilities. Even more important, the self-discipline, concentration, emotional control, and sheer joy that children learn in the act of creation will serve them well all their lives.

# CHAPTER 11

# The Real World of Learning

*A computer puts a literal and psychological screen—a barrier—between the child and the real world.*

—Mary Swift[1]

*…without intimacy with nature, we can confuse crimes against the Earth with technological progress.*

—David Suzuki[2]

On a warm summer's day in August 1995, a group of twelve- and thirteen-year-old students took a field trip to visit a farm near Henderson, Minnesota, a town in the south-central part of the state. Several of the kids were chasing frogs when a thirteen-year-old boy by the name of Jeff Fish caught a peculiar-looking specimen. Describing the incident to a reporter some time later, the teenager said, "When I picked him up I saw that he was missing his right hind leg. My first instinct was that a predator had bitten it off. But I looked him over for sores or scars and I didn't see any, so I showed him to the teacher."[3]

While the teacher examined the frog, her students caught more of the animals. Of the twenty-two frogs collected, eleven had deformities of one kind or another. The students' shaken teacher, Cindy Reinitz, reported their findings to the local wildlife biologist and, eventually, to Minnesota Pollution Control.

The students' discovery turned out to be the first of more than 100 such incidents in Minnesota (and, subsequently, frogs with a range of deformities turned up across Wisconsin, Iowa, South Dakota, Missouri,

California, Texas, Vermont, and along the St. Lawrence River in Quebec, Canada). Numerous amphibians had extra legs, webbed legs, paralyzed legs, and missing eyes. In one horribly memorable case, a frog had an eye growing inside its throat. These deformities have been the subject of a number of conferences, and the water quality of the region has been under constant investigation. Chemical pollutants are seen as the likely culprits, but so far, no single source has been cited as the cause of the deformities. Meanwhile, people in many areas of the state now drink bottled water.

Disturbing as this discovery is, the students learned a valuable lesson, and one that they are unlikely to forget. Their firsthand experience of nature in jeopardy made them understand both the fragility and complexity of the natural world. Something had gone wrong for which there was no obvious cause. There were no neat explanations or easily identifiable solutions. In other words, there were forces at work that were beyond immediate human control.

The environmental challenges which face our own and future generations require that our children grow up sensitive to the forces that shape life on this planet. Teachers know that classroom projects involving living things and field trips help to develop such attitudes. Taking care of the classroom rabbit, fish, or guinea pig gives children a sense of personal responsibility for other forms of life, and trips to a ravine or local conservation area expose urban children to nature.

All this is changing with the use of classroom computers. More and more, children's experience of the natural world is confined to images on a computer screen. Multimedia encyclopedias, Web sites, and computer simulation programs all enable children to visit and experience various types of environments, many of which are far beyond the scope of a one-day excursion from school. Instead of being formed by direct experience, children's perceptions of the natural world are shaped by the technology through which their experiences are mediated. This technology presents a world that is instantly accessible, controllable at will, and subject to arbitrary changes. In the electronic universe consequences can be easily reversed.

The following advertisement for a new electronic atlas is but one example. It begins:

Mother Nature needed 4.5 billion years to create the original. You'll need ten minutes for your version. Rand McNally now brings you the power to shape the world with New Millennium World Atlas Deluxe software. It's the only atlas that lets you create a personalized view of the world.

The slick advertising copy conveys the power-trip mentality that lies behind this computer-generated vision of the earth:

If you're in the mood to explore, New Millennium will let you jump instantly to anywhere in the world. Peer into the eye of a dinosaur. Witness the awesome forces that trigger a volcanic eruption. Navigate the most beautifully detailed 3-D maps available.

The tone is reinforced by the closing words of encouragement: "So go ahead. Take your world for a spin."[4] It's as if the planet was a high-powered, luxury automobile.

One problem with such computer software is that it gives children a false idea of their relationship to the natural world. Because accessing a picture or film clip of a particular animal or habitat is so easy, children gain the impression that nature is conveniently at their fingertips and that its processes can be manipulated or accelerated and served to them in an easy-to-read format. This is poor preparation for the appreciation and understanding the realities of nature because the study of nature requires a good deal of patient observation and, sometimes, considerable hardship. The natural world does not "perform" on demand and much of it is in remote areas that are reached with difficulty and have inhospitable climates. Ironically, programs designed to encourage an interest in nature may have the opposite effect. When confronted with the real thing, children may either be bored or feel threatened, and may well prefer to settle for the screen version.

Computer simulations designed to help children understand the workings of natural (and man-made) systems can be even more misleading than cartoons because they appear to present a realistic model of how such systems actually work. This is, in fact, far from the case. Simulations present only a partial, artfully contrived reality—one for which the programmer determines the variables. The impression given is that there are definite answers, when in reality there may only be hypotheses. Because children, and no doubt many adults, do not appreciate these limitations, they could be led to believe that computer-generated solutions can be applied to issues that, in reality, are far too complex to be resolved in this way.

Learning involves the construction of models from which we form ideas about ourselves and the world around us. These models change through a process of experience and reflection. The problem with computer simulations is that the software designers have already made assumptions about the way the models work, so in using such software, we must rely on someone else's perceptions and judgment. These assumptions are a permanent feature; we cannot change them. Moreover, they are hidden from the user, so we do not even know if they are reasonable or accurate.

Computer simulations present children with situations where they no longer have to consider their real-world experiences and the real-world complexities and constraints with which they live. As Theodore Roszak points out:

> the "universe" which we can create on a computer screen is a small, highly edited simulation of reality. Moreover, it is a universe created by a small, highly edited simulation of *ourselves*. Only one narrow band of our experience is represented in the computer: logical reason. Sensual contact, intuition, inarticulated commonsense judgments, aesthetic taste have been largely, if not wholly, left out. We do not bring the full resources of the self to the computer.[5]

At the same time, simulation programs, especially those for children, contain an element of play. They present human interaction with the environment as a grand experiment, the consequences of which we need not take too seriously because a false move can always be corrected—if the worst happens, one can always start the program again. Although allowing children to exercise their curiosity in a "safe" environment has its merits, this will do little to develop in them a sense of responsibility for their actions. When something goes wrong in the real world, they cannot just close it down and start again.

One must, therefore, question the appropriateness of using simulations with young children. An interesting example is *The Water Game*, a simulation that teaches children about the importance of water and irrigation on a farm in a developing country. Working in groups of two to four, children play the role of a water-carrier who supplies the farm with water. Water is collected from a variety of sources and stored in tanks, which represent particular uses for the water—for washing, for cooking and drinking, for farm animals, and for irrigation of crops. Using keyboard controls, children decide what size of containers to use to collect the water, what sources of water are available, the best route to and from these sources, and how to distribute the water among the various tanks. The object of the game is to carry and distribute enough water so that people, animals, and crops survive. After several simulated days, the results of the children's decisions are revealed in a report that tells how much water has been carried and the state of health of the people, animals, and crops on the farm. The game is designed so that, on the first attempt, the children will fail to keep the farm adequately supplied in order to give them a sense of the "real" difficulties faced by farmers in developing countries.[6]

This simulation clearly has good intentions, and children will no doubt find it an interesting game. But it has serious limitations when measured against the reality it claims to convey. Each team's score is based on the number of gallons successfully carried, the implication being that the more water carried the better. But in a "real" situation other requirements are also extremely important, such as gathering fuel, spreading fertilizer, and weeding crops. The collection and storage of water is only one task. Thus, what really matters is the *optimal* amount of water—enough to nurture the farm while allowing time to meet other essential needs. These other concerns might not be appreciated by the children playing the game. They might well come away with the belief that availability of water is the biggest problem facing farmers in developing countries and have little idea of the other factors affecting the farm's productivity—the effects of the weather (there are times when too *much* rain can be devastating), fuel requirements, pesticide use, and the application of chemical fertilizers.

One must also question whether this kind of simulation on its own is an effective means of teaching children about a way of life that differs so markedly from their own. They would surely learn far more about the complex process of planting, nurturing, and harvesting, and caring for animals if they were to visit a small local farm and see, firsthand, the work involved. Better still, they could grow their own gardens, either in the school yard or in a classroom window box, and do the work themselves. By observing their efforts over time, children would see the effects of changing weather patterns and would come to appreciate the different needs of various plants for water, sunlight, and fertilizer. They would also gain an understanding of the interactions between plant and animal life—for example, the role of bees in pollination. These experiences are far more likely than any computer simulation to lead to an empathetic view of the lives of farmers whose livelihoods depend on the yearly rhythms of the Earth.

Hands-on practical work can also benefit students academically. In a national sample of 24,599 eighth graders, students who conducted science experiments in class, once a week at least, scored significantly higher on a standardized test of science achievement than students who engaged in hands-on activities once a month or less frequently.[7] Further evidence comes from the National Assessment of Educational Progress, whose 1996 report notes that students who worked with living plants obtained higher science scores than those whose assignments excluded hands-on activities.[8]

Although the central role of computer technology in helping us understand natural phenomena is firmly rooted in the public's mind, many scientists now realize that direct observation and practical experience can be of greater value in understanding natural processes than computer-generated models. Brian Carson is a geoscientist who heads up a team of volunteers working to restore the Chapman Creek watershed on the Sunshine Coast north of Vancouver, British Columbia. The river was virtually destroyed by logging and road construction. This caused erosion and landslides, which removed precious soil from the forest and deposited it in the river. Instead of relying on scientific studies and computerized monitoring of the water quality and flow, Carson spends hours walking around the river, learning its secrets by observing its changes. In fact, he and his team have learned that visual observations of the river are crucial to understanding how it flowed before the area was logged. By figuring out how it used to flow, he is, in effect, letting the river tell him what to do—how best to return it to its original course.

Carson also drew on the experiences of people whose knowledge of rivers was based on years of observation. As he told a reporter:

> When I started this project, loggers and old-timers who worked near rivers would tell me things I found unbelievable. Then when I stayed and observed the river continuously, I saw with my own eyes what the locals had reported, and realized they'd been dead right all along. That increased my respect both for nature and for non-scientists.[9]

Although it is not always possible to give children wilderness experiences, a hands-on approach to scientific study takes nothing more than a little imagination on the part of a teacher or parent. For more than twenty years, Kathleen Carroll has worked with inner-city children in Washington, D.C., to help them experience nature in their own backyard. An environmental consultant and a member of the Audobon Natural Society, Carroll regularly takes elementary school students outside the classroom to count the birds, look at insects on a bush or tree growing in the schoolyard, or simply watch a dandelion that has sprouted in a cracked sidewalk. Every neighborhood has birds—pigeons, gulls, sparrows, or the occasional cardinal—and just asking children to observe these creatures can be a transforming experience. "All of a sudden," she says "it opens their eyes."

"Some people have gotten so far from the experience of nature that they think it's a dirty or nasty experience," says Carroll:

> I had the experience of a child who was holding a caterpillar, watching it in rapt fascination, when the child's mother came over and said "that's a nasty, dirty thing." You should have seen the confusion on the child's face.

Intimate experiences of nature are unfortunately all too rare for many children. Those who are in favor of replacing real-world outings with digital "field trips" do not take into account the emotional and intellectual links that must be forged in order for children to care enough about the environment to preserve it.

Being emotionally engaged includes facing up to what some may consider the unpalatable realities of the natural world, not the least of which is the fact that children must get their hands dirty in order to discover the secrets of ecosystems and of the living organisms that inhabit them. Yet computer programs often distance children from the true nature of the material about which they are learning. (Computer software manufactures often advertise the fact that doing experiments on the computer means no "messy spills" to clean up.)

A notable example is the frog dissection kits that can now be purchased or downloaded from the Internet. Instead of dissecting a real frog, which can be messy, children can engage in a scalpel-free dissection. By using the mouse, they can simply point and click, removing organ after organ and, if they wish, putting them back in again. These electronic frogs are shown in 3-D and can be viewed from a variety of angles. The organs are color coded and if a student fails to identify a part correctly or forgets its name, he or she need only point and click and the correct anatomical description will appear on screen.

For those who are squeamish, on-screen dissection offers obvious advantages. They need never experience the smell or feel of an actual frog or the sight of its internal organs. Yet, although these electronic facsimiles save the lives of innocent frogs and sanitize what can be an unpleasant task for sensitive students, both the American Human Anatomy and Physiology Society and the National Association of Biology Teachers have adopted policies strongly in support of real dissection.

They have good reason to take this position. Those who examine biological organisms know that no two specimens of the same species are ever exactly alike. Neither plants nor animals come with color-coded anatomy, and anyone who has ever dissected a frog or examined a seed under a microscope knows only too well that identifying the various parts correctly is not easy. Students must have a lot of visual acumen, which is an ability that must be developed through practical experience. Computer programs may teach students the names of a few organs and their approximate locations, but they are left without an understanding of the far more complex anatomical systems and the intricacy of the links between them.

The use of computer technology, so often seen as a simple solution, can come between students and a proper understanding of the natural world. The acquisition of scientific knowledge does not necessarily depend on high-tech intervention—human observation and experience are far more essential. We seem to have forgotten this simple truth, dazzled as we are by the wonders of the electronic age, yet there are many people for whom it remains a living reality.

The indigenous inhabitants of the Amazon rain forest, for instance, are amazingly knowledgeable about their natural world. They have to be, because they depend on it for survival in a way that many of us, in our thoroughly urbanized existence, would find hard to understand. Even very young children are well-acquainted with a multitude of edible or healing plants.[10] The uses to which various plants are put demonstrates just how sophisticated this knowledge is. For example, one of the staples of the Amazonian Indians' diet is the poisonous root of the yucca plant, which they have learned to prepare in ways that remove its cyanic material. They make a drink from the pomegranate-like fruit of a palm which is rich in vitamin $B_1$—otherwise in scarce supply in their diet. They use drops of a tea made from vine leaves to cure eye infections, and a parasitic plant to stop the blood flow from a wound. They wash themselves and their clothing with plants containing saponins, substances that produce foam when put in water. Indians of the northwestern Amazon use the poison found in several plants to help them catch fish. One such plant is a forest liana, the bark of which is scraped off, softened by soaking, and then either thrown directly into, or placed in a bag and dragged through, the water. The poison affects the function of the gills. The fish are stunned and, seeking oxygen, come to the surface where they are caught. None of the poison is absorbed by the fish, so they are entirely edible.[11]

The Amazonian Indians, in fact, possess an encyclopedic botanical knowledge that few, if any, Western scientists can match. The Indians' uncanny ability to identify a particular kind of plant indicates that their senses are acutely attuned to the botanical riches of their environment. "The forest peoples' acquaintance with plants is subtle as well as extensive," writes Harvard biologist Richard Evans Schultes. "The Indians often distinguish 'kinds' of a plant that appear indistinguishable, even to the experienced taxonomic botanist."[12]

Although this knowledge has been overlooked or ignored in the past, today the United Nations officially recognizes the vast body of knowledge that is not contained in books, but is passed down through generations and gleaned from an intimate contact with the natural environment. Several projects have been undertaken to document indigenous knowledge and integrate it with Western science to gain a better understanding of the Earth's natural systems.

Aboriginal peoples learn about the natural world through observation and direct experience, and this knowledge is passed from one generation to the next so that the longer a people live in an area, the greater their knowledge of it becomes. To take an example from Canada, where the National Aboriginal Forestry Association has documented the forest-related traditional knowledge and practices of several First Nations across the country, the Crees of Eeyou Astchee in northern Quebec have developed a sophisticated system of resource management in which the land is divided into "wildlife harvesting territories," each under the stewardship of a single "tallyman" and his family. The tallyman is responsible for managing the resources of the territory, but in addition to his own knowledge, he depends upon the knowledge of other families using the territory who pass on information about specific sites so that a detailed picture of conditions in the territory can be developed and shared with all the families concerned. The tallyman's accumulated knowledge includes "local seasonal climatic patterns, movement of animals, location of plants, ages of trees, drainage patterns and wildlife habitat preferences" and is vital to maintaining an optimal yield of resources.[13]

This kind of holistic understanding of the environment is in danger of being lost as young Aboriginals absorb, through electronic media, the values of the dominant culture. As for children who live in urban environments in industrialized countries, they are already losing their connections with the natural world in many ways. Many city children cannot accurately name the flowers or shrubs in their local parks or home gardens and are unaware that many of these plants are not native species. Many cannot differentiate between an orange and a tangerine, and even fewer realize that there are dozens of species of, for example, apples, potatoes, and tomatoes, rather than the few, common varieties they normally see. As well, the way in which fruits and vegetables appear year-round in their local grocery stores gives them a sense of a seasonless harvest. When everything is available all the time, the natural constraints of climate and geography no longer seem to matter. Because of this, the simple act of growing a vegetable garden can be a powerful experience for children. Throughout her career, Kathleen Carroll has planted community gardens and invited students to her home to give them the experience of planting, tending, and harvesting vegetables. Children take a lot of pride in what they grow and, as they learn how long a carrot, cucumber, or tomato needs to ripen, their understanding of the process grows. In Carroll's experience, such activities can also change eating habits: "It really opens them up to eating vegetables, since they are so used to just eating fast foods."

Trading computer simulations for hands-on learning can be detrimental in other ways, too. For example, computer simulations dealing with environmental conditions tend to focus on global issues, many of which are far removed from children's personal experiences. As a result, environmental studies are often too abstract for children, who are forced to grapple with large, intractable issues they don't understand. In one case, an eight-year-old girl's response to a school project on endangered animals was to produce a poster showing a carefully drawn and colored elephant beneath which she had written, "Save the Elephant. Don't Buy Ivory Soap."[14] A recent survey found that, despite the attention given to the topic in environmental education materials, 35 percent of fifth-grade students think that global warming is occurring because the sun is moving closer to the earth, and just as many identified the burning of fossil fuel as a likely cause.[15]

Larry Miller and John Olson discovered that when teachers trade a hands-on science activity for a computer simulation, they gain precision and control, but they sacrifice understanding.

We have seen children who—when astounded to see the differences in the results of plant experiments where light, water, and soil are controlled in a simulation—conclude that the computer results rather than their own real-world experiments are correct.[16]

Educators much teach children to have confidence in the evidence of their own senses; it is one of the most important lessons to impart.

Even in the midst of a large city, a sense of being a part of nature can act as a powerful spur to children's imagination and creativity, and making this sense come alive is one of the greatest gifts a teacher can give to her students. Geneticist and environmental activist David Suzuki praised Tokyo teacher Toshiko Toriyama for her ability to do just this.[17] Aware of the fact that so many children, especially those growing up in noisy, polluted urban areas, lack any real understanding of nature and their place in it, Toriyama has her students imagine being an insect such as a praying mantis, laying eggs on a leaf and moving through its life cycle, or a tree growing in the forest that is cut down and taken to market. She derives her inspiration from the writing of Buddhist poet Kenji Miyazawa, whose poetry described the mystery and wonder of the natural world. With Toriyama's guidance, children learn, by invoking their imaginative capabilities, to understand the complex life cycles that bind all living organisms together. Realizing that many children do not understand where their food actually comes from, Toriyama takes her students to visits farms so they can observe the life cycle of pigs, for instance, beginning with their birth and ending when the animals are taken to a slaughterhouse. Only through concrete experiences such as this can children, she believes, come to understand human dependency on other living organisms.

This dependency exists even though our use of technology tends to mask its presence. But human technology need not ignore or, as is often the case, destroy the natural world; it can work in harmony with it. Carroll notes that she uses different kinds of technology—from high to low tech—to assist her and her students in studying the natural world. One of her favorite activities is to take a magnifying glass and ask children to study a wall and look at the minerals it is made of, or to look at insects, their hands, or a violet. "Taking the time to look closely helps kids open their senses." Studying the migration of monarch butterflies is another favorite activity. In order to understand something about their life cycles, she helps children plant milkweed, which serves as food for the butterflies. As the milkweed grows, children observe the butterflies it attracts. Students can watch for the first sighting of a butterfly and then study its migratory cycle. Carroll is not averse to using computers; in fact, she finds it helpful to share information electronically with other students across the country who are also studying the monarch butterfly. She stresses, however, this should only be done in conjunction with students' firsthand observations. "We turn students into scientists," she says, "simply by encouraging them to go outside and become aware of their own immediate environment."

Because so many children never leave the city, Carroll has taught many children who have never studied the night sky. "Most of the kids I teach had never even seen the stars, and they don't have a clue about the planets." Carroll asks these children to study the moon for a month—just to watch it wax and wane. "This is an amazing experience because no one had invited them to look up before." For many children, the sky—indeed all of nature—is simply an abstraction.

To give her students a chance to see more of the natural world, Carroll also founded the Little School program, which provides elementary school children with hands-on activities. (Although Carroll no longer teaches this program, it is still taught.) As part of the program, students from southeast Washington, D.C., visit the Chesapeake Bay and stay overnight. During their stay, students learn about the natural world through immersion in it. They spend time hiking, watching birds, identifying insects, and observing the changing weather patterns. Because so many city children have little acquaintance with nature, their time at Chesapeake Bay is precious and life-changing. Many city children have never walked on a beach or watched waves break on a shore. "Many children," says Carroll, "don't go outside the four-block radius of where they live." Children are captivated by their first unobscured sight of the stars and moon. (For many, the night sky is normally concealed by the lights of the city.) Nothing children can do on a computer can even begin to come close to such experiences. Carroll remembers talking with one boy who visited Chesapeake Bay several years before. When he saw his former teacher he said to her, "The Little

School is the best school. We learn about the islands, the water, the ocean. In the big school there's just all them guns and knives."

The simple experience of just being in nature may have more of an influence on the creative, intellectual, and emotional life of children than can ever be accurately measured. Anthropologist–educator Loren Eiseley recalled that he had been "created" more by the yellow butter-cups he saw on a kindergarten picnic than by any laboratory test tubes he encountered. "It is more important to bathe the spirit in natural influences," said natural history writer John Burroughs, "than to store the mind with facts."

Edith Cobb, a sociologist who analyzed the lives of more than 300 outstanding individuals from the sixteenth through the twentieth centuries, concluded that a strong link exists between genius and the experience of being close to the natural world in childhood. Cobb believed that creativity and constructive thinking were not the result of accumulated information, but rather arose out of what she called "a continued plasticity of response of the whole organism to new infor-mation and in general to the outer world."[18] This kind of thinking, which is highly developed in geniuses, has its genesis in the early years of childhood. Einstein acknowledged that his long walks in nature played a formative role in his thinking; and geneticist Barbara McClintock credits her observations of the unique pattern of corn kernels with her breakthroughs in the structure of DNA. The work of writers such as Emily Dickinson, Julian Huxley, Lawrence Durrell, and Margaret Atwood attests to the importance of close contact with the natural world. During adulthood, creative geniuses return again and again to that period of childhood between the ages of five and twelve when their experiences of the natural world and their place in it gave them an intuitive understanding of what so many have called whole-ness, oneness, or a sense of harmony with nature. Cobb suggests that this preverbal experience of what she terms "aesthetic logic" is the foundation of creative insight. Exposure to nature also sharpens per-ceptual acuity, which is the foundation of any creative act.

Those who are lucky enough to experience the natural world in childhood have advantages over their peers whose only sense of nature is mediated through artificial images. By learning from direct experience to observe and understand the world around them, children not only will develop greater sensory awareness of their surroundings, but also will acquire a wealth of knowledge that they can draw upon all their lives.

## CHAPTER 12

# Finding Technology's Place

*In school, there is no argument or negotiation with the computer.*

—Ursula Franklin[1]

To return to our opening story of Burrville Elementary School in Washington, D.C., you might well wonder what the students did after the First Ladies departed and the new machines were removed. Did the school settle back into low-tech doldrums and did the students resume an accustomed apathy?

Far from it. In fact, Burrville Elementary School has an excellent reputation among schools in the nation's capital, although not for its computer lab. The school is instead known for its extraordinary success in overcoming the chronic underfunding and decay that have made the District of Columbia's schools a national embarrassment.[2] Lack of computer equipment has not hurt the Burrville students. The one-day Internet set-up was a distraction that may have prevented the First Ladies from realizing what really made the school work: the commitment and abilities of the teachers.

As long as technology is seen as the savior of the nation's schools, it will dazzle us with easy answers to complex questions. We will not look at underlying social problems that schools alone cannot solve, and we will overlook those things that make schools work. We will also be blind to the problems that technology causes.

Today's busy parents spend about ten fewer hours with their children each week than they did just a generation ago. Another noisy machine is the last thing a child who has spent his or her early years in the clutches of television, video games, and pop music needs. These children need more contact with people, not more contact with machines. Decreasing class sizes is one way to help children get more time with people—that is, with their teachers.

Author and MIT professor Nicholas Negroponte proclaims that, in the future, "We will socialize in digital neighborhoods in which physical space will be irrelevant and time will play a different role."[3] But children who already get too little attention from parents and who are overlooked in large classes will find life in a "digital neighborhood" a poor substitute. Children need to live in real time in real space with real people. Just as an infant requires a parent in order to feel safe and secure, children require a real social context in which to learn. Online relationships with peers in Moscow or Madrid will not help a child who cannot make friends with a classmate two desks away.

There is no substitute for direct experience. At a conference in Washington, D.C., in the fall of 1998, MIT professor Sherry Terkel made a presentation about children and technology. She told a story of her young daughter who saw a jellyfish for the first time and exclaimed, "But, Mommy, it looks so realistic!" Terkel went on to suggest that we will have to teach children "simulation literacy," so they will be able to tell the difference between real jellyfish—the kind that eat and swim and multiply of their own accord—and those that exist only as colored pixels. This is a sad commentary on the state of childhood.

Schools that encourage hands-on learning—everything from building birdhouses and planting butterfly bushes, to growing vegetables or hiking in conservation areas—will never have to give one moment's consideration to teaching "simulation literacy." Digital field trips are no better (in some cases they may be worse) than television for developing an affinity for science or the natural world in a child who never gets beyond the concrete confines of an inner-city neighborhood.

The widespread use of computers in our schools is a grand

experiment whose outcome is uncertain. Imposing computers on young children is yet another technological innovation that we may live to regret. The fact is, we cannot accurately forecast the long-term effects of regular computer use on children's development.

If there are benefits to be gained from using computers in our schools, they have not yet been realized. "If computers make a difference," says Samuel Salva, former executive director of the National Association of Elementary School Principals, "it has yet to show up in achievement." Computers will probably not improve learning if technology integration proceeds at its current frantic pace. As for teachers, computers have simply added to their already exhausting workload and worsened funding problems.

What has been lacking up to now is a serious public debate about the nature of this technology and what it should, or could, be used for in our children's education. Such a debate is all the more necessary because so many parents and teachers have been seduced by the blandishments of computer companies and software developers. As author and NYU professor Neil Postman says, "Technology may have entered the schools but...technology education [has not]."[4] True computer literacy would teach children (as well as teachers and parents) when it is appropriate to use technology.

Far from creating opportunities for learning, the inappropriate use of computer technology does more harm than good. Judah Schwartz, codirector of Harvard's Educational Technology Center, believes in the judicious use of computers. He warns that because computer technology is more powerful than that of books, "it will be much worse if used badly than books, and will be much more effective in doing damage."

Sadly, the worst use of computers often occurs among those students for whom school computers were to be the great equalizer, providing opportunities unavailable to them in their computerless homes. "There is," says Schwartz, "an implicit racism in the rise of mind-numbing software in inner-city schools. Lock up such software in the closet." Inner-city minority students have been exposed to mind-numbing software and are now living with its consequences in the form of declining math skills.

Our concern about the computerization of elementary school classrooms would not be so acute if we thought that computers would be used only occasionally—perhaps for special projects—and confined to the higher grades or the library. The indications are, however, that the amount of time children spend at computers will only increase. The more computers schools have, the greater the pressure to make use of them.

Rather than put its faith in computer technology, an egalitarian school system would ensure that classes were small enough for all teachers and students to know each other. It would ensure that all children had the opportunity to participate in a daily physical education program, an arts program, and a music program. It would provide well-stocked libraries and librarians to go with them. It would, in short, give every student the opportunity to develop the gifts with which they were born. Where technology does enhance learning—for instance, at Florida's Celebration School—it is usually because the school is so well funded that it does not have to pay for the technology by sacrificing a music program or a teacher's time. But this is not the case for most U.S. schools. The reality is that technology requires trade-offs—trade-offs that are *never* in best interests of our children. The cost of a single computer could pay for a choral music program or a visual arts program for an entire school.

Schools that were concerned with building community would ensure that all children could participate in staging a play, singing in a choir, or creating an art mural. Schools that valued individuality and creativity would ensure that all children visited a real art gallery or museum and took regular field trips. Imagine a school where all children learned the fingering for a recorder instead of a computer keyboard. Instead of a computer on every desk, how about a box of watercolors or a calligraphy pen? What if instead of peering at the pixels on a screen, children could watch the sky through a telescope? What if every child had a chance to plant and harvest vegetables in a community garden, or knew the names of the trees and bushes he or she passed on the way to school?

There are encouraging signs that teachers and parents are beginning to question the use of computers in schools, signs that they are unwilling to make these trade-offs. In New York, technology coordinator Giulia Cox told a *New York Times* reporter, "If someone said to me, you have a choice—you can take your class ratio of 37 to 1 and cut it in half or you can have laptops, I'd choose smaller classes over laptops in a second."[5]

In Missouri, librarians are organizing a conference called Technology: The Dark Side of the Force to examine the impact of computers on student learning and book budgets. Carl Wingo, chair of the computer and information technology committee for the state library association, says the conference is badly needed because the integration of technology has "wreaked havoc with library budgets," creating financial burdens for small libraries.

At the Northville School District near Detroit, Michigan, David Skrbina, a parent of two young children, has begun to speak to other parents and local PTAs to ask them to reconsider the school board's decision to spend $5.3 million on computers. "As a parent, I am most concerned about the long-term psychological and emotional effects of computer technology on my children," he told me.

> Computers mediate and control their experiences, and provide a very limited view on things. I am concerned that they may come to see this limited perspective as normal, or even desirable.... I don't want them to think that their success in any way depends on having access to the appropriate machine.

Skrbina called upon his school board to eliminate all computer use in kindergarten through fifth grade and to use computers in middle school for library searches only.

A broad-based national coalition of parents, scholars, teachers, doctors, and organizations that represent children and families is calling on politicians and computer manufacturers to stop invading the privacy of schoolchildren by collecting personal information from them during school time, and to stop forcing children to watch advertising during school hours. The protest is aimed at the ZapMe! corporation as well as those organizations such as Dell, Microsoft, Gilat, General Electric, NEC America, Toshiba, Xerox, Sylvan Learning Systems, and Yahoo!, that provide ZapMe! with equipment.

And then there's Lakeside School, the elite Seattle private school whose alumni include Bill Gates. Judy Lightfoot, Lakeside's English department chair, has posted on her Web site a 3,500-word essay against the purchase of laptop computers. Lakeside was expected to take part in a $1.7 million state program—The Copernicus Project, in which every student would have a laptop—tied in with the Learning with Laptops campaign being mounted by Toshiba and Microsoft.

A teacher for more than thirty-five years, Lightfoot points out that computers cause distraction in the classroom because students relate more to them than to each other. "They change the atmosphere even if they are closed." Buying them would cost the school annually between $800,000 and $1.6 million—funds that, she told me recently, would be better spent on teachers' salaries, reducing class size, and financial aid to students. "Two things improve student learning," she said, "one is student time-on-task and the other is small classes."

Lightfoot uses her Web site to post her students' work and agrees that computers can aid in the revision process. But overall, she insists, "they don't help students to think better, read better, or write better." Today's children, she maintains, are different than those of previous generations, regardless of whether they are rich or poor:

> Increasingly, I feel students are alienated from themselves. Students have too little time to read or reflect on their own. They have too little time for conversations that allow them to understand themselves and their world.

Politicians and the computer industry have terrorized parents with the belief that their children will need to study computer science to be successful in the labor market, when, in fact, only a small percentage of new jobs will come from high-tech industries. Most new jobs in the next ten years will be created in service industries. More jobs will be created for waiters and waitresses, sales clerks and cashiers than for systems analysts and mathematicians. Skill requirements are changing—most workers can pick up the necessary technical skills on the job in a matter of months. As David Livingstone documents in his book *The Education–Jobs Gap*, we have a greater problem with underemployment and wasted human potential than with a lack of skilled workers. In the ten-year period from 1996–2006, the U.S. Department of Labor proj-ects that the percentage of workers in occupations requiring a college degree will rise by only 1 percent.[6]

In *Technology and Empire*, George Grant writes that "the curriculum is itself chiefly determined by what the dominant classes of the society consider important to be known."[7] The most influential of the domi-nant classes these days is the business elite, and thus we should not be surprised that the corporate agenda looms large in the continuing debate over school curriculums. Although corporate leaders are adept at paying lip service to the need for creativity and better thinking skills, they often have strictly functional requirements in mind. As one educa-tor notes,

> They often *say* that they want critical thinkers and problem solvers...but, as I talk to business leaders, I frequently get the uncomfortable feeling that what they really want are more compliant worker bees.[8]

Joseph Weizenbaum warns against this kind of hollowing-out of education. The teacher, he writes, who sees himself as a mere trainer invites his students to become

> less than fully autonomous persons. He invites them to become mere follow-ers of other people's orders, and finally no better than the machines that might some day replace them in that function.[9]

It is unethical to push students into a high-tech future and fail to give them the critical skills to understand the limitations that *every* technology possesses. That failure may create a generation unable to envision any other future. Envisioning the best future that can be made from present realities is the critical act for any generation. We cannot leave our children and our schools in the hands of the software makers and advertisers. Children's educational needs are best met by first meeting their physical and emotional needs. Nothing is more important for a child in school than his or her relationship with a teacher.

Who among us does not have at least one teacher to thank for igniting an enthusiasm for science, music, or literature? Curiosity is contagious. Good teachers convey their own interests and excitement in learning. They are not just concerned with *what* their students learn but with *why* they should know about certain things and *how* this knowledge can make a difference to them. Only the presence of a sympathetic adult will encourage children to ask the kinds of questions that play a crucial role in their learning. Grasping a few fundamental ideas is more important for a child than having access to a mountain of raw data. Human values must be taught by human beings; a computerized substitute is no substitute at all.

# NOTES

## CHAPTER 1

1. Jane M. Healy, *Endangered Minds: Why Our Children Don't Think* (New York: Simon & Schuster/Touchstone, 1991), p. 345.

2. R. W. Burniske, "The Shadow Play: How the Integration of Technology Annihilates Debate in Our Schools," *Phi Delta Kappan*, October 1998, p. 157.

3. Paul Koring, "Computers Mislead Leaders Wives," *Globe and Mail*, 9 April 1997, p. A1.

4. Quoted in Theodore Roszak, *The Cult of Information*, 2nd ed. (Berkeley: University of California Press, 1994), p. 51.

5. U.S. Congress, Office of Technology Assessment, *Teachers and Technology: Making the Connection*, OTA–HER–616 (Washington, D.C.: GPO, April 1995), "Timeline of Changes in the Prevailing Wisdom of 'Experts' about How Teachers Should Use Computers in Schools," p. 104. Original source: H. J. Becker, "Analysis and Trends of School Use of New Information Technologies," Office of Technology Assessment contractor report (Washington, D.C.: GPO, March 1994).

6. Seymour Papert, *The Children's Machine: Rethinking School in the Age of the Computer* (New York: BasicBooks, 1993), p. 168.

7. Panel on Educational Technology, *Report to the President on the Use of Technology to Strengthen K–12 Education in the United States* (Washington, D.C.: President's Committee of Advisors on Science and Technology, March 1997), p. 20.

8. Quoted in Douglas D. Noble, "Bill of Goods: The Early Marketing of Computer-Based Education and Its Implications for the Present Moment," in *International Handbook of Teachers and Teaching,* vol. II, ed. Bruce J. Biddle et al. (Dordrecht, The Netherlands: Kluwer Academic Publishers, 1997), p. 1364.

9. Seymour Papert, *Mindstorms: Children, Computers, and Powerful Ideas* (New York, BasicBooks, 1980), p. 155.

10. Jerry Mander, *Four Arguments for the Elimination of Television* (New York: Quill, 1978), p. 28.

11. Bill McKibben, *The Age of Missing Information* (New York: Random House, 1992), p. 16.

12. Office of Technology Assessment, p. 92; Software and Information Industry (SIIA), *1999 Education Market Report: K–12* (Washington, D.C.: SIIA, 1999), Executive Summary.

13. According to its home page on the Web, "'NetDay96' is a statewide cooperative effort by California's technology industries, public schools, and communities to install the wires needed to provide at least 20 percent of the state's 13,000 schools with access to the Internet."

14. Paul Lima, "Technophobia," *Toronto Star*, 30 June 1994, p. G5.

15. Military research on educational technology has been driven to a large extent by the need to ensure that military personnel can effectively operate the increasingly sophisticated weapon and defense systems on which the military relies. These systems are in fact seen as man–machine systems, combining human decision-making ability with machine computing power. Douglas D. Noble, *The Classroom Arsenal: Military Research, Information Technology and Public Education* (London: Falmer Press, 1991), p. 36.

16. Noble, *The Classroom Arsenal,* p. 2.

17. Healy, pp. 183, 185.

18. Larry Cuban, *Teachers and Machines: The Classroom Use of Technology Since 1920* (New York: Teachers College Press, 1986). The introduction to this book gives a good overview of the history of technology in the classroom and the futile attempts made to incorporate it into teaching strategies.

19. Cuban, pp. 19–23.

20. Norman Woelfel and Keith Tyler, *Radio and the School* (Yonkers-on-the-Hudson, N.Y.: World Book, 1945), p. 89; cited in Cuban.

21. Quoted in McKibben, p. 204.

22. Cuban, p. 38.

## CHAPTER 2

1. Aaron Falbel, "The Computer as a Convivial Tool," *Mothering*, Fall 1990, p. 96.

2. Quality Education Data (QED); Software and Information Industry Association (SIIA), *1999 Education Market Report: K–12* (Washington, D.C.: SIIA), Executive Summary.

3. SIIA, Executive Summary.

4. Mary Ann Zehr, "Schools Buying More Computer Software, Less Hardware," *Education Week*, 17 February 1999, p. 8.

5. QED; SIIA, Executive Summary.

6. U.S. Congress, Office of Technology Assessment, *Teachers and Technology: Making the Connection*, OTA–EHR–616 (Washington, D.C.: GPO, April 1995), pp. 21, 23.

7. Panel on Educational Technology, *Report to the President on the Use of Technology to Strengthen K–12 Education in the United States* (Washington, D.C.: President's Committee of Advisors on Science and Technology, March 1997), p. 30.

8. Peter West, "Computer Theft Is 'Hidden Cost' of Boom in School Technology," *Education Week*, 5 June 1996, pp. 1, 8–9.

9. Peter West, "Low-Cost Service Should Satisfy Phone-Access Mandate, Group Says," *Education Week*, 15 May 1996, p. 16.

10. Henry Jay Becker, "A Truly Empowering Technology-Rich Education—How Much Will It Cost?," *Educational IRM Quarterly* 3, no. 1 (1993): 31–35.

11. SIIA, Executive Summary.

12. Peter West, "Many Governors Touting Technology As a Magic Bullet," *Education Week*, 13 March 1996, p. 22.

13. Henry Jay Becker, "How Exemplary Computer-Using Teachers Differ from Other Teachers: Implications for Realizing the Potential of Computers in Schools," *Journal of Research on Computing in Education* 26, no. 3 (1994): 297.

14. Office of Technology Assessment, p. 44. The GAO report referred to is *School Facilities: America's Schools Report Differing Conditions*.

15. Kerry A. White, "New Teaching Methods, Technology Add to Space Crunch," *Education Week*, 2 October 1996, p. 12. The GAO report referred to is *School Facilities: America's Schools Not Designed or Equipped for 21st Century*.

16. Reported in *Quality Counts '99, Education Week* in collaboration with the Pew Charitable Trusts, 11 January 1999.

17. White, p. 12.

18. Todd Oppenheimer, "The Computer Delusion," *Atlantic Monthly*, July 1997, p. 46.

19. Douglas D. Noble, "Bill of Goods: The Early Marketing of Computer-Based Education and Its Implications for the Present Moment," in *International Handbook of Teachers and Teaching*, vol. II, ed. Bruce J. Biddle et al. (Dordrecht, The Netherlands: Kluwer Academic Publishers, 1997), p. 1361.

20. Jerry Borrell, "America's Shame: How We've Abandoned Our Children's Future," *Macworld*, September 1992, p. 25.

21. Gary Wolf, "Steve Jobs: The Next Insanely Great Thing," *Wired*, February 1996, p. 158.

## CHAPTER 3

1. Alfred North Whitehead, "Technical Education and Its Relation to Science and Literature," in *The Aims of Education*, ed. Alfred North Whitehead (New York: Free Press, 1967), p. 50.

2. This view is held by those who advocate an extreme version of computer functionalism, according to John Searle, professor of philosophy at the University of California at Berkeley. John R. Searle, "Consciousness and the Philosophers," *New York Review of Books*, 6 March 1997, p. 44.

3. Seymour Papert, *Mindstorms: Children, Computers, and Powerful Ideas* (New York: Basic Books, 1980), p. vi.

4. Papert, *Mindstorms*, p. viii.

5. Seymour Papert, *The Children's Machine: Rethinking School in the Age of the Computer* (New York: BasicBooks, 1993), p. 33.

6. Papert, *Mindstorms*, p. 9.

7. *The Ontario Curriculum, Grades 1–8, Mathematics* (Toronto: Ministry of Education, 1997), p. 47.

8. Rina Cohen, "Implementing Logo in the Grade Two Classroom: Acquisition of Basic Programming Concepts," *Journal of Computer-Based Instruction* 14, no. 2 (1987): 124–132. Another study involving grade two students abandoned "free-discovery" learning in favor of a "guided discovery" approach when researchers determined that the three-month period of the study would not be long enough for students to attain any significant programming ability. Lloyd P. Rieber, "LOGO and Its Promise: A Research Report," *Educational Technology* 27, no. 2 (1987): 12–16.

9. Peter Cope and Malcolm Simmons, "Children's Exploration of Rotation and Angle in Limited Logo Microworlds," *Computers and Education* 16, no. 2 (1991): 140.

10. Janet K. Keller, "Characteristics of Logo Instruction Promoting Transfer of Learning: A Research Review," *Journal of Research on Computing in Education* 23, no. 1 (1990): 58–59.

11. A similar transition occurred in a two-year study of the use of Logo at the Center for Children and Technology at Bank Street College in New York. The teachers involved began by seeing Logo as an environment for learning general problem-solving skills, but by the second year they saw Logo mainly as a way for students to learn about computers and computer programming. Curt Dudley-Marling and Ronald D. Owston, "Using Microcomputers to Teach Problem Solving: A Critical Review," *Educational Technology* 28, no. 7 (1988): 30.

12. Theodore Roszak, *The Cult of Information*, 2nd ed. (Berkeley: University of California Press, 1994), p. 85.

13. See, for example, Gavriel Salomon and D. N. Perkins, "Transfer of Cognitive Skills from Programming: When and How?" *Journal of Educational Computing Research* 3, no. 2 (1987): 149–169; and D. N. Perkins and Gavriel Salomon, "Are Cognitive Skills Context-Bound?" *Educational Researcher* 18, no. 1 (1989): 16–25.

14. See, for example, Douglas H. Clements and Bonnie K. Nastasi, "Effects of Computer Environments on Social–Emotional Development: Logo and Computer-Assisted Instruction," *Computers in the Schools* 2, no. 2/3 (1985): 11–31.

15. David Elkind, "The Impact of Computer Use on Cognitive Development in Young Children: A Theoretical Analysis," *Computers in Human Behavior* 1, no. 2 (1985): 139.

16. Linda R. Krasnor and John O. Mitterer, "Logo and the Development of General Problem-Solving Skills," *Alberta Journal of Educational Research* 30, no. 2 (1984): 138.

17. Papert, *Mindstorms*, p. 21.

18. Ronald Kotulak, *Inside the Brain: Revolutionary Discoveries of How the Mind Works* (Kansas City, Mo.: Andrews and McMeel, 1996), p. 5.

19. Linda Jacobson, "Study: High-Quality Child Care Pays Off," *Education Week*, 28 April 1999, p. 9.

20. Tiffany Field, "Preschoolers in America Are Touched Less and Are More Aggressive than Preschoolers in France," *Early Child Development and Care* 151 (1999): 11–17.

21. Pat Wolfe and Ron Brandt, "What Do We Know from Brain Research," *Educational Leadership*, November 1998, p. 13.

22. Maria Montessori, *The Absorbent Mind* (New York: Dell Publishing, 1984), p. 46.

23. George Butterworth, "Starting Point," *Natural History*, May 1997, pp. 14–16.

24. Kotulak, p. 7.

25. The sorting task involved deciding whether objects should be placed either inside or outside the house. Vickie M. Brinkley and J. Allen Watson, "Effects of Microworld Training Experience on Sorting Tasks by Young Children," *Journal of Educational Technology Systems* 16, no. 4 (1987–1988): 349–364.

26. Lilian G. Katz and Sylvia C. Chard, *Engaging Children's Minds: The Project Approach* (Norwood, N.J.: Ablex, 1989), pp. 18–19 (emphasis in original).

27. Anne E. Cunningham and Keith E. Stanovich, "Early Spelling Acquisition: Writing Beats the Computer," *Journal of Educational Psychology* 82, no. 1 (1990): 159.

28. John A. Livingston, *The Rogue Primate* (Toronto: Key Porter Books, 1994), p. 122.

29. John Davy, "Mindstorms in the Lamplight," in *The Computer in Education: A Critical Perspective*, ed. Douglas Sloan (New York: Teachers College Press, 1985), p. 12.

30. Papert, *Mindstorms*, p. 118.

31. Theresa H. Escobedo and Ambika Bhargava, "A Study of Children's Computer-Generated Graphics," *Journal of Computing in Childhood Education* 2, no. 4 (1991): 21–22.

32. N. Miller and L. Malamed, "Neuropsychological Correlates of Academic Achievement" (poster presentation, International Neuropsychological Society, Vancouver, B.C., February 1989).

33. Diane Ackerman, *A Natural History of the Senses* (New York: Random House, 1990), p. xv.

34. Jane M. Healy, *Endangered Minds: Why Our Children Don't Think* (New York: Simon & Schuster, 1991), p. 144.

35. Healy, pp. 138, 144 (emphasis in original).

36. G. N. Getman, "Computers in the Classroom: Bane or Boon?" *Academic Therapy* 18, no. 5 (1983): 519.

37. Papert, *Mindstorms*, p. 11.

38. Bill Gates, *The Road Ahead* (New York: Penguin Books, 1995), p. 217.

## CHAPTER 4

1. D. LaMont Johnson and Cleborne D. Maddux, "The Birth and Nurturing of a New Discipline," *Computers in the Schools*, 8, no. 1/2/3 (1991): 9.

2. *Home PC*, June 1994, pp. 40–41.

3. See for example, James A. Kulik, Chen-Lin C. Kulik, and Robert L. Bangert-Drowns, "Effectiveness of Computer-Based Education in Elementary Schools," *Computers in Human Behavior* 1, no. 1 (1985): 59–74; Richard P. Niemiec and Herbert J. Walberg, "Computers and Achievement in the Elementary Schools," *Journal of Educational Computing Research* 1, no. 4 (1985): 435–440; Richard Niemiec et al., "The Effects of Computer Based Instruction in Elementary Schools: A Quantitative Analysis," *Journal of Research on Computing in Education* 20, no. 2 (1987): 85–103; M. D. Roblyer, W. H. Castine, and F. J. King, "A Review of Recent Research," *Computers in the Schools* 5, no. 3/4 (1988): 11–149 (This research team examined several previous reviews as well as conducting one of their own.); Chen-Lin C. Kulik and James A. Kulik, "Effectiveness of Computer-Based Instruction: An Updated Analysis," *Computers in Human Behavior* 7, no. 1–2 (1991): 75–94; Yuen-Kuang Cliff Liao and George W. Bright, "Effects of Computer Programming on Cognitive Outcomes:

A Meta-Analysis," *Journal of Educational Computing Research* 7, no. 3 (1991): 251–268; Alice W. Ryan, "Meta-Analysis of Achievement Effects of Microcomputer Applications in Elementary Schools," *Educational Administration Quarterly* 27, no. 2 (1991): 161–184; Ahmad Khalili and Lily Shashaani, "The Effectiveness of Computer Applications: A Meta-Analysis," *Journal of Research on Computing in Education* 27, no. 1 (1994): 48–61; Claire M. Fletcher-Flinn and Breon Gravatt, "The Efficacy of Computer Assisted Instruction (CAI): A Meta-Analysis," *Journal of Educational Computing Research* 12, no. 3 (1995): 219–242; and Yuen-kuang Cliff Liao, "Effects of Hypermedia versus Traditional Instruction on Students' Achievement: A Meta-Analysis," *Journal of Research on Computing in Education* 30, no. 4 (1998): 341–359.

4. Kulik and Kulik, pp. 75, 80. The 254 studies cover learners of all ages, from kindergarten to adult students. Of these, 48 studies involved elementary school students.

5. Roblyer, Castine, and King.

6. Roblyer, Castine, and King, pp. 113–114.

7. Henry Jay Becker, "Computer-Based Integrated Learning Systems in the Elementary and Middle Grades: A Critical Review and Synthesis of Evaluation Reports," *Journal of Educational Computing Research* 8, no. 1 (1992): 1–41.

More recently, the New York City Public Schools ILS project, which ran from 1989 to 1993 and involved thousands of students in the third, fourth, and fifth grades failed to produce the expected improvements in math and reading. The researchers evaluating the project concluded that the results "were at best mixed and at worst negative." Harold L. Miller, Jr., "The New York City Public Schools Integrated Learning Systems Project: Evaluation and Meta-Evaluation," ch. 3, "Quantitative Analyses of Student Outcome Measures," *International Journal of Educational Research* 27, no. 2 (1997): 135.

8. Douglas D. Noble, "The Educational Engineer Meets Wayne's World," *Rethinking Schools* 8, no. 2 (1993): 15.

9. The authors of one study believe that "it is essential that students spend a substantial portion of their day working on the computers. Our studies suggest that each student must spend a minimum of 30 minutes per subject per day on the computers to achieve significant learning gains." Lani M. Van Dusen and Blaine R. Worthen, "Can Integrated Instructional Technology Transform the Classroom?" *Educational Leadership*, October 1995, p. 30.

10. For example, an analysis of 65 studies of the effects of computer programming found that although the effects on students' performance were "slightly positive," the studies less than three months long showed more positive results than those of longer duration. (Liao and Bright, p. 257.) A possible explanation for this difference is that the students did better in the shorter studies because the novelty of programming would have worn off before the end of the longer studies. The University of Michigan research review mentioned earlier recorded similar results, although in this case computer-based instruction was found to be "especially effective when the duration of treatment was limited to four weeks or less." (Kulik and Kulik, p. 88.)

11. Kathy A. Krendl and Mary Broihier, "Student Responses to Computers: A Longitudinal Study," *Journal of Educational Computing Research* 8, no. 2 (1992): 215–227.

12. Keiko T. Miyashita, "Effect of Computer Use on Attitudes among Japanese First- and Second-Grade Children," *Journal of Computing in Childhood Education* 5, no. 1 (1994): 72–83.

13. A meta-analysis of computer-based instruction in U.S. colleges found a significant effect in favor of computer-based instruction when different teachers taught the computer-based and conventional classes, but that far less difference in results existed when the same teacher taught both types of classes. Therefore, we can reasonably suppose that the same would hold true for younger students in school. Gavriel Salomon and Howard Gardner, "The Computer as Educator: Lessons from Television Research," *Educational Researcher* 15, no. 1 (1986): 14.

14. Don Tapscott, "A Data Tonic for Schooling and Medicine," *Globe and Mail*, 25 May 1994, p. A11.

15. *San Jose Mercury News*, "Exploring the Link between Academic Achievement and Investment in Classroom Technology," 21 November 1995.

16. Christopher H. Schmitt, "Computers in Schools: Do Students Improve?" *San Jose Mercury News*, 14 January 1996, p. 8A. The strong link between poorer school districts and improved achievement with computer use suggests that students from disadvantaged backgrounds may get a moral boost from having access to new equipment. Gleaming new computers and fancy software may give students, especially those who feel neglected, a feeling of greater control over their own lives and a sense, however brief, of being valued.

17. Harold Wenglinsky, *Does It Compute?: The Relationship between Educational Technology and Student Achievement in Mathematics* (Princeton, N.J.: Educational Testing Service, 1999).

18. Larry Miller and J. Dale Burnett, "The Role of Case Studies in Studying Computer Technology in Education" (paper presented at the Sixteenth Annual World Association for Case Method Research Conference, Caceres, Extremadura, Spain, July 1999), p. 7.

19. Herbert Kohl, *Basic Skills: A Plan for Your Child, A Program for All Children* (Boston: Little, Brown, 1982), p. 16. For an excellent discussion on testing and the bell curve, see pp. 12–17, 217–231.

20. William Hynes, "Kudos to Our Classrooms," *Globe and Mail*, 11 August 1996, p. D1.

21. Charles M. Achilles, Jeremy D. Finn, and Helen P. Bain, "Using Class Size to Reduce the Equity Gap," *Educational Leadership*, December 1997–January 1998, p. 40.

22. James H. Wiebe and Nancy J. Martin, "The Impact of a Computer-Based Adventure Game on Achievement and Attitudes in Geography," *Journal of Computing in Childhood Education* 5, no. 1 (1994): 61.

23. Sharon McCoy Bell, "World Processing: The Magic of Carmen Sandiego," *Home PC*, June 1994, pp. 68, 70.

## CHAPTER 5

1. Bruno Bettelheim and Karen Zelan, *On Learning to Read: The Child's Fascination with Meaning* (New York: Knopf, 1982), p. 5.

2. Foreword by Chester E. Finn, Jr., Assistant Secretary, Office of Educational Research and Improvement, U.S. Department of Education, to *Becoming a Nation of Readers: What Parents Can Do* (Indianapolis, Ind.: D. C. Heath, March 1988), p. iii.

3. Ontario Ministry of Education, *Literacy for Life: Report on Partnerships for Children's Literacy* (Toronto: Queen's Printer for Ontario, 1991), p. 7.

4. Child psychologist Margaret Donaldson points out that young children do not necessarily realize "that the flow of speech, which they have been producing and interpreting unreflectingly for years, is composed of *words*." Margaret Donaldson, *Children's Minds* (London: Fontana Press, 1986), p. 97 (emphasis in original).

5. Marilyn Jager Adams, *Beginning to Read: Thinking and Learning about Print* (Cambridge, Mass.: MIT Press, 1990), p. 321.

6. Reported in Ronald Kotulak, *Inside the Brain: Revolutionary Discoveries of How the Mind Works* (Kansas City, Mo.: Andrews and McMeel, 1996), p. 32. Janellen Huttenlocher of the University of Chicago made the comment with reference to early television watching, but with television and multimedia computers rapidly converging, it could just as well apply to early computer use.

Studies conducted in Manchester and London, England, by Dr. Sally Ward, a leading authority on children's speech development, demonstrate the shortcomings of voices from the screen. Her studies found that television can be a major factor in delaying speech development in children younger than age three. Children who spent too much time watching television were prevented from learning to talk by the constant noise from the television set. The children, however, soon recovered if parents turned off the television and spent more time talking to them.

7. Margaret Donaldson, "Speech and Writing and Modes of Learning," in *Awakening to Literacy*, ed. Hillel Goelman, Antoinette Oberg, and Frank Smith (Portsmouth, N.H.: Heinemann, 1984), p. 174.

8. Frank Smith, "The Creative Achievement of Literacy," in *Awakening to Literacy*, p. 144.

9. Yetta Goodman, "The Development of Initial Literacy," in *Awakening to Literacy*, p. 102.

10. Quoted in Robert Darnton, "The New Age of the Book," *The New York Review*, 18 March 1999, p. 5.

11. R. C. Anderson et al., *Becoming a Nation of Readers: The Report of the Commission on Reading* (Pittsburgh, Pa.: National Academy of Education, 1985), p. 23; Adams, p. 86.

12. Larry Miller and John Olson, "Literacy Research Oriented Toward Features of Technology and Classrooms," in *Handbook of Literacy and Technology*, ed. D. Reinking (in press), p. 351.

13. See Bruno Bettelheim and Karen Zelan, "Why Children Don't Like to Read," *The Atlantic Monthly*, November 1981, pp. 25–31.

14. Hilary McLellan, "Hyper Stories: Some Guidelines for Instructional Designers," *Journal of Research on Computing in Education* 25, no. 1 (1992): 31.

15. Personal communication from Celia Lottridge.

16. Smith, "The Creative Achievement of Literacy," p. 152 (emphasis in original).

17. Laura D. Goodwin et al., "Cognitive and Affective Effects of Various Types of Microcomputer Use by Preschoolers," *American Educational Research Journal* 23, no. 3 (1986): 348–356; Dolores A. Gore et al., "A Study of Teaching Reading Skills to the Young Child Using Microcomputer Assisted Instruction," *Journal of Educational Computing Research* 5, no. 2 (1989): 179–185; Anne E. Cunningham and Keith E. Stanovich, "Early Spelling Acquisition: Writing Beats the Computer," *Journal of Educational Psychology* 82, no. 1 (1990): 159–162. The first of these studies involved children between the ages of three and five, the second children age five, and the third children in the first grade.

In Goodwin et al. three software programs were used: *The Stickybear ABC, Alphabet Zoo–ABC Time*, and *Early Games–Match Letters and Alphabet*. All of these programs are intended for children between ages three and six and all claim to teach letter matching and recognition. In Gore et al. the software programs used were *Charlie Brown ABC's* (Random House); *Memory: A First Step* (Sunburst Communications); *Sesame Street Letter Go Round* (CBS Software); *Kinder Koncepts Reading* (Queque Inc.); *Easy as ABC* (Springboard Software); *First Letter Fun* (MECC); *Preschool I.Q. Builder* (Program Design Inc); *Stickybear ABC's* (Weekly Reader Software); *Early Games for Young Children* (Learning Tools); *Early Elementary 1* (Compu-Tations Inc).

18. John Schacter, *Reading Programs that Work: A Review of Programs for Pre-kindergarten to 4th Grade* (Santa Monica, Calif.: Milken Family Foundation, 1999), p. 19.

19. The five stations are:

1. Computer Station. Children learn phonemes (the sounds of spoken language) by listening to and repeating key words. One activity has them fill in blanks in words with the correct phonemes.

2. Work Journal Station. This provides further practice with phonemes. Children listen to prerecorded lessons using headphones and fill in blanks in a workbook.

3. Writing–Typing Station. Children write words they have learned by typing on the computer or using pencil and paper. They can continue a story, start a new one, print a story, or read a story previously written.

4. Listening–Library Station. Stories are read to children at reduced speeds while they

follow along in a written version.

5. Make Words Station. Children use various materials–sticks, clay, wire, and paper cutouts–to form words, letters, and sentences.

20. Douglas D. Noble, "A Bill of Goods: The Early Marketing of Computer-Based Education and Its Implications for the Present Moment" (draft ms, April 1995), p. 102. A substantially revised version, *WTR 2000*, has recently been published, but no evaluations are currently available.

21. For example, studies involving kindergarten students in California, first-grade students in Georgia, and second-grade students in Iowa indicated that the program had little or no effect on the children's reading and writing. Balwant Singh, "IBM's *Writing to Read* Program: The Right Stuff or Just High Tech Fluff?," paper presented at the Annual Meeting of the Florida Educational Research Association, November 1991, referred to in Nancy R. Preston, "ERIC Research Abstracts," *Journal of Computer-Based Instruction* 19, no. 4 (1992): 138. A study of the use of *WTR* in British Columbia found no significant difference in children's reading readiness at the end of the first full year of implementation compared with previous years. Betty Collis, Lloyd Ollila, and Kathleen Ollila, "*Writing to Read*: An Evaluation of a Canadian Installation of a Computer-Supported Initial Language Environment," *Journal of Educational Computing Research* 6, no. 4 (1990): 416.

22. Kathy A. Krendl and Russell B. Williams, "The Importance of Being Rigorous: Research on *Writing to Read*," *Journal of Computer-Based Instruction* 17, no. 3 (1990): 84.

23. "Often as many as three or four adults are present with only 15 students in the lab during *Writing to Read* instruction." Krendl and Williams, p. 81. With another class of "almost 30 students" three adults staffed the lab—"the paraprofessional who ran the lab, the classroom teacher, and the paraprofessional from the class." Dorothy Huenecke, "An Artistic Criticism of a Computer-Based Reading Program," *Educational Technology* 32, no. 7 (1992): 55.

24. As recommended in Richard C. Overbaugh, "Word Processors and Writing-Process Software: Introduction and Evaluation," *Computers in Human Behavior* 8, no. 1 (1992): 142.

25. Collis, Ollila, and Ollila, p. 416.

26. Huenecke, pp. 56, 55. Huenecke observed children using the *WTR* program from the spring of their kindergarten year until the end of their first-grade year.

27. Jeanne Chall, *Learning to Read: The Great Debate* (New York: McGraw-Hill, 1967), p. 270 (emphasis in original).

28. Bettelheim and Zelan, *On Learning to Read*, p. 236.

29. Jane M. Healy, *Endangered Minds: Why Our Children Don't Think* (New York: Simon & Schuster/Touchstone, 1991), p. 210.

## CHAPTER 6

1. Natalie Goldberg, *Writing Down the Bones* (Boston: Shambhala, 1986), p. 15.

2. This description appears in Herbert H. Wideman et al., *The Development of Children's Writing in a High Computer Access Environment: A Three Year Study*, Technical Report 94–3 (Toronto, Ont.: Centre for the Study of Computers in Education, York University, November 1994), p. 122.

3. One researcher has suggested that "the most significant effect of computers on children's writing may be that they increase the amount of peer collaboration in classrooms.... Cooperation among children is important because of its positive effects on children's affective, social and intellectual development." David K. Dickinson, "Cooperation, Collaboration, and a Computer: Integrating a Computer into a First-Second Grade Writing Program, *Research in the Teaching of English* 20, no. 4 (1986): 358.

4. Thomas T. Barker, "Computers and the Instructional Context," in Deborah H.

Holdstein and Cynthia L. Selfe (eds.), *Computers and Writing: Theory, Research, Practice* (New York: Modern Language Association of America, 1990), p. 16.

5. Colette Daiute of Harvard University, writing in the mid-1980s, noted that research to date had not provided any overwhelming evidence that children aged nine to thirteen produced more text, or better text, using computers than they did with pen and paper. Colette Daiute, *Writing and Computers* (Reading, Mass.: Addison-Wesley, 1985), pp. 170–171.

Nearly ten years later, an analysis of the results of 28 studies of students' writing indicated slightly more positive effects. Researchers found that two-thirds of these studies "concluded that access to word processing during writing instruction improved the quality of students' writing," although the author notes that overall the improvement was "fairly small." [Robert L. Bangert-Drowns, "The Word Processor as an Instructional Tool: A Meta-Analysis of Word Processing in Writing Instruction," *Review of Educational Research* 63, no. 1 (1993): 77, 87.] Nine studies were conducted in which word processors were used to provide remedial writing instruction, and these yielded the most positive results.

Positive results are also reported in Margarie Montague, "Computers and Writing Process Instruction," *Computers in the Schools* 7, no. 3 (1990): 5–20; Ronald D. Owston, Sharon Murphy, and Herbert H. Wideman, "On and Off Computer Writing of Eighth Grade Students Experienced in Word Processing," *Computers in the Schools* 8, no. 4 (1991): 67–87; Ronald D. Owston, Sharon Murphy, and Herbert H. Wideman, "The Effects of Word Processing on Students' Writing Quality and Revision Strategies," *Research in the Teaching of English* 26, no. 3 (1992): 249–276; and Wideman et al. In the second of these studies the authors speculate that having become used to writing with computers, students may have had negative attitudes toward writing by hand, and this may have had an effect on students' performance: "…it could be that the students' extensive and relatively positive experience with word processing reduced their willingness to write and revise by hand since it made handwritten effort seem more onerous by comparison…" (p. 84).

Negative or inconclusive results are reported in Ruth J. Kurth, "Using Word Processing to Enhance Revision Strategies during Student Writing Activities," *Educational Technology* 27, no. 1 (1987): 13–19; Aviva Freedman and Linda Clarke, *The Effect of Computer Technology on Composing Processes and Written Products of Grade 8 and Grade 12 Students* (Toronto: Ontario Ministry of Education, 1988); Edward L. Shaw, Jr., Ann K. Nauman, and Debbie Burson, "Comparisons of Spontaneous and Word Processed Compositions in Elementary Classrooms: A Three-Year Study," *Journal of Computing in Childhood Education* 5, no. 3/4 (1994): 319–327; Lois Mayer Nichols, "Pencil and Paper versus Word Processing: A Comparative Study of Creative Writing in the Elementary School," *Journal of Research on Computing in Education* 29, no. 2 (1996): 159–166; and Edward W. Wolfe et al., "A Study of Word Processing Experience and Its Effects on Student Essay Writing," *Journal of Educational Computing Research* 14, no. 3 (1996): 269–283. In the last study, involving tenth-grade students, the negative effects were confined to students with little computer experience. However, in Nichols, "Pencil and Paper versus Word Processing," the sixth-grade students had all received a year and a half word processing instruction.

In her review of the research, Marilyn Cochran-Smith concludes that "using word processing, in and of itself, generally does not improve the overall quality of students' writing." Marilyn Cochran-Smith, "Word Processing and Writing in Elementary Classrooms: A Critical Review of Related Literature," *Review of Educational Research* 61, no. 1 (1991): 114.

6. Shaw, Nauman, and Burson, p. 325.

7. Evidence of positive effects on students' attitudes to writing is reported in Kurth; Owston, Murphy, and Wideman, "On and Off Computer Writing of Eighth Grade Students Experienced in Word Processing"; Lori Seawel et al., "A Descriptive Study Comparing Computer-Based Word Processing and Handwriting on Attitudes and Performance of Third and Fourth Grade Students Involved in a Program Based on a Process Writing

Approach," *Journal of Computing in Childhood Education* 5, no. 1 (1994): 43–59; and W. Michael Reed, "Assessing the Impact of Computer-Based Writing Instruction," *Journal of Research on Computing in Education* 28, no. 4 (1996): 418–437. Little change in attitudes is reported in Margaret A. Moore and Stuart A. Karabenick, "The Effects of Computer Communications on the Reading and Writing Performance of Fifth-Grade Students," *Computers in Human Behavior* 8, no. 1 (1992): 27–38.

8. One researcher has suggested that "attitude toward writing itself may not be the chief determinant of engagement in word processing. Students may become more enthusiastic about word processing, not because of more positive attitudes toward writing, but because they enjoy working on the computer." Bangert-Drowns, p. 88.

9. Reported in Daiute, *Writing and Computers*, p. 43.

10. Jessica Kahn and Pamela Freyd, "Touch Typing for Young Children: Help or Hindrance?" *Educational Technology* 30, no. 2 (1990): 41.

11. Cochran-Smith, p. 145.

12. Colette Daiute, "Physical and Cognitive Factors in Revising: Insights from Studies with Computers," *Research in the Teaching of English* 20, no. 2 (1986): 141–159; Elana Joram et al., "The Effects of Revising with a Word Processor on Written Composition," *Research in the Teaching of English* 26, no. 2 (1992): 167–193; and Wolfe et al. In this last study, the students who had a medium or high level of comfort and experience with word processing wrote essays of about the same length on the computer as they did by hand.

13. Wideman et al. Students' writing folders were evaluated each spring, and researchers gave separate scores for the meaning and content of a text and for the surface features of the writing, such as grammar, spelling, use of words, typographical errors, and length. This study is also discussed in Ronald D. Owston and Herbert W. Wideman, "Word Processors and Children's Writing in a High-Computer-Access Setting," *Journal of Research on Computing in Education* 30, no. 2 (1997): 202–220.

14. Wideman et al., p. 142. In one of the classes using computers, the students, as part of a special project, each had the use of their own PowerBook laptop computer. It's quite possible that the provision of a laptop computer for each student created a new relation between the students and their work. The report states that their teacher "became more intensely involved with what students were doing with their PowerBooks. She showed more excitement in class, and was more prepared to advise, monitor, question and make changes to student work." And the students responded. They were

> thrilled that the teacher had enough confidence in them as mature people and competent users by eventually allowing them to take the PowerBooks home. Although the exercise was planned as part of the pilot project, the students interpreted it as but another reflection of their status as special students. (Wideman et al., p. 142)

The fact that the students could take their laptops home added to the time they could spend on their projects. It is surely not a coincidence that the students in this class wrote far more than any other class in either school, on average producing texts that were twice as long.

15. The following excerpts are fairly typical of the writing done by the three students. *Low rated:*

> Then behind Jim there was Grendel, Grendel "said, lets see you take on my baby Lobo" Jim "said OK unless you want to see your baby get his but kicked" Go fight him Lobo" OK daddy" Lobo took out a knife come on Lobo lets fight fare and square, ok in two seconds Jim wiped Lobo out the window and he landed in the mail box.... (Wideman et al., p. 170)

*Average rated:*

Time was running out because there was an old saying that if you were on Mercury for about 2–3 days you could get this disease or you could get a very very very bad cold and you would have to [The text is broken this way in the original.]

go to this special shooting star "which is really a special hospital" and get stunned by a needle as long as a keyboard and where ever you got stunned by the needle it would bleed and bleed and bleed. I was just hoping so bad that someone would just come and pick me up and I would never have to go back to this eerie,frightening, [sic] weird place ever again. Anyway I tried to get up but it was just impossible to get up after I had tried about fifty times to see if I could get up for the 56th time and I finally got up thank goodness for getting up. (Wideman et al., p. 172)

*High rated:*

I slowly edge closer to the window. I can see the moon, it looks alone, like me. I crawl away from the window again, my leg still hurting from being thrown into my new prison. The ground is cold and slippery, with a layer of dust. I felt something crawling up my arm. I scream and brush it away. I slowly stand up, and limp over to the window. There was something comforting about it. I stared out into the darkness, feeling to confused and scared to think. Tall shadows of trees stretched out across the bare land, that seemed to carry on forever. They seemed so free. A cool breeze scurried the dirt, and lifted the hair on my shoulders. I closed my eyes. The comfort was gone. The muffled sound of restless leaves, sounded like slow, dragging footsteps. I shivered. (Wideman et al., p. 177)

Unfortunately none of the work done by students using traditional pen and paper was included for comparison.

16. Chris Breese, Anita Jackson, and Terry Prince, "Promise in Impermanence: Children Writing with Unlimited Access to Word Processors," *Early Child Development and Care* 118 (1996): 67–91. With the students in this study the benefits of using word processors showed up almost immediately.

17. Quoted in Kathleen Kennedy Manzo, "U.S. Students Lack Writing Proficiency," *Education Week*, 6 October 1999, p. 18.

18. Bill Wresch, "What I Learned in Wabeno," *Computers in Human Behavior* 8, no. 1 (1992): 11 (emphasis added). Wresch is author of the *Writer's Helper* software program.

19. Gene Wilburn, "Kids' Programs Put the Accent on Fun," *Toronto Star*, 12 May 1994, p. G6. We would like to think that the last sentence contained a touch of humor, but this does not seem to be the case.

20. Blaine H. Moore and Helen Caldwell, "Drama and Drawing for Narrative Writing in Primary Grades," *Journal of Educational Research* 8, no. 2 (1993): 100–110.

21. Theodore Roszak, *The Cult of Information*, 2nd ed. (Berkeley: University of California Press, 1994), p. 80 (emphasis in original).

22. Wideman et al., p. 122.

23. Owston, Murphy, and Wideman, "The Effects of Word Processing on Students' Writing Quality and Revision Strategies," p. 264.

24. Michael Peacock and Chris Breese, "Pupils with Portable Writing Machines," *Educational Review* (U.K.) 42, no. 1 (1990): 48.

25. Several researchers have pointed out that little research supports the claim that word processors improve the quality of writing because they make revisions easier. Joram et al. cites a number of studies indicating that word processing revisions tend to consist mainly of surface changes "and other revising activities that are typical of immature writ-

ers" (pp. 168–169). The author of another paper points out that few studies of revision with word processing "report increased quality." Gail E. Hawisher, "The Effects of Word Processing on the Revision Strategies of College Freshmen," *Research in the Teaching of English* 21, no. 2 (1987): 146.

26. Owston, Murphy, and Wideman, "The Effects of Word Processing on Students' Writing Quality and Revision Strategies." The drafts and final versions of the first two students were both about 200 words in length. One of these students did divide her draft into three paragraphs in the final version, which indicates some concern about the structure of her piece, but otherwise she merely corrected eight typographical errors (two of these being identical), combined two sentences that had previously been correctly separated, and failed to address five grammatical mistakes. The other student corrected five typographical errors (two of them identical) and missed two others. With so few changes being made, one wonders just how these two students spent their time at the revision stage.

27. Daiute, "Physical and Cognitive Factors in Revising," pp. 156, 153.

28. Freedman and Clarke, p. 100.

## CHAPTER 7

1. Michael Heim, *The Metaphysics of Virtual Reality* (New York: Oxford University Press, 1993), p. 145.

2. Gary Chapman, "Push to Trade Class Textbooks for Laptop PCs Is a Misuse of Technology," *Los Angeles Times*, 15 June 1998.

3. Pierre Lacerte, "Internet: The Badly Connected School," *L'Actualité*, 1 October 1998, p. 18.

4. John W. Merck Jr., "Mesozoic Errors," *The Sciences*, September/October 1995, pp. 40–43.

5. Paul Roberts, "Virtual Grub Street, Sorrows of a Multimedia Hack," *Harper's*, June 1996, pp. 73–74.

6. *Technology Counts '99: Building the Digital Curriculum, Education Week* in collaboration with the Milken Exchange on Education Technology, 23 September 1999, p. 7

7. Nancy Trejos, "Lamenting Libraries," *Washington Post*, 31 January 2000, p. B01.

8. Trejos, p. B01.

9. Thomas A. Childers, "California's Reference Crisis," *Library Journal*, 15 April 1994, p. 33.

10. Gary Marchionini, "Hypermedia and Learning: Freedom and Chaos," *Educational Technology* 28, no. 11 (1988): 9.

## CHAPTER 8

1. Personal communication.

2. Personal communication.

3. Gary Ruskin, "Why They Whine: How Corporations Prey On Our Children," *Mothering*, November–December 1999, p. 42.

4. David Leonhardt and Kathleen Kerwin, "Hey Kid, Buy This," *Business Week*, 30 June 1997, p. 62. Another source indicates that in the United States children between ages three and twelve control about $47 billion of spending a year. ["Shop for Little Horrors," *The Economist*, 5 June 1997, p. 66.]

5. Erica Gruen's remarks were also reported in "Children Get Growing Online Attention: Marketers Discuss How to Make Connections with the New Wave of Interactive Kids," *Interactive Marketing News*, 10 November 1995, p. 2.

6. Ruskin, p. 41

7. Jeremy Hoey, "Web Free?" *Adbusters*, Autumn 1997, p. 61.

8. Kathryn Montgomery and Shelley Pasnik, *The Web of Deception: Threats to Children from Online Marketing* (Washington, D.C.: Center for Media Education, 1996).

9. Center for Media Education, *Alcohol and Tobacco on the Web: New Threats to Youth* (Washington, D.C.: Center for Media Education, 1997), p. 29.

10. Center for Media Education, *An Update of Children's Web Sites' Information Collection Practices* (Washington, D.C.: Center for Media Education, 1997), p. 2.

11. Anne Reilly Dowd, "Protect Your Privacy," *Money*, August 1997, p. 112.

12. *FTC News*, 16 July 1996, pp. 2, 3.

13. Michael Brody, "Children in Cyberspace: Targets for Corporate Marketers," *Psychiatric News*, 7 February 1997, p. 13.

14. David Lazarus, "Firm Says Kids Visit Questionable Web Sites at School," *San Francisco Chronicle*, 6 September 1999.

15. Jef I. Richards et al., "The Growing Commercialization of Schools: Issues and Practices" *Annals, AAPSS*, 557 (May 1998): 152–153.

16. Written Testimony on Channel One, Jim Metrock, Commercial Alert, Washington, D.C., 1999.

17. Elizabeth Bell, "Questions Raised about School's Computer Deal Bill Would Let Parents Block Marketing to Kids," *San Francisco Chronicle*, 11 October 1999.

18. "Free School Computers Blur Line Between Student and Consumer, Critics Say," Nando Media and Associated Press, 6 December 1998.

19. Some preschoolers may spend up to one-third of their waking hours in front of the television. Stephen Kline, *Out of the Garden: Toys and Children's Culture in the Age of TV Marketing* (Toronto: Garamond Press, 1993), p. 17. According to the American Medical Association, "The amount of time spent in front of a television or video screen is the single biggest chunk of time in the waking life of an American child." American Medical Association, "Physician Guide to Media Violence," July 1996, p. 9.

In the United States, the FTC guidelines restricting children's television advertising time to nine minutes per hour on Saturday and Sunday morning have been relaxed. The Children's Television Act of 1990 increased commercial time to ten minutes per hour on weekends and twelve minutes per hour on weekday. Kline, pp. 214–18.

20. Kline, p. 141.

21. By creating their fantasies for them, advertising limits children's imaginative responses to problems they experience in their lives. Their imagination is so crowded with characters and plots from commercials that these become a touchstone for children in talking about and determining their behavior. In other words, children are being culturally conditioned to the point that they cannot express their feelings without the mediation of their favorite on-screen characters.

Michael Brody has an extensive collection of character figures he uses in his medical practice. His stock includes everything from Barney and Baby Bop, the Little Mermaid, Teenage Mutant Ninja Turtles, and the Power Rangers to oldies such as Cinderella, Mickey Mouse, Donald Duck, Batman, and Spiderman. When children come to him for treatment, he finds that he must use these figures in order to put the children at ease. Such characters, he has found, figure prominently in the imaginative life of his young patients. In many respects, one can say that a child is inhabited by the characters he or she chooses as role models, and in Brody's experience many children choose fantasy characters as role models. Unfortunately, the coping strategies these role models have in dealing with difficulties in their lives are not necessarily ones that are available to children, and they certainly do not constitute viable options or strategies for dealing with daily life.

## CHAPTER 9

1. Emil Pascarelli and Deborah Quilter, *Repetitive Strain Injury: A Computer User's Guide* (New York: John Wiley, 1994), p. 3.

2. Jane Greening and Bruce Lynn, "Vibration Sense in the Upper Limb in Patients with Repetitive Strain Injury and a Group of At-Risk Office Workers," *International Archives of Occupational and Environmental Health* 71, no. 1, (1998): 29–34.

3. Deborah Quilter, "Computer Injuries: The Next Generation," *VDT News*, November/December 1995, p. 8.

4. Alison Dickie, "Computer Caution: This Machine Could Be Hazardous to Your Child's Health," *Home and School Magazine*, May 1995, pp. 37–38.

5. Abby Fung, "RSI Attacks the Next Generation," *Boston Globe*, 13 October 1998.

6. Shawn Oates, Gary W. Evans, and Alan Hedge, "An Anthropometric and Postural Risk Assessment of Children's School Computer Work Environments," *Computers in the Schools* 14, no. 3/4(1988): 58.

7. Oates, Evans, and Hedge, pp. 59, 62.

8. Kathryn L. Laeser, Lorraine E. Maxwell, and Alan Hedge, "The Effect of Computer Workstation Design on Student Posture," *Journal of Research on Computing in Education* 31, no. 2 (1998): 173–188.

9. Factors specific to the VDT that can cause eyestrain include:

*Glare*: Glare associated with VDTs can come from the reflection of artificial or natural light from white paper placed near the screen and even from white clothing worn by the person at the keyboard. Glare can reduce the contrast between characters/images and their background, making them harder to distinguish. Antiglare screens can address this problem, but they reduce character/image sharpness and make the screen darker. Compensating for this by increasing the brightness tends to reduce sharpness even more.

*Resolution and color problems*: Lack of sharpness can lead to excessive and futile efforts by the eye to bring characters into focus. Unusual fonts with small or tightly spaced characters impair legibility and create problems in distinguishing among characters. Too many colors on the screen simultaneously can be visually confusing, and colors widely separated on the spectrum can blur together, owing to their differing focal points.

*Flicker*: Commonly known as "flicker," the scan-line refresh rate is the number of times per second an image is redrawn on the screen. Many see a potential source of eyestrain in the instability of flicker at lower refresh rates, suggesting that higher refresh rates produce a more stable image and thus reduce eyestrain. However, Alan Kennedy and Wayne Murray of the University of Dundee in Scotland write that they "have evidence that disturbances to eye movement control occur at, or above, refresh rates of 100Hz, well beyond the point at which users report a display as appearing stable." Kennedy and Murray found the eye makes an increasing number of small corrective movements as the refresh rate increases, and this may impair reading performance and contribute to visual fatigue.

*Jitter*: Individual characters on VDTs can also oscillate. This "jitter" can lead to poor legibility and may be one of the main causes of the vision problems VDT workers experience, according to Dr. Kjell Hansson Mild of Sweden's National Institute of Occupational Health (NIOH). Dr. Mild notes that EMFs below a certain frequency cause movement in characters on the screen that cannot be seen with the naked eye. Other researchers at NIOH have shown that on-screen "jitter" may be caused by EMFs from other nearby electrical sources and not the VDT itself. They argue that building wiring, or electrical devices such as low-voltage lamps and microfiche readers, can distort characters displayed on VDTs.

10. W. Jaschinski-Kruza, "Transient Myopia after Visual Work," *Ergonomics* 27, no. 11 (1984): 81–89; H. Yoshikawa and I. Hara, "A Case of Rapidly Developed Myopia among VDT Workers," *Japanese Journal of Industrial Health* 31, no. 1 (1989): 24–25.

11. Shirley Palmer, "Does Computer Use Put Children's Vision at Risk?," *Journal of Research and Development in Education* 26, no. 2 (1993): 59–65.

12. Ken Schroeder, "Eyeing Computer Eye Pain," *Education Digest* 64, no. 2 (1998): 70.

13. Marian C. Fish and Shirley C. Feldman, "Learning and Teaching in Microcomputer Classrooms: Reconsidering Assumptions," *Computers in the Schools* 7, no. 3 (1990): 91.

14. Warren E. Hathaway, *The Effects of Type of School Lighting on Physical Development and School Performance of Children* (Edmonton: Alberta Department of Education, March 1994),

pp. 1–19. The two-year project, which involved 327 children in grades five and six at five Edmonton-area schools, tested the scholastic development and physical development of children who were exposed to full-spectrum lighting versus those whose classrooms were lit by high-energy sodium-vapor lights.

15. The study was cited in William D. Graf et al., "Video Game-Related Seizures: A Report on 10 Patients and a Review of the Literature." *Pediatrics* 93, no. 4 (1994): 551–556. In December 1997 a television cartoon based on Nintendo's popular Pocket Monster caused about 500 Japanese children to suffer epileptic seizures after an explosion followed by a five-second flash from the eyes of the most popular character.

16. Researchers have identified emissions of the following chemicals from computers and VDTs: n-Butanol, 2-Butanone, 2-Butoxyethanol, Caprolactam, Cresol, Dimethylbenzene, Ethylbenzene, Heptadecane, Hexanedioic acid, Ozone, Phenol, Phosphoric acid, Toluene, Xylene, Butyl 2-methylpropyl phthalate, Decamethyl cylcopentasiloxane, Dodecamethyl cyclohexasiloxane, 2-Ethoxyethylacetate, 4-Hydroxy benzaldehyde, 2-Methyl-2-propenoic acid, and 2-tetra-butylazo-2-methyozy-4-methyl-pentane. Cited in Environmental Protection Agency, *Office Equipment: Design, Indoor Air Emissions, and Pollution Prevention Opportunities*, March 1995.

17. Environmental Protection Agency.

18. An interdisciplinary study by the Office Illness Project in northern Sweden found 450 cases of mucosal and dermatological symptoms among the 5,986 office workers surveyed.

19. For years electric utility companies and computer manufacturers denied that any effect, deleterious or otherwise, occurred from low-level exposure to EMFs. But epidemiological studies have led many scientists, both inside and outside the industry, to accept that these fields do affect living organisms. Denver researchers Nancy Wertheimer and Ed Leeper were the first to discover a link between childhood leukemia and EMFs among children living in homes located near electrical transformers. The mortality rate from leukemia for children living near these transformers was two to three times higher than the rate among the general population. Other findings, including three pooled studies from Denmark, Finland, and Sweden by Drs. Anders Ahlbom, Mari Feychting, Jorgen Olson, and Pia Verkasalo, concluded that evidence "support[ed] the hypothesis that exposure to magnetic fields of the type generated by transmission lines has some etiological role in the development of leukemia in children." They reported a doubling of the risk of childhood leukemia for long-term residential exposures greater than 2 mG. Anders Ahlbom et al., "Electromagnetic Fields and Childhood Cancer," *The Lancet* 34, no. 8882 (20 November 1993): 1295–1296.

20. Indira Nair and Jun Zhang, "Distinguishability of the Video Display Terminal (VDT) as a Source of Magnetic Field Exposure," *American Journal of Industrial Medicine* 28, no. 1 (1995): 23–29.

21. Russel J. Reiter and Jo Robinson, *Melatonin: Your Body's Natural Wonder Drug* (New York: Bantam Books, 1995), p. 170.

22. "The exposure of humans or animals to light (visible electromagnetic radiation) at night rapidly depresses pineal melatonin production and blood melatonin levels. Likewise, the exposure of animals to various pulsed static and extremely low frequency magnetic fields also reduces melatonin levels. Because it is a potent oncostatic agent and prevents both the initiation and promotion of cancer, reduction of melatonin, at night, by any means, increases cells' vulnerability to alteration by carcinogenic agents. Thus, if in fact artificial electromagnetic field exposure increases the incidence of cancer in humans, a plausible mechanism could involve a reduction in melatonin which is the consequence of such exposures."
Russel J. Reiter, "Melatonin Suppression by Static and Extremely Low Frequency Electromagnetic Fields: Relationship to the Reported Increased Incidence of Cancer," *Reviews on Environmental Health* 10, no. 3–4 (1994): 171.

23. C. Chociolko and W. Leiss, *Risk and Responsibility* (Montreal/Kingston: McGill-Queen's University Press, 1994).

24. Millicent Lawton, "More Children Becoming Overweight, Study Finds," *Education Week*, 11 October 1995, p. 6.

25. Robert C. Klesges, Mary L. Shelton, and Lisa M. Klesges, "Effects of Television on Metabolic Rate: Potential Implications for Childhood Obesity," *Pediatrics* 91, no. 2 (1993): 281.

26. Janetta A. Wilson, "Computer Laboratory Workstation Dimensions: Scaling Down for Elementary School Children," *Computers in the Schools* 8, no. 4 (1992): 41–48.

27. Proponents see virtual reality (VR) as having great potential to improve education: taking field trips without leaving the classroom is an often-cited example.

Early forms of VR have been in use since the 1950s as flight simulators, and a broad range of associated health problems have been documented, including excessive salivation, fatigue, headaches, nausea, vomiting, coordination problems, and finally dramatic disorientation. Flashbacks are also commonly reported. The July 1995 issue of *Technology Review* reported that young people seem more susceptible to these wide-ranging symptoms.

The most common explanation for such simulator sickness is that the senses are confused, not knowing how to choose between the subject's actual situation and what they think they are seeing. Robert Kennedy, a psychologist with the Orlando branch of Essex Corporation, suggests that 30 percent of all people who use simulators of some kind display symptoms of motion sickness, such as cold sweats, nausea, and vomiting. One of Kennedy's studies finds that 14 percent of helicopter pilots trained in a simulator reported symptom of motion sickness lasting longer than six hours. Sega canceled its $200 home Genesis 16 VR game when it discovered that 40 percent of users were experiencing simulator sickness.

Those for whom VR was first developed take simulator sickness seriously. NASA and the U.S. Air Force, Army, Navy, and Marines—none will let those suffering from simulator sickness fly or drive until 24 hours after the symptoms subside.

Although the effects of simulator sickness are thoroughly documented, they are rarely mentioned in discussions of the technology. According to Kennedy, "it is not until after the design is frozen that the effect of a game on humans is considered."

## CHAPTER 10

1. Charles Fowler, Strong *Arts, Strong Schools: The Promising Potential and Shortsighted Disregard of the Arts in American Schooling* (New York: Oxford University Press, 1996), p. 43.

2. Nan Elsasser, Executive Director, Working Classroom, Inc., Albuquerque, New Mexico. Quoted in Judith Humphreys Weitz, *Coming Up Taller: Arts and Humanities Programs for Children and Youth at Risk* (Washington, D.C.: President's Committee on the Arts and the Humanities, 1996), p. 29. Working Classroom, Inc., is a multidisciplinary arts program offering visual arts, theater, and creative-writing workshops.

3. Robert J. Sternberg, "Successful Intelligence: An Expanded Approach to Understanding Intelligence," February 1997, pp. 3, 4.

4. Sternberg, p. 21.

5. Daniel Goleman, *Emotional Intelligence* (New York: Bantam Books, 1995), p. 80.

6. Goleman, pp. 81–82. "The third of children who at four grabbed for the marshmallow most eagerly had an average verbal score of 524 and quantitative (or 'math') score of 528; the third who waited longest had average scores of 610 and 652, respectively—a 210-point difference in total score."

7. Goleman, p. 160.

8. Goleman, p. 237.

9. Robert Sylwester, "Art for the Brain's Sake," *Educational Leadership*, November 1998, pp. 31–35.

10. Carol Seefeldt, "Art—A Serious Work," *Young Children*, March 1995, p. 41.

11. Seefeldt, p. 41.

12. Patricia Greenfield, Dorathea Farrar, and Jessica Beagles-Roos, "Is the Medium the Message?: Effects of Radio and Television on Imagination," *Journal of Applied Developmental Psychology* 7, no. 3 (1986): 201–218.

13. Todd Oppenheimer, "The Computer Delusion," *Atlantic Monthly*, July 1997, p. 52.

14. Donald F. Roberts, et al., *Kids & Media @ the New Millennium: A Comprehensive National Analysis of Children's Media Use* (Menlo Park, Calif.: Kaiser Family Foundation Report, November 1999), pp. 70, 71.

15. Fowler, pp. 138–139.

16. Nancy Welch et al., *Schools, Communities, and the Arts: A Research Compendium* (Washington, D.C.: National Endowment for the Arts, 1995), pp. 13–15; Richard L. Luftig, *The Schooled Mind: Do the Arts Make a Difference? Year 2, An Empirical Evaluation of the Hamilton Fairfield SPECTRA+ Program, 1992–1994* (Oxford, Ohio: Center for Human Development, Learning, and Teaching, Miami University, n.d.).

17. Blaine H. Moore and Helen Caldwell, "Drama and Drawing for Narrative Writing in Primary Grades," *Journal of Educational Research* 8, no. 2 (1993): 100–110. Quoted in Nancy Welch et al., pp. 46, 47.

18. Reported in Welch et al., pp. 16–18.

19. Amy Wilson, "No More Magic Flute?" *Psychology Today*, January/February 2000, p. 77.

20. Wilson, p. 77.

21. Fowler, pp. 163–164.

22. Ontario Arts Council, *The Arts and the Quality of Life: The Attitudes of Ontarians* (Toronto: Ontario Arts Council, 1995), p. 28.

23. The survey was conducted for the National Endowment for the Arts and was known as the Survey of Public Participation in the Arts (SPPA92). Bergonzi and Smith's analysis is reviewed in Welch et al., pp. 111–112.

## CHAPTER 11

1. Mary Swift, "Computers in Pre-School Centres?" *Australian Journal of Early Childhood*, 10, no. 3 (1985): 22.

2. David Suzuki, "A Buddhist Way to Teach Kids Ecology," *Toronto Star*, 18 June 1994, p. C2.

3. William Souder, "Deformed Frogs Rattle Experts," *Toronto Star*, 5 October 1996, p. C6.

4. *Natural History*, November 1997, p. 3.

5. Theodore Roszak, *The Cult of Information*, 2nd ed. (Berkeley: University of California Press, 1994), pp. 70–71.

6. *The Water Game* (CWD Software, 1989) is featured in a study by Peter Kutnick and David Marshall, "Development of Social Skills and the Use of the Microcomputer in the Primary School Classroom," *British Educational Research Journal*, 19, no. 5 (1993): 517–533. The students taking part in the study were between the ages of nine and ten.

7. Patricia M. Stohr-Hunt, "An Analysis of Frequency of Hands-On Experience and Science Achievement," *Journal of Research in Science Teaching*, 33, no. 1 (1996): 101–109.

8. Linda Jacobson, "Long-Term Achievement Study Shows Gains, Losses," *Education Week*, 3 September 1997, p. 12.

9. Bill Atkinson, "The Prince of Muddy Waters," *Globe and Mail*, 3 May 1997, p. D5.

10. By contrast few of our children would recognize, say, chamomile by its shape, color, or smell, or know that it can settle an upset stomach or that it is useful for soothing rashes. Yet this medicinal plant can be found growing in many North American cities. On

the other hand, many of our children would know the whereabouts of the nearest pharmacy, although they would not necessarily be able to pick out the appropriate cure (assuming it were available over the counter) when they got there.

11. Richard Evans Schultes, "Burning the Library of Amazonia," *The Sciences,* March/April 1994, pp. 24, 30.

12. Schultes, p. 24.

13. National Aboriginal Forestry Association, "Aboriginal Forest-Based Ecological Knowledge in Canada," Canadian Forest Service, Natural Resources Canada (30 August 1996), pp. 42–43. The paper presents case studies on the Algonquins of Barriere Lake, Quebec; the Gitxsan, of northwestern British Columbia; the Nuu-Chah-Nulth of Clayoquot Sound, Vancouver Island; the Cree, Dene, and Metis of northeastern Alberta; and the Crees of Eeyou Astchee in northern Quebec.

14. Reported in Kathleen deBettencourt, "Learning the Facts of Life about Planet Earth," *Education Week,* 14 July 1999, p. 34

15. deBettencourt, p. 34

16. Larry Miller and John Olson, "How Computers Live in Schools," *Educational Leadership,* October 1995, p. 75.

17. Suzuki, p C2.

18. Edith Cobb, "The Ecology of Imagination in Childhood," *Daedalus,* 88 (1959): 538.

## CHAPTER 12

1. Ursula Franklin, *The Real World of Technology* (Toronto: CBC Enterprises, 1991), p. 51.

2. Paul Koring, "Computers Mislead Leaders' Wives," *Globe and Mail,* 9 April 1997, p. A1.

3. Nicholas Negroponte, *Being Digital* (New York: Vintage Books, 1996), p. 7.

4. Neil Postman, *The End of Education* (New York: Knopf, 1995), p. 189.

5. Mike Romano, "...with Liberty and Laptops for All?" *New York Times,* 26 February 1998.

6. Richard Rothstein, "Calculus for Waitresses? A 'New Economy' Myth," *New York Times,* 27 October 1999.

7. George Grant, *Technology and Empire* (Toronto: Anansi, 1969), p. 113.

8. Cleborne D. Maddux, "The Merger of Education and the Private Sector: Panacea or Pandora's Box?" *Computers in the Schools,* 9, no. 2/3 (1991): 33.

9. Joseph Weizenbaum, *Computer Power and Human Reason: From Judgment to Calculation,* (1984; reprint, Harmondsworth: Penguin Books, 1993), p. 279.

# BIBLIOGRAPHY

**BOOKS**

Ackerman, Diane. *A Natural History of the Senses.* New York: Random House, 1990.

Adams, Marilyn Jager. *Beginning to Read: Thinking and Learning About Print.* Cambridge, Mass.: MIT Press, 1990.

Bettelheim, Bruno. *The Uses of Enchantment.* New York: Vintage Books, 1977.

Bettelheim, Bruno, and Zelan, Karen. *On Learning to Read: The Child's Fascination with Meaning.* New York: Knopf, 1982.

Bormann, F. Herbert, and Kellert, Stephen R. (eds). *Ecology, Economics, Ethics: The Broken Circle.* New Haven, Conn./London: Yale University Press, 1991.

Bowers, C.A. *The Cultural Dimensions of Educational Computing: Understanding the Non-Neutrality of Technology.* New York: Teachers College Press, 1988.

Brod, Craig. *Technostress: The Human Cost of the Computer Revolution.* Reading, MA: Addison-Wesley, 1984.

Capra, Fritjof. *The Web of Life.* New York: Anchor Books, 1996.

Chall, Jeanne S. *Learning to Read: The Great Debate.* New York: McGraw-Hill, 1967.

Cooley, Mike. *Architect or Bee?: The Human Price of Technology.* New ed. London: Hogarth Press, 1987.

Cuban, Larry. *Teachers and Machines: The Classroom Use of Technology Since 1920.* New York: Teachers College Press, 1986.

Daiute, Colette. *Writing and Computers.* Reading, Mass.: Addison-Wesley, 1985.

Donaldson, Margaret. *Children's Minds.* London: Fontana Press, 1986.

Fowler, Charles. *Strong Arts, Strong Schools: The Promising Potential and Shortsighted Disregard of the Arts in American Schooling.* New York: Oxford University Press, 1996.

Franklin, Ursula. *The Real World of Technology.* Toronto: CBC Enterprises, 1991.

Gardner, Howard. *Frames of Mind: The Theory of Multiple Intelligences.* New York: Basic Books, 1983.

Gates, Bill. *The Road Ahead.* New York: Penguin Books, 1995.

Goelman, Hillel; Oberg, Antoinette; and Smith, Frank (eds). *Awakening to Literacy.* Portsmouth, N.H.: Heinemann, 1984.

Goleman, Daniel. *Emotional Intelligence.* New York: Bantam Books, 1995.

Healy, Jane M. *Endangered Minds: Why Our Children Don't Think.* New York: Simon & Schuster/Touchstone, 1991.

———. *Failure to Connect: How Computers Affect Our Children's Minds — for Better and Worse.* New York: Simon & Schuster, 1998.

Heim, Michael. *The Metaphysics of Virtual Reality.* New York: Oxford University Press, 1993.

Hunt, Morton. *The Universe Within: A New Science Explores the Human Mind.* New York: Simon & Schuster, 1982.

Jacoby, Russell, and Glauberman, Naomi (eds). *The Bell Curve Debate: History, Documents, Opinions.* New York: Times Books, 1995.

Kagan, Jerome. *The Nature of the Child.* New York: Basic Books, 1984.

Katz, Lilian G., and Chard, Sylvia C. *Engaging Children's Minds: The Project Approach.* Norwood, N.J.: Ablex Publishing, 1989.

Kline, Stephen. *Out of the Garden: Toys and Children's Culture in the Age of TV Marketing.* Toronto: Garamond Press, 1993.

Kotulak, Ronald. *Inside the Brain: Revolutionary Discoveries of How the Mind Works.* Kansas City, Mo.: Andrews and McMeel, 1996.

Livingston, John A. *The Rogue Primate.* Toronto: Key Porter Books, 1994.

Livingstone, David. *The Education-Jobs Gap.* Boulder, Colo.: Westview Press, 1998.

Mander, Jerry. *Four Arguments for the Elimination of Television.* New York: Quill, 1978.

———. *In the Absence of the Sacred.* San Francisco: Sierra Club Books, 1992.

McGuinness, Diane. *When Children Don't Learn: Understanding the Biology and Psychology of Learning Disabilities.* New York: Basic Books, 1985.

McKibben, Bill. *The Age of Missing Information.* New York: Random House, 1992.

Montessori, Maria. *The Absorbent Mind.* New York: Dell Publishing, 1984.

Nabham, Gary Paul, and Trimble, Stephen. *The Geography of Childhood.* Boston, Mass.: Beacon Press, 1994.

Negroponte, Nicholas. *Being Digital.* New York: Vintage Books, 1996.

Noble, David. *Progress Without People.* Toronto: Between the Lines Press, 1995.

Noble, Douglas D. "A Bill of Goods: The Early Marketing of Computer-Based Education and Its Implications for the Present Moment." In vol. 2 of *International Handbook of Teachers and Teaching,* edited by Bruce J. Biddle et al. Dordrecht, The Netherlands: Kluwer Academic Publishers, 1997, pp. 1321-1385.

————. *The Classroom Arsenal: Military Research, Information Technology and Public Education.* London: Falmer Press, 1991.

Norman, Donald A. *Things That Make Us Smart: Defending Human Attributes in the Age of the Machine.* Reading, Mass.: Addison-Wesley, 1993.

Quilter, Deborah. *The Repetitive Strain Injury Recovery Book.* New York: Walker & Co., 1998.

Papert, Seymour. *Mindstorms: Children, Computers, and Powerful Ideas.* New York: Basic Books, 1980.

————. "Teaching Children Thinking." In *The Computer in the School: Tutor, Tool, Tutee,* edited by Robert P. Taylor. New York: Teachers College Press, 1980.

————. *The Children's Machine: Rethinking School in the Age of the Computer.* New York: Basic Books, 1993

Pascarelli, Emil, and Quilter, Deborah. *Repetitive Strain Injury: A Computer User's Guide.* New York: John Wiley, 1994.

Pearlman, Robert. "Can K-12 Education Drive on the Information Superhighway?" In National Research Council, *The Changing Nature of Telecommunications/Information Infrastructure.* Washington, D.C.: National Academy Press, 1995.

Penrose, Roger. *The Emperor's New Mind.* London: Vintage Books, 1989.

Perkins, David. *Smart Schools: From Training Memories to Educating Minds.* New York: Free Press, 1992.

Postman, Neil. *The Disappearance of Childhood* (with a new preface by the author). New York: Vintage Books, 1994

————. *The End of Education: Redefining the Value of School.* New York: Knopf, 1995.

————. *Technopoly: The Surrender of Culture to Technology.* New York: Knopf, 1992.

Reiter, Russel J., and Robinson, Jo. *Melatonin: Your Body's Natural Wonder Drug.* New York: Bantam Books, 1995

Restack, Richard. *The Brain Has a Mind of Its Own.* New York: Harmony Books, 1991.

Roszak, Theodore. *The Cult of Information.* 2nd ed. Berkeley: University of California Press, 1994.

Sanders, Barry. *A Is for Ox: The Collapse of Literacy and the Rise of Violence in an Electronic Age*. New York: Vintage Books, 1995.

Setzer, Valdemar. *Computers in Education*. Edinburgh: Floris Books, 1989.

Siegler, Robert S. *Children's Thinking*. 2nd ed. Englewood Cliffs, N.J.: Prentice Hall, 1991.

Sloan, Douglas (ed). *The Computer in Education: A Critical Perspective*. New York: Teachers College Press, 1985.

Smith, Frank. *Reading*. 2nd ed. Cambridge: Cambridge University Press, 1985.

———. *Understanding Reading: A Psycholinguistic Analysis of Reading and Learning to Read*. 2nd. ed. New York: Rinehart and Winston, 1978.

———. *Writing and the Writer*. Hillsdale, N.J.: Lawrence Erlbaum, 1982.

Stoll, Clifford. *Silicon Snake Oil*. New York: Doubleday, 1995.

Turkle, Sherry. *The Second Self: Computers and the Human Spirit*. New York: Simon & Schuster/Touchstone, 1985.

Weikart, Phyllis, and Carlton, Elizabeth B. *Foundations in Elementary Education Movement*. Ypsilanti, Mich.: High/Scope Press, 1995.

Weizenbaum, Joseph. *Computer Power and Human Reason: From Judgment to Calculation* (reprinted with new preface). Harmondsworth: Penguin Books, 1993.

## REPORTS

Anderson, R.C., et al. *Becoming a Nation of Readers: The Report of the Commission on Reading*. Pittsburgh, Penn.: National Academy of Education, 1985.

Center for Media Education. *Alcohol and Tobacco on the Web: New Threats to Youth*. Washington, D.C.: Center for Media Education, 1997.

———. *An Update of Children's Web Sites' Information Collection Practices*. Washington, D.C.: Center for Media Education, 1997.

Childers, Thomas *A. Reference Performance in California Public Libraries, 1994-95*. Philadelphia, Penn.: College of Information, Science, and Technology, Drexel University, 1995.

*Computers in Education: A Critical Look*. Invitational Symposium, University of California, Berkeley, June 3-5, 1995. Summary of discussions and conclusions synthesized by Fritjof Capra. Berkeley, Calif.: Center for Ecoliteracy.

*Education Week* in collaboration with the Milken Exchange on Education Technology. *Technology Counts '99: Building the Digital Curriculum. Education Week*, 23 September 1999.

Emmett, Terry S., and Roberts, Lily. *California's Investment in Site-Based Educational Technology: Volume I, Evaluation of the Model Technology Schools Levels I and*

II; Volume II, Evaluation of the School-Based Educational Technology Grant Projects. Research, Evaluation, and Technology Division, California Department of Education, February 1995.

Exploring the Link Between Academic Achievement and Investment in Classroom Technology. San Jose Mercury News, 21 November 1995.

Freedman, Aviva, and Clarke, Linda. The Effect of Computer Technology on Composing Processes and Written Products of Grade 8 and Grade 12 Students. Toronto: Ontario Ministry of Education, 1988.

Hathaway, Warren E. The Effects of Type of School Lighting on Physical Development and School Performance of Children. Edmonton: Alberta Department of Education, March 1994.

Luftig, Richard L. The Schooled Mind: Do the Arts Make a Difference? Year 2, An Empirical Evaluation of the Hamilton Fairfield SPECTRA+ Program, 1992-1994. Oxford, Ohio: Center for Human Development, Learning, and Teaching, Miami University, n.d.

Montgomery, Kathryn, and Pasnik, Shelley. The Web of Deception: Threats to Children from Online Marketing. Washington, D.C.: Center for Media Education, 1996.

National Aboriginal Forestry Association. "Aboriginal Forest-Based Ecological Knowledge in Canada." Canadian Forest Service, Natural Resources Canada, August 1996.

Nye, Barbara. Project Challenge Fifth-Year Summary Report: An Initial Evaluation of The Tennessee Department of Education "At-Risk" Student/Teacher Ratio Reduction Project in Sixteen Counties, 1989-90 through 1993-94. Nashville, Tenn.: Center of Excellence for Research and Policy on Basic Skills, Tennessee State University, 1995.

————. The Lasting Benefits Study: A Continuing Analysis of the Effect of Small Class Size in Kindergarten Through Third Grade on Student Achievement Test Scores in Subsequent Grade Levels. Nashville, Tenn.: Center of Excellence for Research and Policy on Basic Skills, Tennessee State University, 1995.

Panel on Educational Technology. Report to the President on the Use of Technology to Strengthen K-12 Education in the United States. Washington, D.C.: President's Committee of Advisors on Science and Technology, March 1997.

Roberts, Donald F., et al. Kids and Media @ the New Millennium: A Comprehensive National Analysis of Children's Media Use. Menlo Park, Calif.: The Henry J. Kaiser Family Foundation, November 1999.

Schacter, John. Reading Programs that Work: A Review of Programs for Pre-kindergarten to 4th Grade. Santa Monica, Calif.: Milken Family Foundation, 1999.

Software and Information Industry Association (SIIA), 1999 Education Market Report: K-12. Washington, D.C.: SIIA, 1999.

U.S. Congress, Office of Technology Assessment. *Teachers and Technology: Making the Connection,* OTA–EHR–616. Washington, D.C.: U.S. Government Printing Office, April 1995.

U.S. Environmental Protection Agency. *Office Equipment: Design, Indoor Air Emissions, and Pollution Prevention Opportunities.* Washington, D.C., March 1995.

Welch, Nancy, et al. *Schools, Communities, and the Arts: A Research Compendium.* Washington, D.C.: National Endowment for the Arts, June 1995.

Wellburn, Elizabeth. *Information, Telecommunications and Learning: A Review of the Research Literature.* British Columbia Education Technology Centre, 1991.

Wenglinsky, Harold. *Does It Compute? The Relationship Between Educational Technology and Student Achievement in Mathematics.* Princeton, N.J.: Educational Testing Service, 1999.

Wideman, Herbert H., et al. *The Development of Children's Writing in a High Computer Access Environment: A Three Year Study.* North York, Ont.: Centre for the Study of Computers in Education, York University, Technical Report 94-3, November 1994.

## UNPUBLISHED PAPERS

Noble, David. "Digital Diploma Mills:  Part I, The Automation of Higher Education," October 1997.

Sternberg, Robert J. "Successful Intelligence: An Expanded Approach to Understanding Intelligence," February 1997.

## ARTICLES

Achilles, Charles M. "Students Achieve More in Smaller Classes." *Educational Leadership,* February 1996, 76-77.

————.; Finn, Jeremy D.; and Bain, Helen P. "Using Class Size to Reduce the Equity Gap." *Educational Leadership,* December 1997-January 1998, 40-43.

Apple, Michael W. "The New Technology: Is It Part of the Solution or Part of the Problem in Education?" *Computers in the Schools* 8, no. 1/2/3 (1991): 59-81.

Bangert-Drowns, Robert L. "The Word Processor as an Instructional Tool: A Meta-Analysis of Word Processing in Writing Instruction." *Review of Educational Research* 63, no. 1 (1993): 69-93.

Becker, Henry Jay. "A Model for Improving the Performance of Integrated Learning Systems: Mixed Individualized/Group/Whole Class Lessons, Cooperative Learning, and Organizing Time for Teacher-Led Remediation of Small Groups." *Educational Technology* 32, no. 9 (1992): 6-15.

————. "A Truly Empowering Technology-Rich Education — How Much Will It Cost?," *Educational IRM Quarterly* 3, no. 1 (1993): 31-35.

————. "Computer-based Integrated Learning Systems in the Elementary and Middle Grades: A Critical Review and Synthesis of Evaluation Reports." *Journal of Educational Computing Research* 8, no. 1 (1992): 1-41.

————. "How Exemplary Computer-Using Teachers Differ from Other Teachers: Implications for Realizing the Potential of Computers in Schools." *Journal of Research on Computing in Education* 26, no. 3 (1994): 291-321.

————. "Mindless or Mindful Use of Integrated Learning Systems." *International Journal of Educational Research* 21, no. 1 (1994): 65-79.

————. "The Importance of a Methodology that Maximizes Falsifiability: Its Applicability to Research About Logo." *Educational Researcher* 16, no. 5 (1987): 11-16.

————, and Hativa, Nira. "History, Theory and Research Concerning Integrated Learning Systems." *International Journal of Educational Research* 21, no. 1 (1994): 5-12.

Bennett, Neville. "Class Size in Primary Schools: Perceptions of Headteachers, Chairs of Governors, Teachers and Parents." *British Educational Research Journal* 22, no. 1 (1996): 33-56.

Berg, Susan, et al. "Exemplary Technology Use in Elementary Classrooms." *Journal of Research on Computing in Education* 31, no. 2 (1998): 111-122.

Bettelheim, Bruno, and Zelan, Karen. "Why Children Don't Like to Read." *The Atlantic Monthly,* November 1981, 25-31.

Bigelow, Bill. "On the Road to Cultural Bias: A Critique of *The Oregon Trail* CD-ROM." *Language Arts* 74 (February 1997): 84-93.

Blatchford, Peter; Goldstein, Harvey; and Mortimore, Peter. "Research on Class Size Effects: A Critique of Methods and a Way Forward." *International Journal of Educational Research* 29 (1998): 691-710.

Borrell, Jerry. "America's Shame: How We've Abandoned Our Children's Future." *Macworld,* September 1992, 25-30.

Bradsher, Monica, and Hagan, Lucy. "The Kids Network: Student-Scientists Pool Resources." *Educational Leadership,* October 1995, 38-43.

Breese, Chris; Jackson, Anita; and Prince, Terry. "Promise in Impermanence: Children Writing with Unlimited Access to Word Processors." *Early Child Development and Care* 118 (1996): 67-91.

Breivik, Patricia Senn. Information Literacy: When Computers Aren't Enough." *Learning & Leading with Technology,* February 1996, 65-67.

Brinkley, Vickie M., and Watson, J. Allen. "Effects of Microworld Training Experience on Sorting Tasks by Young Children." *Journal of Educational Technology Systems* 16, no. 4 (1987-88): 349-364.

Brouwer, Peter. "Hold On a Minute Here: What Happened to Critical Thinking in the Information Age?" *Journal of Educational Technology Systems* 25, no. 2 (1996–97): 189–197.

Brown, A. Howard. "Driving Lessons for the Information Superhighway, or the Information Cul-de-Sac." *Learning & Leading with Technology,* October 1995, 16–17.

Brown, John Seeley. "Process versus Product." *Journal of Educational Computing Research* 1, no. 2 (1985): 179–201.

Bruer, John T. "Brain Science, Brain Fiction." *Educational Leadership,* November 1998, 14–18.

————. "Education and the Brain: A Bridge Too Far." *Educational Researcher* 26, no. 8 (1997): 4–16.

Buckley, Robert B. "What Happens When Funding Is Not an Issue?" *Educational Leadership,* October 1995, 64–66.

Budin, Howard R. "Technology and the Teacher's Role." *Computers in the Schools* 8, no. 1/2/3 (1991): 15–26.

Burgstahler, Sheryl. "Surfing the Internet with the Younger Set." *Learning & Leading with Technology,* February 1999, 25–29.

Burniske, R.W. "The Shadow Play: How the Integration of Technology Annihilates Debate in Our Schools." *Phi Delta Kappan,* October 1998, 155–157.

Campbell, Robert J. "HyperMinds for HyperTimes: The Demise of Rational, Logical Thought?" *Educational Technology* 38 no. 1 (1998): 24–31.

"Canadian Perspectives on *The Bell Curve.*" Special issue of *The Alberta Journal of Educational Research* 41, no. 3 (1995).

Childers, Thomas A. "California's Reference Crisis." *The Library Journal,* 15 April 1994, 32–35.

Clarke-Stewart, K. Alison. "Reading with Children." *Journal of Applied Developmental Psychology* 19, no. 1 (1998): 1–14.

Clements, Douglas H., and Nastasi, Bonnie K. "Effects of Computer Environments on Social-Emotional Development: Logo and Computer-Assisted Instruction." *Computers in the Schools* (Special Double Issue: Logo in the Schools) 2, no. 2/3 (1985): 11–31.

Clements, Douglas H.; Nastasi, Bonnie K.; and Swaminathan, Sudha. "Young Children and Computers: Crossroads and Directions from Research." *Young Children,* January 1993, 56–64.

Clements, Douglas H., and Sarama, Julie. "Research on Logo: A Decade of Progress." *Computers in the Schools* 14, no. 1/2 (1997): 9–46.

Cobb, Edith. "The Ecology of Imagination in Childhood." *Daedalus* 88 (1959): 537–548.

Cochran-Smith, Marilyn. "Word Processing and Writing in Elementary Classrooms: A Critical Review of Related Literature." *Review of Educational Research* 61, no. 1 (1991): 107–155.

Cohen, Rina. "Implementing Logo in the Grade Two Classroom: Acquisition of Basic Programming Concepts." *Journal of Computer-Based Instruction* 14, no. 2 (1987): 124–132.

Collis, Betty; Ollila, Lloyd; and Ollila, Kathleen. "Writing to Read: An Evaluation of a Canadian Installation of a Computer-Supported Initial Language Environment." *Journal of Educational Computing Research* 6, no. 4 (1990): 411–427.

Cope, Peter, and Simmons, Malcolm. "Children's Exploration of Rotation and Angle in Limited Logo Microworlds." *Computers and Education* 16, no. 2 (1991): 133–141.

Cunningham, Anne E., and Stanovich, Keith E. "Early Spelling Acquisition: Writing Beats the Computer." *Journal of Educational Psychology* 82, no. 1 (1990): 159–162.

Daiute, Colette. "Physical and Cognitive Factors in Revising: Insights from Studies with Computers." *Research in the Teaching of English* 20, no. 2 (1986): 141–159.

Dickinson, David K. "Cooperation, Collaboration, and a Computer: Integrating a Computer into a First-Second Grade Writing Program." *Research in the Teaching of English* 20, no. 4 (1986): 357–378.

Dickinson, David K., and DiGisi, Lori Lyman. "The Many Rewards of a Literacy-Rich Classroom." *Educational Leadership,* March 1998, 23–26.

Dillon, Thomas W., and Emurian, Henry H. "Some Factors Affecting Reports of Visual Fatigue Resulting from Use of a VDU." *Computers in Human Behavior* 12, no. 1 (1996): 49–59.

Dockterman, David A. "Interactive Learning: It's Pushing the *Right* Buttons." *Educational Leadership,* October 1995, 58–59.

Dudley-Marling, Curt, and Owston, Ronald D. "Using Microcomputers to Teach Problem Solving: A Critical Review." *Educational Technology* 28, no. 7 (1988): 27–33.

Dybdahl, Claudia S.; Shaw, Donna Gail; and Blahous, Emily. "The Impact of the Computer on Writing: No Simple Answers." *Computers in the Schools* 13, no. 3/4 (1997): 41–53.

Editorial. "Avoiding Cyberspace Junk Through Teaching Responsibility." *Computers in the Schools* 13, no. 3/4 (1997): 1–4.

Elkind, David. "The Impact of Computer Use on Cognitive Development in Young Children: A Theoretical Analysis." *Computers in Human Behavior* 1, no. 2 (1985): 131–141.

Ely, Donald P. "Computers in Schools and Universities in the United States of America." *Educational Technology* 33, no. 9 (1993): 53–57.

Eraut, Michael. "Groupwork with Computers in British Primary Schools." *Journal of Educational Computing Research* 13, no. 1 (1995): 61–87.

Escobedo, Theresa H., and Bhargava, Ambika. "A Study of Children's Computer-Generated Graphics." *Journal of Computing in Childhood Education* 2, no. 4 (1991): 3–25.

Eurich-Fulcer, Rebecca, and Schofield, Janet Ward. "Wide-area Networking in K-12 Education: Issues Shaping Implementation and Use." *Computers and Education* 24, no. 3 (1995): 211–220.

Falbel, Aaron. "The Computer as a Convivial Tool." *Mothering,* Fall 1990, 91–96.

Fatouros, Cherryl. "Young Children Using Computers: Planning Appropriate Learning Experiences." *Australian Journal of Early Childhood* 20, no. 2 (1995): 1–6.

Fay, Anne Louise, and Mayer, Richard E. "Children's Naive Conceptions and Confusions About Logo Graphics Commands." *Journal of Educational Psychology* 79, no. 3 (1987): 254–268.

Fernandez, Melanie. "Electronic Versus Paper: Do Children Learn from Stories on the Computer?." *Learning & Leading with Technology,* May 1999, 32–34.

Field, Tiffany. "Preschoolers in America Are Touched Less and Are More Aggressive than Preschoolers in France." *Early Child Development and Care* 151 (1999): 11–17.

Fish, Marian C., and Feldman, Shirley C. "Learning and Teaching in Microcomputer Classrooms: Reconsidering Assumptions." *Computers in the Schools* 7, no. 3 (1990): 87–96.

Fletcher-Flinn, Claire M., and Gravatt, Breon. "The Efficacy of Computer Assisted Instruction (CAI): A Meta-Analysis." *Journal of Educational Computing Research* 12, no. 3 (1995): 219–242.

Fletcher-Flinn, Claire M., and Suddendorf, Thomas. "Do Computers Affect 'The Mind'?." *Journal of Educational Computing Research* 15, no. 2 (1996): 97–112.

Futoran, Gail Clark; Schofield, Janet Ward; and Eurich-Fulcer, Rebecca. "The Internet as a K-12 Educational Resource: Emerging Issues of Information Access and Freedom." *Computers and Education* 24, no. 3 (1995): 229–236.

Getman, G.N. "Computers in the Classroom: Bane or Boon?" *Academic Therapy* 18, no. 5 (1983): 517–524.

Ginther, Dean W., and Williamson, James D. "Learning Logo: What Is Really Learned?" *Computers in the Schools* (Special Double Issue: Logo in the Schools) 2, no. 2/3 (1985): 73–78.

Goodwin, Laura D., et al. "Cognitive and Affective Effects of Various Types of Microcomputer Use by Preschoolers." *American Educational Research Journal* 23, no. 3 (1986): 348–356.

Gore, Dolores A., et al. "A Study of Teaching Reading Skills to the Young Child Using Microcomputer Assisted Instruction." *Journal of Educational Computing Research* 5, no. 2 (1989): 179–185.

Greenfield, Patricia; Farrar, Dorathea; and Beagles-Roos, Jessica. "Is the Medium the Message?: Effects of Radio and Television on Imagination." *Journal of Applied Developmental Psychology* 7, no. 3 (1986): 201–218.

Hadler, Nortin M. "Arm Pain in the Workplace: A Small Area Analysis." *Journal of Occupational Medicine,* February 1992, 113–118.

Hargreaves, Linda; Galton, Maurice; and Pell, Anthony. "The Effects of Changes in Class Size on Teacher-Pupil Interaction." *International Journal of Educational Research* 29 (1998): 779–795.

Harris, Judith B. "Information Is Forever in Formation; Knowledge Is in the Knower: Global Connectivity in K-12 Classrooms." *Computers in the Schools* 12, no. 1/2 (1996): 11–22.

Haugland, Susan. "Children's Home Computer Use: An Opportunity for Parent/Teacher Collaboration." *Early Childhood Education Journal* 25, no. 2 (1997): 133–135.

Hawisher, Gail. "The Effects of Word Processing on the Revision Strategies of College Freshmen." *Research in the Teaching of English* 21, no. 2 (1987): 145–159.

Heller, Rachelle S. "The Role of Hypermedia." *Journal of Research on Computing in Education* 22, no. 4 (1990): 431–444.

Henniger, Michael L. "Computers and Preschool Children's Play: Are They Compatible?" *Journal of Computing in Childhood Education* 5, no. 3/4 (1994): 231–239.

Hickey, M. Gail. "Computer Use in Elementary Classrooms: An Ethnographic Study." *Journal of Computing in Childhood Education* 4, no. 3/4 (1993): 219–228.

Hoko, J. Aaron. "SIS: A Futuristic Look at How Computerized Classroom Can Enhance Rather than Diminish Teachers' Pedagogical Power." *Computers in the Schools* 6, no. 1/2 (1989): 135–143.

Huenecke, Dorothy. "An Artistic Criticism of a Computer-Based Reading Program." *Educational Technology* 32, no. 7 (1992): 53–57.

Irwin, Martha E. "Connections: Young Children, Reading, Writing, and Computers." *Computers in the Schools* 4, no. 1 (1987): 37–51.

Jaschinski-Kruza, W. "Transient Myopia after Visual Work." *Ergonomics* 27, no. 11 (1984): 1181–1189.

Johnson, D. LaMont. "The Electronic Reader: A Paradigm Shift." (Editorial), *Computers in the Schools* 12, no. 3 (1996): 1–4.

Johnson, D. LaMont, and Maddux, Cleborne D. "The Birth and Nurturing of a New Discipline." *Computers in the Schools* 8, no. 1/2/3 (1991): 5–14.

Johnston, Callum B. "Interactive Storybook Software: Effects on Verbal Development in Kindergarten Children." *Early Child Development and Care* 132 (1997): 33–44.

Jonassen, David H. "Designing Structured Hypertext and Structured Access to Hypertext." *Educational Technology* 28, no. 11 (1988): 13–16.

Jones, Ithel. "The Effect of a Word Processor on the Written Composition of Second-Grade Pupils." *Computers in the Schools* 11, no. 2 (1994): 43–54.

————. "The Effect of Computer-Generated Spoken Feedback on Kindergarten Students' Written Narratives." *Journal of Computing in Childhood Education* 9, no. 1 (1998): 43–56.

Jones, Ithel, and Pellegrini, A.D. "The Effects of Social Relationships, Writing Media, and Microgenic Development on First-Grade Students' Written Narratives." *American Educational Research Journal* 33, no. 3 (1996): 691–718.

Joram, Elana, et al. "The Effects of Revising with a Word Processor on Written Composition." *Research in the Teaching of English* 26, no. 2 (1992): 167–193.

Kahn, Jessica, and Freyd, Pamela. "Touch Typing for Young Children: Help or Hindrance?" *Educational Technology* 30, no. 2 (1990): 41–45.

Karger, Howard Jacob. "Children and Microcomputers: A Critical Analysis." *Educational Technology* 28, no. 12 (1988): 7–11.

Kaufman, Roger. "The Internet as the Ultimate Technology and Panacea." *Educational Technology* 38, no. 1 (1998): 63–64.

Kearsley, Greg. "Educational Technology: A Critique." *Educational Technology* 38, no. 2 (1998): 47–51.

Keller, Janet K. "Characteristics of Logo Instruction Promoting Transfer of Learning: A Research Review." *Journal of Research on Computing in Education* 23, no. 1 (1990): 55–71.

Kinzer, Charles, et al. "Different Logo Learning Environments and Mastery: Relationships Between Engagement and Learning." *Computers in the Schools* (Special Double Issue: Logo in the Schools) 2, no. 2/3 (1985): 33–43.

Klimpston, Richard D., et al. "The Effects of Integrating Computers Across a Primary Grade Curriculum." *Journal of Computing in Childhood Education* 2, no. 2 (1990/91): 31–45.

Krasnor, Linda R., and Mitterer, John O. "Logo and the Development of General Problem-Solving Skills." *The Alberta Journal of Educational Research* 30, no. 2 (1984): 133-144.

Kraut, R. et al. "Internet Paradox: A Social Technology that Reduces Social Involvement and Psychological Well-Being?" *American Psychologist* 53, no. 9 (1998): 1017-1031.

Krendl, Kathy A., and Broihier, Mary. "Student Responses to Computers: A Longitudinal Study." *Journal of Educational Computing Research* 8, no. 2 (1992): 215-227.

Krendl, Kathy A., and Williams, Russell B. "The Importance of Being Rigorous: Research on Writing to Read." *Journal of Computer-Based Instruction* 17, no. 3 (1990): 81-86.

Kulik, Chen-Lin C., and Kulik, James A. "Effectiveness of Computer-Based Instruction: An Updated Analysis." *Computers in Human Behavior* 7, nos 1-2 (1991): 75-94.

Kulik, James A.; Kulik, Chen-Lin C.; and Bangert-Drowns, Robert L. "Effectiveness of Computer-Based Education in Elementary Schools." *Computers in Human Behavior* 1, no. 1 (1985): 59-74.

Kurth, Ruth J. "Using Word Processing to Enhance Revision Strategies During Student Writing Activities." *Educational Technology* 27, no. 1 (1987): 13-19.

Kutnick, Peter, and Marshall, David. "Development of Social Skills and the Use of the Microcomputer in the Primary School Classroom." *British Educational Research Journal* 19, no. 5 (1993): 517-533.

Laeser, Kathryn L.; Maxwell, Lorraine E.; and Hedge, Alan. "The Effect of Computer Workstation Design on Student Posture." *Journal of Research on Computing in Education* 31, no. 2 (1998): 173-188.

Lafer, Stephen. "Audience, Elegance, and Learning via the Internet." *Computers in the Schools* 13, no. 1/2 (1997): 89-97.

Lee, William B., and Kazlauskas, Edward John. "The Ecole Moderne: Another Perspective on Educational Technology." *Educational Technology* 35, no. 2 (1995): 14-20.

Levin, Diane E., and Carlsson-Page, Nancy. "The Mighty Morphin Power Rangers: Teachers Voice Concern." *Young Children,* September 1995, 67-72.

Liao, Yuen-Kuang Cliff. "Effects of Hypermedia Versus Traditional Instruction on Students' Achievement: A Meta-Analysis." *Journal of Research on Computing in Education* 30, no. 4 (1998): 341-359.

Liao, Yuen-Kuang Cliff, and Bright, George W. "Effects of Computer Programming on Cognitive Outcomes: A Meta-Analysis." *Journal of Educational Computing Research* 7, no. 3 (1991): 251-268.

Linn, Marcia C. "The Cognitive Consequences of Programming Instruction in Classrooms." *Educational Researcher* 14, no. 5 (1985): 14–16, 25–29.

Maddux, Cleborne D. "Barriers to the Successful Use of Information Technology in Education." *Computers in the Schools* 14, no. 3/4 (1998): 5–11.

————. "Logo: Scientific Dedication or Religious Fanaticism in the 1990s?" *Educational Technology* 29, no. 2 (1989): 18–23.

————. "Preface" to *Computers in the Schools* (Special Issue: Assessing the Impact of Computer-Based Instruction) 5, no. 3/4 (1988): 1–10.

————. "The Internet: Educational Prospects — and Problems." *Educational Technology* 34, no. 7 (1994): 37–42.

————. "The Merger of Education and the Private Sector: Panacea or Pandora's Box?" *Computers in the Schools* 9, no. 2/3 (1993): 23–34.

————. "The Newest Technology Crisis: Teacher Expertise and How to Foster It." *Computers in the Schools* 13, no. 3/4 (1997): 5–12.

————. "The State of the Art in Web-Based Learning." *Computers in the Schools* 12, no. 4 (1996): 63–71.

————. "The World Wide Web and the Television Generation." *Computers in the Schools* 12, no. 1/2 (1996): 23–30.

Maddux, Cleborne D., and Johnson, D. LaMont. "Logo: A Retrospective." *Computers in the Schools* 14, no. 1/2 (1997): 1–8.

Marchionini, Gary. "Hypermedia and Learning: Freedom and Chaos." *Educational Technology* 28, no. 11 (1988): 8–12.

Matthew, Kathryn. "A Comparison of the Influence of Interactive CD-ROM Storybooks and Traditional Print Storybooks on Reading Comprehension." *Journal of Research on Computing in Education* 29, no. 3 (1997): 263–275.

Mavrogenes, Nancy A., and Bezruczko, Nikolaus. "Influences on Writing Development." *Journal of Educational Research* 86, no. 4 (1993): 237–245.

McCarty, Paul J. "Four Days That Changed the World (and other amazing Internet stories)." *Educational Leadership,* October 1995, 48–50.

McKenzie, Jamie. "Grazing the Net: Raising a Generation of Free-Range Students." *Phi Delta Kappan,* September 1998, 26–31.

McLellan, Hilary. "Hyper Stories: Some Guidelines for Instructional Designers." *Journal of Research on Computing in Education* 25, no. 1 (1992): 28–49.

Mehlinger, Howard D. "School Reform in the Information Age." *Phi Delta Kappan,* February 1996, 400–407.

Meyer, Maggie. "The GREENing of Learning: Using the Eighth Intelligence." *Educational Leadership,* September 1997, 32–34.

Miller, Harold L., Jr. et al. "The New York City Public Schools Integrated Learning Systems Project: Evaluation and Meta-Evaluation." *International Journal of Educational Research* 27, no. 2 (1997): 89-184.

Miller, Larry, and Burnett, Dale J. "The Role of Case Studies in Studying Computer Technology in Education." Paper Presented at the Sixteenth Annual World Association for Case Method Research Conference, Caceres, Extremadura, Spain, July 1999.

Miller, Larry, and Olson, John. "How Computers Live in Schools." *Educational Leadership,* October 1995, 74-77.

Miyashita, Keiko T. "Effect of Computer Use on Attitudes Among Japanese First- and Second-Grade Children." *Journal of Computing in Childhood Education* 5, no. 1 (1994): 73-82.

Montague, Margarie. "Computers and Writing Process Instruction." *Computers in the Schools* 7, no. 3 (1990): 5-20.

Moore, Blaine H., and Caldwell, Helen, "Drama and Drawing for Narrative Writing in Primary Grades." *Journal of Educational Research* 8, no. 2 (1993): 100-110.

Moore, Margaret A., and Karabenick, Stuart A. "The Effects of Computer Communications on the Reading and Writing Performance of Fifth-Grade Students." *Computers in Human Behavior* (Special Issue: Computer Use in the Improvement of Writing) 8, no. 1 (1992): 27-38.

Moursund, David. "Some 'Hidden' Costs of Computers." *Learning & Leading with Technology,* April 1998, 4-5.

―――. "The 15% Solution." *Learning & Leading with Technology,* March 1999, 4-5.

"NAEYC Position Statement: Technology and Young Children — Ages Three through Eight." *Young Children,* September 1996, 11-16.

NAEYC/IRA. "Learning to Read and Write: Developmentally Appropriate Practices for Young Children." *A joint position statement of the* International Reading Association (IRA) *and the* National Association for the Education of Young Children (NAEYC), *Young Children,* July 1998, 30-46.

Nair, Indira, and Zhang, Jun. "Distinguishability of the Video Display Terminal (VDT) as a Source of Magnetic Field Exposure." *American Journal of Industrial Medicine* 28, no. 1 (1995): 23-29.

Newberger, Julee J. "New Brain Development Research — A Wonderful Window of Opportunity to Build Public Support for Early Childhood Education!" *Young Children,* May 1997, 4-9.

Nichols, Lois Mayer. "Pencil and Paper Versus Word Processing: A Comparative Study of Creative Writing in the Elementary School." *Journal of Research on Computing in Education* 29, no. 2 (1996): 159-166.

Niemiec, Richard, et al. "The Effects of Computer Based Instruction in Elementary Schools: A Quantitative Synthesis." *Journal of Research on Computing in Education* 20, no. 2 (1987): 85–103.

Niemiec, Richard P.; Sikorski, Christian; and Walberg, Herbert J. "Learner-Control Effects: A Review of Reviews and a Meta-Analysis." *Journal of Educational Computing Research* 15, no. 2 (1996): 157–174.

Niemiec, Richard P., and Walberg, Herbert J. "Comparative Effects of Computer-Assisted Instruction: A Synthesis of Reviews." *Journal of Educational Computing Research* 3, no. 1 (1987): 19–37.

―――. "Computers and Achievement in the Elementary Schools." *Journal of Educational Computing Research* 1, no. 4 (1985): 435–440.

Noble, Douglas D. "The Educational Engineer Meets Wayne's World." *Rethinking Schools* 8, no. 2 (1993): 14–15.

Oates, Shawn; Evans, Gary W.; and Hedge, Alan. "An Anthropometric and Postural Risk Assessment of Children's School Computer Work Environments." *Computers in the Schools* 14, no. 3/4 (1998): 55–63.

O'Neil, John. "On Technology and Schools: A Conversation with Chris Dede." *Educational Leadership,* October 1995, 6–12.

Oppenheimer, Todd. "The Computer Delusion." *The Atlantic Monthly,* July 1997, 45–62.

Overbaugh, Richard C. "Word Processors and Writing-Process Software: Introduction and Evaluation." *Computers in Human Behavior* (Special Issue: Computer Use in the Improvement of Writing) 8, no. 1 (1992): 121–148.

Owston, Ronald D. "The World Wide Web: A Technology to Enhance Teaching and Learning?" *Educational Researcher* 26, no. 2 (1997): 27–33.

Owston, Ronald D.; Murphy, Sharon; and Wideman, Herbert H. "On and Off Computer Writing of Eighth Grade Students Experienced in Word Processing." *Computers in the Schools* 8, no. 4 (1991): 67–87.

―――. "The Effects of Word Processing on Students' Writing Quality and Revision Strategies." *Research in the Teaching of English* 26, no. 3 (1992): 249–276.

Owston, Ronald D., and Wideman, Herbert H. "Word Processors and Children's Writing in a High-Computer-Access Setting." *Journal of Research on Computing in Education* 30, no. 2 (1997): 202–220.

Palmer, Shirley. "Does Computer Use Put Children's Vision at Risk?" *Journal of Research and Development in Education* 26, no. 2 (1993): 59–65.

Parr, Judy M. "When Pens Are Passe: Students Reflect on Written Composition." *Journal of Research on Computing in Education* 27, no. 2 (1994–95): 221–230.

Peacock, Michael, and Beard, Roger. " 'Almost an Invincible Repugnance'?: Word Processors and Pupil Writers." *Educational Review* 49, no. 3 (1997): 283-294.

Peacock, Michael, and Breese, Chris. "Pupils with Portable Writing Machines." *Educational Review* (U.K.) 42, no. 1 (1990): 41-56.

Pennington, Martha C. "Computer-Assisted Writing on a Principled Basis: The Case Against Computer-Assisted Text Analysis for Non-proficient Writers." *Language and Education* 7, no. 1 (1993): 43-59.

Perkins, D.N., and Salomon, Gavriel. "Are Cognitive Skills Context-Bound?" *Educational Researcher* 18, no. 1 (1989): 16-25.

Pica, Rae. "Beyond Physical Development: Why Young Children Need to Move." *Young Children,* September 1997, 4-11.

Pool, Carolyn R. "A New Digital Literacy: A Conversation with Paul Glister." *Educational Leadership,* November 1997, 6-11.

Reed, W. Michael. "Assessing the Impact of Computer-Based Writing Instruction." *Journal of Research on Computing in Education* 28, no. 4 (1996): 418-437.

Reeves, Thomas C. " 'Future Schlock,' 'The Computer Delusion,' and 'The End of Education': Responding to Critics of Educational Technology." *Educational Technology* 38, no. 5 (1998): 49-53.

Reiter, Russel J. "Melatonin Suppression by Static and Extremely Low Frequency Electromagnetic Fields: Relationship to the Reported Increased Incidence of Cancer." *Reviews on Environmental Health* 10, no. 3-4 (1994): 171-186.

Rieber, Lloyd P. "LOGO and Its Promise: A Research Report." *Educational Technology* 27, no. 2 (1987): 12-16.

Roberts, Paul. "Virtual Grub Street: Sorrows of a Multimedia Hack." *Harper's,* June 1996, 71-77.

Robertson, J. "Paradise Lost: Children, Multimedia and the Myth of Interactivity." *Journal of Computer Assisted Learning* 14, no. 1 (1998): 31-39.

Roblyer, M.D. "Predictions and Realities: The Impact of the Internet on K-12 Education." *Leading & Learning with Technology,* September 1997, 54-56.

Roblyer, M.D.; Castine, W.H.; and King, F.J. "A Review of Recent Research." *Computers in the Schools* (Special Issue: Assessing the Impact of Computer-Based Instruction) 5, no. 3/4 (1988): 11-115.

Rothstein, Russell I., and McKnight, Lee. "Technology and Cost Models of K-12 Schools on the National Information Infrastructure." *Computers in the Schools* 12, no. 1/2 (1996): 31-57.

Rowell, Patricia M.; Gustafson, Brenda J.; and Guilbert, Sandra M. "Problem-Solving Through Technology: An Interpretive Dilemma." *The Alberta Journal of Educational Research* 43, no. 2/3 (1997): 86-98.

Ryan, Alice W. "Meta-analysis of Achievement Effects of Microcomputer Applications in Elementary Schools." *Educational Administration Quarterly* 27, no. 2 (1991): 161–184.

Salomon, Gavriel. "Of Mind and Media: How Culture's Symbolic Forms Affect Learning and Thinking." *Phi Delta Kappan,* January 1997, 375–380.

Salomon, Gavriel, and Gardner, Howard. "The Computer as Educator: Lessons from Television Research." *Educational Researcher* 15, no. 1 (1986): 13–19.

Salomon, Gavriel, and Perkins, D.N. "Transfer of Cognitive Skills from Programming: When and How?" *Journal of Educational Computing Research* 3, no. 2 (1987): 149–169.

Schofield, Janet Ward. "Computers and Classroom Social Processes — A Review of the Literature." *Social Science Computer Review* 15, no. 1 (1997): 27–39.

Schrum, Lynne. "Educators and the Internet: A Case Study of Professional Development." *Computers and Education* 24, no. 3 (1995): 221–228.

Schultes, Richard Evans. "Burning the Library of Amazonia." *The Sciences,* March/April 1994, 24–30.

Schwartz, Judah L. "Intellectual Mirrors: A Step in the Direction of Making Schools Knowledge-Making Places." *Harvard Educational Review* 59, no. 1 (1989): 51–61.

Seawel, Lori, et al. "A Descriptive Study Comparing Computer-Based Word Processing and Handwriting on Attitudes and Performance of Third and Fourth Grade Students Involved in a Program Based on a Process Writing Approach." *Journal of Computing in Childhood Education* 5, no. 1 (1994): 43–59.

Seefeldt, Carol. "Art — A Serious Work." *Young Children,* March 1995, 39–45.

Shade, Daniel D. "Are You Ready to Teach Young Children in the 21st Century?" *Early Childhood Education Journal* 24, no. 1 (1996): 43–44.

Shavelson, Richard J., and Salomon, Gavriel. "Information Technology: Tool and Teacher of the Mind." *Educational Researcher* 14, no. 5 (1985): 4.

Shaw, Edward L. Jr.; Nauman, Ann K.; and Burson, Debbie. "Comparisons of Spontaneous and Word Processed Compositions in Elementary Classrooms: A Three-Year Study." *Journal of Computing in Childhood Education* 5, no. 3/4 (1994): 319–327.

Shilling, Wynne A. "Young Children Using Computers to Make Discoveries About Written Language." *Early Childhood Education Journal* 24, no. 4 (1997): 253–259.

Shore, Ann, and Johnson, Marilyn F. "Integrated Learning Systems: A Vision for the Future." *Educational Technology* 32, no. 9 (1992): 36–39.

Siegel, Linda S. "Does the IQ God Exist?" *The Alberta Journal of Educational Research* 41, no. 3 (1995): 283–288.

Smith, Ann. "Young Children and Reading: What Does the Research Tell Us?" *Australian Journal of Early Childhood* 23, no. 4 (1998): 12-17.

Smith, Frank. "When Irresistible Technology Meets Irreplaceable Teachers." *Language Arts* 76, no. 5 (1999): 414-421.

Sparkes, R.A. "An Investigation of Year 7 Pupils Learning CONTROL LOGO." *Journal of Computer Assisted Learning* 11, no. 3 (1995): 182-191.

Stohr-Hunt, Patricia M. "An Analysis of Frequency of Hands-On Experience and Science Achievement." *Journal of Research in Science Teaching* 33, no. 1 (1996): 101-109.

Swift, Mary. "Computers in Pre-School Centres?" *Australian Journal of Early Childhood* 10, no. 3 (1985): 22-23.

Sylwester, Robert. "Art for the Brain's Sake." *Educational Leadership,* November 1998, 31-35.

Tan, Annette, and Nicholson, Tom. "Flashcards Revisited: Training Poor Readers to Read Words Faster Improves Their Comprehension of Text." *Journal of Educational Psychology* 89, no. 2 (1997): 276-288.

Tetenbaum, Toby Jane, and Mulkeen, Thomas A. "Computers as an Agent for Educational Change." *Computers in the Schools* 2, no. 4 (1985): 91-103.

Underwood, J., et al. "Are Integrated Learning Systems Effective Learning Support Tools?" *Computers and Education* 26, no. 1-3 (1996): 33-40.

Vaidya, Sheila, and McKeeby, John. "Computer Turtle Graphics: Do They Affect Children's Thought Processes?" *Educational Technology* 24, no. 9 (1984): 46-47.

Van Dusen, Lani M., and Worthen, Blaine R. "Can Integrated Instructional Technology Transform the Classroom?" *Educational Leadership,* October 1995, 28-33.

————. "The Impact of Integrated Learning System Implementation on Student Outcomes: Implications for Research and Evaluation." *International Journal of Educational Research* 21, no. 1 (1994): 13-24.

Van Horne, Royal. "Bad Ideas: Technology Integration and Job-Entry Skills." *Phi Delta Kappan,* January 1997, 417-418.

Vesel, Judith H. "Using Teleconversations to Explore Social Issues." *Learning & Leading with Technology,* February 1996, 27-30.

White, Mary-Alice. "Are ILSs Good Education?" *Educational Technology* 32, no. 9 (1992): 49-50.

White, Steven H., and Kuhn, Troy. "A Comparison of Elementary Students' Information Recall on Text Documents, Oral Reading, and Multimedia Presentations." *Journal of Computing in Childhood Education* 8, no. 1 (1997): 15-21.

Wiebe, James H. "At-Computer Programming Success of Third-Grade Students." *Journal of Research on Computing in Education* 24, no. 2 (1991): 214–229.

Wiebe, James H., and Martin, Nancy J. "The Impact of a Computer-Based Adventure Game on Achievement and Attitudes in Geography." *Journal of Computing in Childhood Education* 5, no. 1 (1994): 61–71.

Weinberger, Norman M. "The Music in Our Minds." *Educational Leadership,* November 1998, 36–40.

Witz, Klaus G. "Science with Values and Values for Science Education." *Journal of Curriculum Studies* 28, no. 5 (1996): 597–612.

Wolfe, Edward W., et al. "A Study of Word Processing Experience and Its Effects on Student Essay Writing." *Journal of Educational Computing Research* 14, no. 3 (1996): 269–283.

Wolfe, Pat, and Brandt, Ron. "What Do We Know from Brain Research?" *Educational Leadership,* November 1998, 8–13.

Wresch, Bill. "What I Learned in Wabeno." *Computers in Human Behavior* (Special Issue: Computer Use in the Improvement of Writing) 8, no. 1 (1992): 9–16.

Yelland, Nicola. "Young Children's Attitudes to Computers and Computing." *Australian Journal of Early Childhood* 20, no. 2 (1995): 20–25.

Yoshikawa, H., and Hara, I. "A Case of Rapidly Developed Myopia among VDT Workers." *Japanese Journal of Industrial Health* 31, no. 1 (1989): 24–25.

Zane, Thomas, and Frazer, Connell G. "The Extent to Which Software Developers Validate Their Claims." *Journal of Research on Computing in Education* 24, no. 3 (1992): 410–419.

# INDEX